Nick Vandome

Laptops for Seniors

Windows 10 Creators Update edition

In easy steps is an imprint of In Easy Steps Limited
16 Hamilton Terrace · Holly Walk · Leamington Spa
Warwickshire · United Kingdom · CV32 4LY
www.ineasysteps.com

Notice of Liability
Every effort has been made to ensure that this book contains accurate and current information. However, In Easy Steps Limited and the author shall not be liable for any loss or damage suffered by readers as a result of any information contained herein.

Trademarks
Microsoft® and Windows® are registered trademarks of Microsoft Corporation. All other trademarks are acknowledged as belonging to their respective companies.

In Easy Steps Limited supports The Forest Stewardship Council (FSC), the leading international forest certification organization. All our titles that are printed on Greenpeace approved FSC certified paper carry the FSC logo.

Printed and bound in the United Kingdom

ISBN 978-1-84078-781-8

Contents

3 Getting Up and Running 57

4 Working with Apps 75

5 The Online World 91

1 Choosing a Laptop

More and more computer users are now using laptops because of their convenience and portability. This chapter looks at some of the issues to consider when buying a laptop, and how to ensure you buy the right one for your needs. It also covers the elements of a laptop and some of the accessories you will need.

A Brief History of Laptops

Modern computers have come a long way since the days of mainframe computers, which took up entire rooms and were generally only the domain of large educational establishments or government organizations. Before microprocessors (the chips that are used to run modern-day computers), these mainframe computers were usually operated by punchcards: the operators programmed instructions via holes in a punchcard and then waited for the results, which could take hours or days.

Apple has an excellent range of laptops, running its macOS operating system. However, the majority of this book deals with "IBM-compatible" laptops, as they are known. These types of laptops are the most common, and run on the Windows operating system.

The first personal computers, i.e. ones in which all of the computing power was housed in a single box, started to appear in the early 1970s, and the first machine that bore any resemblance to modern personal computers was called the Datapoint 2200. The real breakthrough for personal computers came with the introduction of microprocessors – small chips that contained all of the necessary processing power for the computer. After this, the industry expanded at a phenomenal rate with the emergence of major worldwide companies such as Microsoft, Apple, IBM, Dell and Intel.

But even as personal computers were being developed for a mass-market audience, there was a concerted drive to try to create a portable computer so that people could take their own computer with them wherever they went. Even in the fast-moving world of technology, the timescale for shrinking a computer from the size of a large room to the size of a small briefcase was a dramatic one.

The New icon pictured above indicates a new or enhanced feature introduced on laptops with the Windows 10 Creators Update.

First portable computers

With most types of technology, we are obsessed with the idea of making the item as small as possible, whether it is a music player, a telephone or a computer. However, the first portable computers bore little resemblance to the machines that we now know as laptops. At the beginning of the 1980s there were a few portable computers released, but most of them were bulky, had very small screens and could not run on internal batteries. The most popular of these was called the Osborne 1, which was released in 1981. Although this was the size of a small suitcase and had a minuscule amount of computing power compared with modern machines, it proved a big success as it enabled people to carry their computers around with them for the first time.

The machine that first used the term "laptop" was called the Gavilan SC, which was developed in 1983 and introduced in 1984. This had the big advantage of being able to run on an internal battery, and it was also one of the first portable computers that appeared with the now-universal "clamshell" design, where the monitor folded down over the keyboard.

Because of their size and weight, the first portable computers, such as the Osborne 1, were known rather unflatteringly as "luggables".

In the late 1980s, companies such as Kyocera, Tandy, Olivetti, NEC, IBM, Toshiba, Compaq and Zenith Data Systems began developing fast and more powerful laptops, and it is in this period that the growth of laptops really began to take off.

In 1991, Apple introduced its PowerBook range of laptops, and in 1995 the introduction of Windows 95 provided an operating system for IBM-compatible laptops.

Laptops have now become an integral part of the computer market, and in many areas sales have outstripped those of desktop computers. Also, they are more than capable of comfortably meeting the computing needs of most computer users. Add to this their portability (which has reached a stage where you no longer need to worry about causing yourself an injury in order to carry one around), and it is clear why laptops have become so popular.

Mobility is now an essential part of computing, and when Windows 8 was released it was aimed firmly at the mobile world. However, this caused some issues, particularly with users of desktop and laptop computers. Windows 10 has gone a long way to addressing these issues, partly by reinstalling a number of features that are aimed more at users with a traditional keyboard and mouse. This shows that laptops still have an important role to play, and will continue to do so.

Laptops v. Desktops

When considering buying a laptop computer, one of the first considerations is how it will perform in comparison with a desktop computer. In general, you will pay more for a laptop with similar specifications to a desktop. The reason for this is purely down to size: it is more expensive to fit the required hardware into a laptop than the more generous physical capacity of a desktop computer. However, with modern computing technology and power, even laptops with lower specifications than their desktop cousins will be able to handle all but the most intensive computing needs of most home users. The one situation where laptops will need to have as high a specification as possible is if you are going to be doing a lot a video downloading and editing, such as converting and editing old family movies.

Another issue with laptops is battery power, which is required to keep them operating when they are removed from a mains electrical source. Obviously, this is not an issue that affects desktops.

Some of the issues to consider when looking at the differences between laptops and desktops are:

- **Portability**. Laptops easily win over desktops in this respect, but when looking at this area it is worth thinking about how portable you actually want your computer to be. If you want to mainly use it in the home, then you may think that a desktop is the answer. However, a laptop gives you portability in the home too, which means that you can use your computer in a variety of locations within the home and even in the garden, if desired.
- **Power**. Even the most inexpensive laptops have enough computing power to perform most of the tasks that the majority of users require. However, if you want to have the same computing power as the most powerful desktops, then you will have to pay a comparatively higher price.
- **Functionality**. Again, because of their size, desktops have more room for items such as DVD writers, multi-card readers and webcams. These can be included with laptops, but this can also increase the price and the weight of the laptop.

Types of Laptops

To meet the needs of the different types of people who use laptops there are several variations that are available:

- **Netbooks**. These are the ultimate in small laptops, but have less power and functionality than larger options. They generally have screens that are approximately 10 inches (measured diagonally from corner to corner) and are best suited for surfing the web and sending email, although they can also do productivity tasks.
- **Ultrabooks**. These are very light and slim laptops that still have significant power and functionality. They have screens of approximately 13 inches, and weigh as little as 1.2 kg. They are an excellent option if you are going to be using your laptop a lot while traveling.
- **Notebooks**. These are the most common types of laptops as they have a good combination of size, weight and power. They generally have screens that are approximately 13-17 inches and weigh approximately 2-3.5 kg. Notebooks are an excellent option for using in the home and also while traveling.
- **Desktop replacements**. These are larger, heavier laptops that can be used in the home instead of a desktop computer. They are more powerful than other types of laptops, but the downside is that they are not as portable. They generally have screens that are up to approximately 17-19 inches, and weigh approximately 4-6 kg.
- **Hybrids**. With the proliferation of touchscreen mobile computing devices such as smartphones and tablet computers, manufacturers have been looking at ways to incorporate this functionality into laptops. This has resulted in the development of touchscreen laptops and hybrid devices, which can be used both as a laptop and a tablet. This is done by including a keyboard that can be hidden (by having a sliding, detachable or revolving screen) so that the device can quickly be converted into a touchscreen tablet. These devices are becoming increasingly popular.

Netbooks usually have a slimmed-down version of the full Windows operating system, due to limits of their memory and architecture.

A lot of the weight in a laptop is taken up by peripherals such as DVD writers, card readers and webcams. The more of these that a laptop has, the heavier it is likely to be.

Laptop Jargon Explained

Since laptops are essentially portable computers, much of the jargon is the same as for a desktop computer. However, it is worth looking at some of this jargon and the significance it has in terms of laptops:

- **Processor**. Also known as the central processing unit, or CPU, this refers to the processing of digital data as it is provided by programs on the computer. The more powerful the processor, the quicker the data is interpreted.
- **Memory**. This closely relates to the processor and is also known as random-access memory, or RAM. Essentially, this type of memory manages the programs that are being run and the commands that are being executed. The more memory there is, the quicker programs will run. With more RAM, they will also be more stable and less likely to crash. In the current range of laptops, memory is measured in megabytes (MB) or gigabytes (GB).
- **Storage**. This refers to the amount of digital information that the laptop can store. In the current range of laptops, storage is measured in gigabytes. There are no external signs of processor or memory on a laptop but the details are available from within the This PC option, which is accessed from the File Explorer.

Memory can be thought of as a temporary storage device, as it only keeps information about the currently-open programs. Storage is more permanent, as it keeps the information even when the laptop has been turned off.

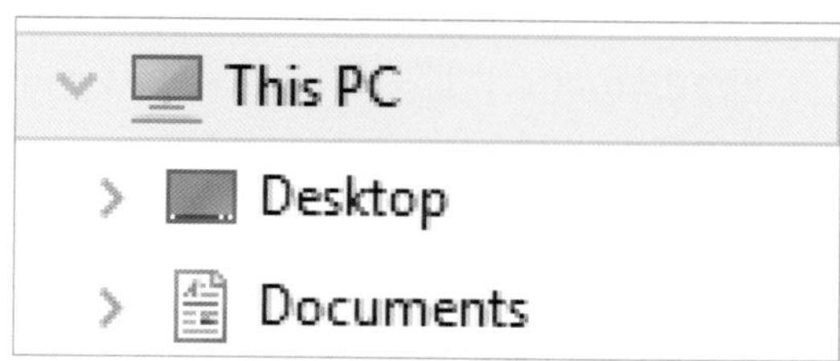

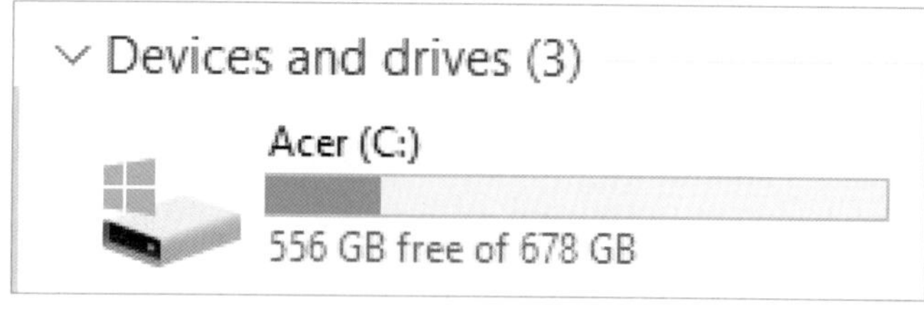

- **Optical drive**. This is a drive on the laptop that is capable of reading information from, and copying it to, a disc such as a CD or a DVD. Some modern laptops have internal optical drives such as CD writers or DVD writers.

External optical drives can also be connected to a laptop through a USB cable.

- **Connectivity**. This refers to the different types of media device to which the laptop can be connected. These include card readers for memory cards from digital cameras, USB devices such as music players, and USB flashdrives for backing up files or storing items.
- **Graphics card**. This is a device that enables images, video and animations to be displayed on the laptop. It is also sometimes known as a video card. The faster the graphics card, the better the quality the relevant media will be displayed at. In general, very fast graphics cards are really only needed for intensive multimedia applications such as video games or videos.

For more on using wireless technology, see page 155.

- **Wireless**. This refers to a laptop's ability to connect wirelessly to a network – i.e. another computer or an internet connection. In order to be able to do this, the laptop must have a wireless card, which enables it to connect to a network or high-speed internet connection.
- **Ports**. These are the parts of a laptop into which external devices can be plugged, using a cable such as a USB. They are usually located on the side of the laptop, and there can be two or three of each.
- **Pointing device**. This is the part of the laptop that replaces the traditional mouse as a means of moving the cursor on the screen. Most pointing devices are in the form of a touch pad, where a finger on a pad is used to move the cursor. An external mouse can also be connected to the laptop and used in the conventional way.

USB stands for Universal Serial Bus, and is a popular way of connecting external devices to computers.

- **Webcam**. This is a type of camera that is fitted into the laptop, and can be used to take still photographs, or communicate via video with other people.

Size and Weight

The issues of size and weight are integral to the decision to buy a laptop. In addition to getting a machine with enough computing power, it is also important to ensure that the screen is large enough for your needs and that it is light enough for you to carry around comfortably.

Size

The main issue with the size of a laptop is the dimensions of the screen. This is usually measured in inches, diagonally from corner to corner. The range for the majority of laptops currently on the market is approximately 12-17 inches, with some more powerful models going up to 19 inches.

When considering the size of screen it is important to think about how you are going to use your laptop:

- If you are going to use it mainly for functions such as letter writing and sending email, then a smaller screen might suffice.
- If you are going to use it mainly for functions such as surfing the web or editing and looking at photographs, then you may feel more comfortable with a larger screen.
- If you, or anyone else, is going to be using it for playing games and watching videos, then the larger the screen, the better.

Looking at material on a smaller screen can be more tiring on the eyes as, by default, it is displayed proportionally smaller than on a larger screen. It is possible to change the size of the screen display, but this will lead to less material being displayed on the screen. See page 52 to see how to change the screen resolution.

Weight

Unless you are buying a laptop to replace a desktop, weight should not be too much of an issue, as most models are similar in this respect. However, make sure you physically feel the laptop before you buy it.

If you are going to be traveling a lot with your laptop, then a lighter, ultrabook type may be the best option. When considering this, take into account the weight of any type of case that you will use to carry the laptop, as this will add to the overall weight.

Getting Comfortable

Since you will probably be using your laptop in more than one location, the issue of finding a comfortable working position can be vital, particularly as you cannot put the keyboard and monitor in different positions as you can with a desktop computer. Whenever you are using your laptop try to make sure that you are sitting in a comfortable position, with your back well supported, and that the laptop is in a position where you can reach the keyboard easily and also see the screen without straining.

Working comfortably at a laptop involves a combination of a good chair, good posture and good positioning of the laptop.

Despite the possible temptation to do so, avoid using your laptop in bed, on your lap, or where you have to slouch or strain to reach the laptop properly:

If possible, the best place to work at a laptop is at a dedicated desk or workstation.

Seating position

The ideal way to sit at a laptop is with an office-type chair that offers good support for your back. Even with these types of chairs it is important to maintain a good body position so that your back is straight and your head is pointing forwards.

If you do not have an office-type chair, use a chair with a straight back and place a cushion behind you for extra support and comfort, as required.

One of the advantages of office-type chairs is that the height can usually be adjusted, and this can be a great help in achieving a comfortable position.

...cont'd

Laptop position

When working at your laptop it is important to have it positioned so that both the keyboard and the screen are in a comfortable position. If the keyboard is too low, then you will have to slouch or strain to reach it:

Take regular breaks when working with a laptop, and stop working if you experience aches, or pins and needles in your arms or legs.

If the keyboard is too high, your arms will be stretching. This could lead to pain in your tendons:

The ideal setup is to have the laptop in a position where you can sit with your forearms and wrists as level as possible while you are typing on the keyboard:

Adjusting the screen

Another factor in working comfortably at a laptop is the position of the screen. Unlike with a desktop computer, it is not feasible to have a laptop screen at eye level, as this would result in the keyboard being in too high a position. Instead, once you have achieved a comfortable seating position, open the screen so that it is approximately 90 degrees from your eyeline:

Find a comfortable body position and adjust your laptop's position to this, rather than vice versa.

One problem with laptop screens is that they can reflect glare from sunlight or indoor lighting:

Most modern laptops have screens with an anti-glare coating. However, even this will not be very effective against bright sunlight that is shining directly onto the screen.

If this happens, either change your position or block out the light source, using some form of blind or shade. Avoid squinting at a screen that is reflecting glare as this will quickly give you a headache.

Carrying a Laptop

As laptops are designed for mobility, it is safe to assume that they will have to be carried around at some point. Because of the weight of even the lightest laptops, it can be uncomfortable to carry a laptop for an extended period of time. To try to minimize this, it is important to follow a few rules:

If you are carrying your laptop for a long period of time make sure that you take regular breaks, otherwise you may cause yourself a strain or an injury.

- Carry the laptop with a carry case that is designed for this task (or a double-strapped backpack).
- Carry the laptop on one side of your body and move it from side to side if necessary.

- Do not cross the strap over your shoulders, and try not to carry too many other items at the same time.

If you place your laptop with another piece of luggage, make sure that you keep it with you at all times, so as to minimize the chance of theft.

If you are traveling with your laptop you might be able to incorporate it into your luggage, particularly if it can be moved on wheels.

Keyboard and Touch Pad

Laptops have the same basic data input devices as desktop computers, i.e. a keyboard and a mouse. A laptop keyboard is very similar to a desktop one, although it is best to try the action of the keys before you buy a particular laptop, to ensure that they are not too "soft", i.e. that there is enough resistance when they are pressed.

One of the main differences between a laptop and a desktop computer is the mouse (or pointing device) that controls the on-screen cursor. In the early days of laptops, some of them had a small control stick to move the cursor. However, these have been almost universally replaced by touch pads, which are small, sensitive, square or rectangular pads that are activated by stroking a finger over them to move the cursor. It sometimes takes a bit of practice to get used to them, but after a little experience they can be as effective as a traditional mouse. When using a keyboard or touch pad, avoid having your fingers too high:

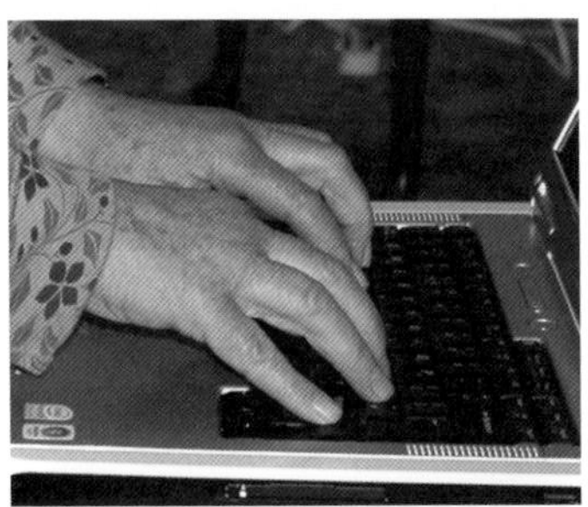

Instead, keep your hands and fingers as flat as possible over the keyboard and the touch pad:

Laptop keyboards contain the same functionality as any standard computer keyboard. However, most manufacturers have keyboards with functions that are specific to their own laptops.

Using an External Mouse

Not everyone likes touch pads as a means of moving the cursor on a laptop, and it is true they can sometimes be slightly fiddly and prone to erratic movement if the control is too jerky. The good news is that it is possible to use a conventional mouse with a laptop to move the cursor.

A mouse can be connected to a laptop via one of the suitable sockets (ports) at the back or side of the laptop. These are usually in the form of USB ports:

It is certainly worth persevering with a laptop's touch pad, even if it seems very frustrating at first. Once you have found the correct pressure to apply, it will become much easier to control.

Once the mouse has been connected to the laptop it can be used in exactly the same way as with a desktop computer. In some cases it is possible to add a wireless mouse, which can be used without the need for a cable:

Ports and Slots

Most laptops have a slightly bewildering array of sockets and slots for connecting external devices. These sockets are known as ports, and they come in a variety of shapes and sizes for different devices and uses:

- **USB**. This is a method for connecting a variety of external devices such as digital cameras, digital music players, scanners and printers. The latest standard in widespread use is USB 3.0, and this has largely replaced parallel and serial ports in terms of connecting devices such as printers or an external mouse.
- **USB Type-C**. This is the latest type of USB port, for devices with a USB Type-C cable. The port is thinner than a standard USB one and is reversible, so that the end of the cable can be inserted both ways, rather than a single way as for standard USB ports.
- **Ethernet**. This can be used as a cable connection to your internet router, rather than using a Wi-Fi connection.
- **HDMI (High-Definition Multimedia Interface)**. This can be used to connect to compatible digital devices, including high-definition TVs. This enables you to view whatever is on your laptop screen on a television, and is a good option for watching movies or displaying photos.
- **Memory card readers**. These are used for downloading photos from memory cards from digital cameras or smartphones. Some laptops only have an SD card slot, since these are most commonly used. If you need to attach a multi-card reader for different types of memory card, this can be done using a USB port.

The main slot on some laptops is:

- **CD/DVD players or re-writers**. These can be used to play music CDs or watch videos on a DVD. They can also be used to copy data to blank CDs or DVDs. This is a good option for backing up items that you want to keep, such as photos.

Laptops with USB 3.0 ports can still be used with USB 2.0 (or earlier) devices, but they will also work with any USB 3.0 devices.

Not all laptops have a CD/DVD player, although external CD/DVD drives can be connected.

The Wonder of Wireless

For anyone who has struggled with a tangle of computer cables and wires, the advent of wireless technology has been one of the great computing breakthroughs of recent years.

Wireless technology does exactly what the name suggests: it allows a wireless-enabled computer to communicate with other similarly-enabled devices, such as other computers, printers or an internet connection. First of all, the devices have to be set up as a network, i.e. they have to be linked together so that they know they should be communicating with each other. Once this has been done, files can be shared or sent to the printer, and the internet browsed, all without the need to connect the devices using a cable.

One concern about hotspots is security. This is because if you can access a network wirelessly, someone else could then also access your laptop and data. Many hotspots have software in place to try to stop this.

In order to be part of a wireless network, a laptop must have a wireless capability. Most modern laptops come with wireless cards already installed; otherwise, they can be installed in any available expansion slot.

Hotspots

One of the great growth areas of wireless technology is hotspots. These are public areas that have been set up to distribute the internet wirelessly. This means that anyone with a wireless card in their laptop can, if they are within a certain range, access the internet in a variety of public places. These include:

- Coffee shops
- Airports
- Hotels
- Libraries
- Supermarkets

For more details about Wi-Fi and networks, see Chapter Nine.

Hotspots operate using Wi-Fi technology, which is the method by which the signal from the network is transferred to individual users. Most hotspots have a limited range of approximately 100 yards. Some are free to use, while others charge a fee, depending on usage.

Cleaning a Laptop

Like most things, laptops benefit greatly from a little care and attention. The two most important areas to keep clean are the screen and the keyboard.

Cleaning the screen

All computer screens quickly collect dust and fingerprints, and laptops are no different. If this is left too long it can make the screen harder to read, causing eye strain and headaches. Clean the screen regularly with the following cleaning materials:

- A lint-free cloth, similar to the type used to clean camera lenses (it is important not to scratch the screen in any way).
- An alcohol-free cleaning fluid that is recommended for computer screens.
- Screen wipes, again that are recommended for use on computer screens.

The outer casing of a laptop can be cleaned with the same fluid as used for the screen. Equally effective can be a duster or a damp (but not wet) cloth and warm water. Keep soap away from laptops if possible.

Cleaning the keyboard

Keyboards are notorious for accumulating dust, fluff and crumbs. One way to solve this problem is to turn the laptop upside down and very gently shake it to loosen any foreign objects. Failing this, a can of condensed air can be used with a narrow nozzle to blow out any stubborn items that remain lodged in the keys.

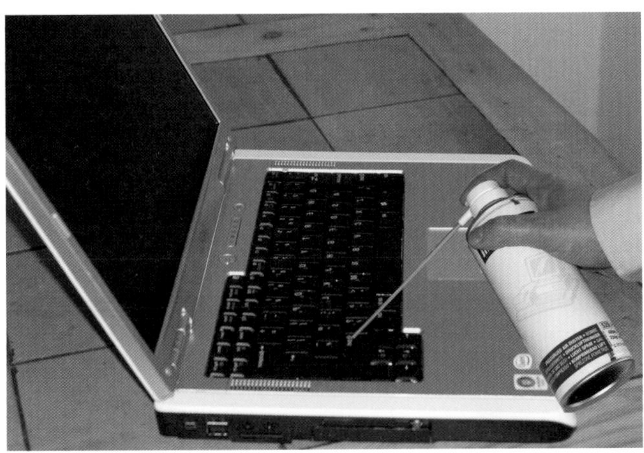

Choosing a Carry Case

When you are transporting your laptop it could be placed in any convenient bag, such as a backpack, a duffle bag or even a large handbag. However, there are several advantages to using a proper laptop carry case:

- It will probably be more comfortable when you are carrying it, as it is designed specifically for this job.
- The laptop will be more secure, as it should fit properly in the case.
- You should be able to keep all of your laptop accessories together in one case.

When choosing a carry case, look for one that fits your laptop well and has a strap to keep it secure inside:

Also, make sure that there are enough additional spaces and pockets for accessories, such as cables and an external mouse. Finally, choosing a case with a padded shoulder strap will be of considerable benefit if you have to carry your laptop for any length of time.

A laptop case should also be lockable, either with its own internal lock, or with a fastening through which a padlock can be put.

Spares and Accessories

Whenever you are going anywhere with your laptop, there are always spares and accessories to consider. Some of these are just nice things to have, while others could be essential to ensure that you can still use your laptop if anything goes wrong while you are on your travels. Items to consider for putting in your laptop case include:

- **Spare battery**. This is probably the most important spare if you are going to be away from home for any length of time, and particularly if you think you may be unable to access a power supply for a period of time, and so be unable to charge your laptop battery. Like all batteries, laptop batteries slowly lose power over time and do not keep their charge for as long as when they are new. It is a good idea to always keep an eye on how much battery power you have left and, if you are running low, try to conserve as much energy as possible. Although laptop batteries are bulky and heavy, carrying a spare could mean the difference between frustration and relief, if you are left with no battery power and no charging options.
- **Power cable**. This is the cable that can be used to power the laptop when it is not being run on battery power. It usually consists of a cable and a power adapter, which makes it rather bulky and heavy. Whenever possible, this should be used rather than the internal battery, and it should be kept with the laptop at all times.

For more information on batteries, see Chapter Ten.

...cont'd

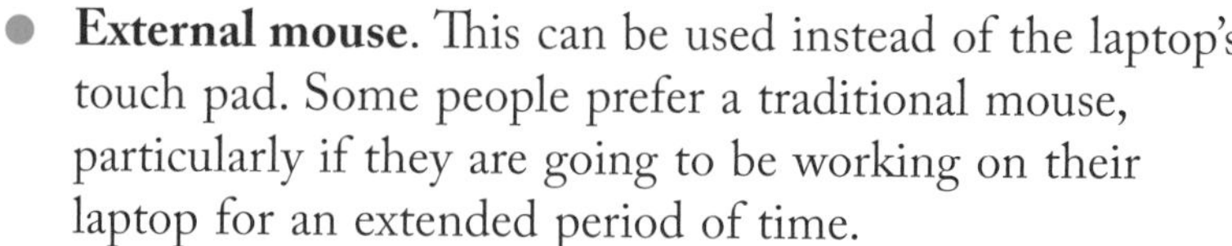

- **External mouse**. This can be used instead of the laptop's touch pad. Some people prefer a traditional mouse, particularly if they are going to be working on their laptop for an extended period of time.

It is important that headphones are comfortable to wear for an extended period of time. In general, the types that fit over the ears are more comfortable than the "bud" variety that is inserted into the ear.

- **Multi-card reader**. If you do not have a built-in multi-card reader (see page 21), an external one can be used to download photos from a digital camera memory card. This will connect via a USB port.
- **Headphones**. These can be used to listen to music or films if you are in the company of other people and you do not want to disturb them. They can also be very useful if there are distracting noises coming from other people.
- **USB flashdrive**. This is a small device that can be used to copy data to and from your laptop. It connects via a USB port and is about the size of a packet of chewing gum. It is an excellent way of backing up files from your laptop when you are away from home.

Backing up (see page 181) is the process of copying folders and files from your laptop onto an external device for safekeeping in case the folders and files on the laptop are deleted or corrupted.

- **Cleaning material**. The materials described on page 23 can be taken to ensure your laptop is always in tip-top condition for use.
- **DVDs/CDs**. Video or music DVDs and CDs can be taken to provide mobile entertainment, and blank ones can be taken to copy data onto, similar to using a USB flash drive.

2 Around a Laptop

This chapter shows how to quickly become familiar with your laptop, and Windows 10. It gives an overview of Windows 10 so that you can become comfortable with this new environment and confidently use the Start menu, the Start button, the Taskbar and the Desktop. It also looks at personalizing Windows 10 to exactly the way you want it.

Opening Up and Turning On

The first step towards getting started with a new laptop is to open it ready for use. The traditional clamshell design keeps the screen and keyboard together through the use of an internal clip or connector. This can be released by a button on the exterior of the laptop, which is usually positioned at the front or side. Some laptops have a magnetic connection between the screen and the main body.

Open the screen of your laptop carefully, so as not to put any unnecessary pressure on the connection between the screen and the main body of the laptop.

Once the screen has been opened, it can then be positioned ready for use. The screen should stay in any position in which it is placed:

Press the Power button with one firm, definite motion. If you accidentally press it twice in quick succession, the laptop may turn on and then shut down immediately afterwards.

The Power button for turning on a laptop, ready for use, is usually located near to the keyboard:

The laptop can be turned on by pushing this button firmly. The laptop will then probably make a sound, to indicate that it has been turned on, and begin loading the operating system (the software that is used to run and manage all of the laptop's apps, folders and files). Once the laptop has completed its startup procedure, the opening screen should be displayed. At this point the laptop is ready for use.

Most laptops will take a couple of minutes to start up and be fully ready to use.

Touchscreen Laptops

Windows 10 is the latest operating system from Microsoft, and this will be installed on most new laptops. It is optimized for touchscreen use, so it is ideal for using with laptops with touchscreen capability and also with Windows 10 tablets.

Touchscreen laptops still have a traditional keyboard but navigation can also be done by tapping, swiping and pinching on the screen. Some of the functions that can be performed on a touchscreen laptop are:

- Activate a button, such as Done or OK, by tapping on it. Apps on the Windows 10 interface can also be accessed by tapping on them from the Start menu.
- Move up and down long pages by swiping in the required direction, e.g. to navigate around web pages.
- Zoom in and out of pages by pinching inwards, or outwards, with thumb and forefinger (if the open app has this functionality). It is most commonly used for zooming in and out of web pages.

Touchscreen laptops are a realistic option for users who want to get the most out of the functionality of Windows 10. Some laptop manufacturers to look at are:

- Acer
- Dell
- HP
- Lenovo
- Sony
- Toshiba

A number of touchscreen models can also be converted into tablet mode, either by revolving the screen or by detaching the keyboard. There are also some hybrid models, with a detachable screen that can be used as either a tablet, or a traditional laptop with the keyboard attached.

The latest version of Windows 10 is the Creators Update edition. This is the edition used in this book but, in general, it will be referred to as Windows 10.

The Microsoft Surface Pro tablet also runs on Windows 10, and it is a realistic option in terms of replacing a regular laptop.

About Windows 10

The latest version of Windows (*at the time of printing*) was released in April 2017:

- 2017 – Windows 10 Creators Update, which can be used to upgrade any existing version of Windows 10.

All major computer operating systems (OS) undergo regular upgrades to new versions. In terms of Microsoft Windows, Windows 8 was one of the most radical updates to the user interface (UI) and introduced a number of new features, for both desktop and mobile versions of Windows. However, it was not met with universal approval as it did not fully meet the needs of desktop users and those with mobile devices.

It is possible to synchronize Windows 10 so that all of your settings and apps will be available over multiple devices through an online Microsoft Account.

With Windows 10, a lot of the problems with Windows 8 were addressed: the familiar Start menu was reinstated to return to a similar UI to earlier versions of Windows; there was a greater consolidation between desktop and mobile devices running Windows 10; and the operation of apps was standardized. In a sense, this was a case of going back one step in order to go forwards two steps, and Windows 10 has succeeded in creating a familiar environment, coupled with a range of innovative and useful features.

Windows 10 Creators Update

The intention for Windows 10 has always been to produce incremental updates, rather than waiting a period of time for the next major update. This is the reason why it is unlikely that there will be a Windows 11: instead, there will be regular online updates to Windows 10. The Windows 10 Creators Update marks the second anniversary of the release of the software. It contains a number of improvements and refinements but, in keeping with the Windows 10 ethos, it is an incremental update rather than a major new operating system, although it contains a comprehensive range of new features. The Creators Update is delivered online through the Windows Update function in the Settings app. A registered version of Windows 10 has to be installed in order for the Creators Update to be downloaded (or a license can be bought when downloading the Creators Update).

Obtaining Windows 10

Windows 10 is a departure by Microsoft in that it is promoted as an online service, rather than just a stand-alone operating system. This means that by default, Windows 10 is obtained and downloaded online, with subsequent updates and upgrades provided on a regular basis.

The original version of Windows 10 was a free upgrade if it was downloaded and installed by July 2016. Windows 10 can now be bought from the Microsoft website, or through software retailers. A registered version of Windows 10 has to been installed before the free Creators Update can be downloaded.

If a laptop is running Windows 7 or 8, it can be upgraded to the Creators Update if a Windows 10 license is bought.

The three main options for obtaining the Windows 10 Creators Update are:

- **Use Windows Update** – Replace an older version of Windows 10, retaining the installed applications and settings. This can be done through the **Settings** app (select **Update & Security** > **Windows Update** and click on the **Check for updates** button).
- **Microsoft website** – Visit the software download page on the Microsoft website (**microsoft.com/en-us/software-download/windows10**) to use the **Update Assistant** to download the Windows 10 Creators Update.
- **Pre-install** – Buy a new laptop with the Windows 10 Creators Update already installed.

Some of the steps that the installation will go through are:

- **Personalize**. These are settings that will be applied to your version of Windows 10.
- **Microsoft Account**. You can set up a Microsoft Account during installation.
- **Privacy**. Certain privacy settings can be applied during the setup process for the Windows 10 Creators Update.

...cont'd

About Creators Update

Although the Creators Update is still under the Windows 10 banner, there is a range of significant additions and enhancements from the early versions of the operating system. Some of these include:

These features are new or updated in the Windows 10 Creators Update.

- **Enhanced Settings**. The Settings app has been updated to include more options and, also, more of the items in the Windows Control Panel have been migrated to the Settings app so that they can be found in one place. One example of this is the Themes option, which can be used to apply personalized themes across the whole of Windows 10.
- **Gaming Settings**. There is a new Settings category for Gaming and there is also a new Game Bar that is a virtual games controller that can be activated when playing games with the Windows 10 Creators Update.
- **Start menu folders**. The Start menu has been enhanced, with the option of creating folders on the Start menu so that several items can be stored and accessed within one menu tile.

- **Cortana commands**. Cortana, the Windows 10 personal digital assistant, has new voice commands for turning off, sleeping or restarting a PC; and also, a greater range of apps now support Cortana.
- **Edge tabs**. The Microsoft Edge web browser has enhanced tabs functions, whereby they can be grouped together and also previewed by moving the cursor over a tab.
- **Share menu**. The Share menu has been redesigned to display apps with which certain items can be shared, and this is available from the Share button in a range of apps.

3D in the Creators Update

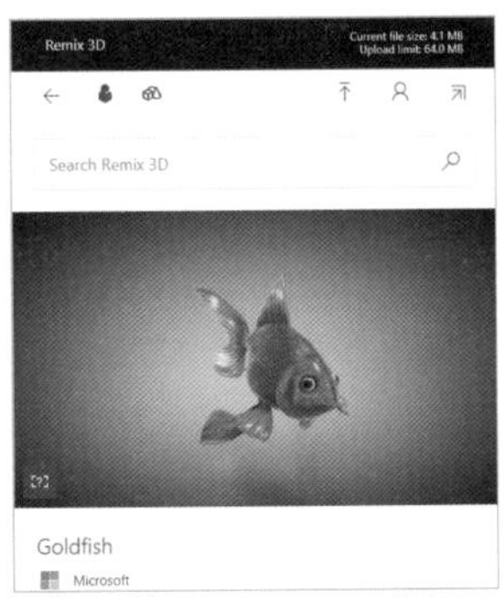

3D features prominently in the Windows 10 Creators Update, with a new app, Paint 3D, for creating your own 3D pictures. It also contains the Remix 3D section, which is a Microsoft website where 3D objects from other users can be viewed and downloaded for use in your own projects.

Other 3D enhancements include being able to upload and view 3D images in the Edge web browser, and 3D models can be used in PowerPoint for transitions between slides.

Items created in Paint 3D can be used in a Mixed Reality environment using the HoloLens headset.

Mixed Reality

Developing the 3D theme further, the Windows 10 Creators Update also includes a number of Mixed Reality (MR) features. Mixed Reality is the combining of the real and virtual worlds to create a unique user experience. This is usually done through the use of a Mixed Reality headset, and the Microsoft one is called HoloLens. When this is worn, 3D objects and holograms can be viewed within the user's actual environment, i.e. you can view an array of objects while still viewing the physical elements of a room in your home. However, the HoloLens is expensive, and Microsoft is addressing this by developing a range of Mixed Reality headsets with other manufacturers.

The Windows 10 Creators Update includes a **Mixed Reality Portal** app that gives a useful overview of using Mixed Reality with the Windows 10 Creators Update.

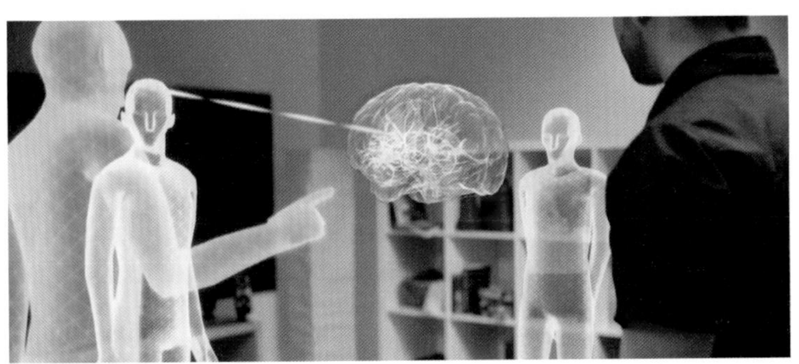

Mixed Reality requires PCs with higher processor and graphics-card capabilities than for general computing.

The Start Button

In the Windows 10 Creators Update, the Start button works in a similar way to most early versions of Windows, with some enhancements.

Using the Start button

The Start button provides access to the apps on your Windows 10 PC and also to the enhanced Start menu:

1. Click on the **Start** button in the bottom left-hand corner of the screen

2. The **Start** menu is displayed
3. The left-hand side of the Start menu contains links to frequently-used apps, a list of quick links to items such as the Power button, and an alphabetic list of all of the apps on the computer

The items on the Start menu can be customized from the **Personalization** > **Start** section of the Settings app.

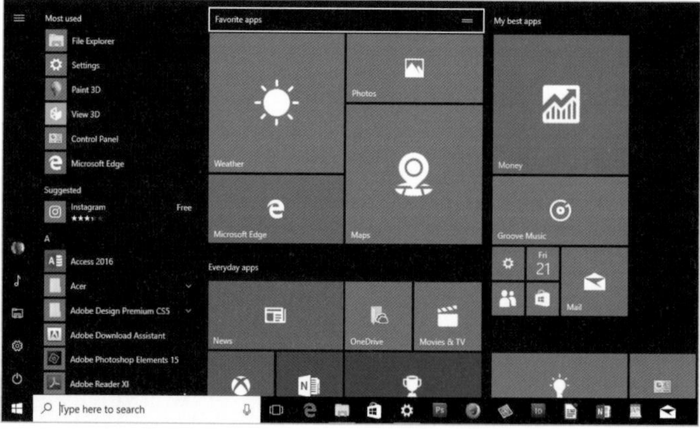

4. The right-hand side of the Start menu is where apps can be pinned so that they are always available. This is displayed as a collection of large, colored tiles
5. Other items can also be accessed from the Start button by right-clicking on it

Click on the **Power** button on the Start menu to access options for Sleep, Shut down or Restart.

Start button functionality

In addition to accessing the Start menu, the Start button can also be used to access the Power User menu, by right-clicking on it:

1. Right-click on the **Start** button to view the Power User menu

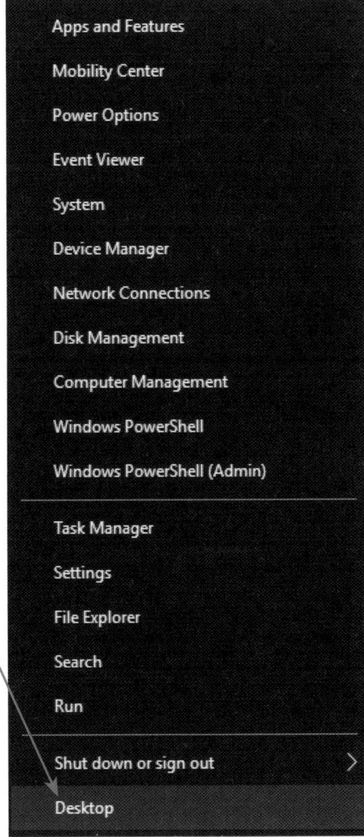

2. Click on the relevant buttons to view items including the **Desktop** and other popular locations such as the **File Explorer**

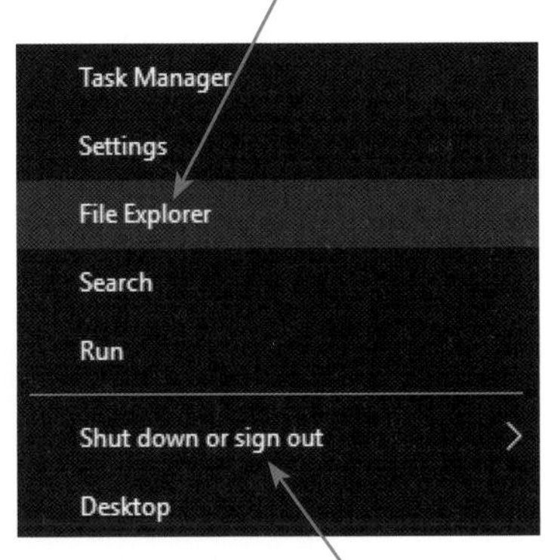

3. Click on the **Shut down or sign out** button to access the options

The Power User menu in Step 1 has a number of options for accessing system functions, such as Windows PowerShell and Disk Management.

The Start Menu

The Start menu in Windows 10 is where you can access areas within your computer, perform certain functions and also access apps from a variety of locations. Some of the default items on the Start menu can be customized to a certain extent (under **Settings** > **Personalization** > **Start**), and there is considerable functionality here:

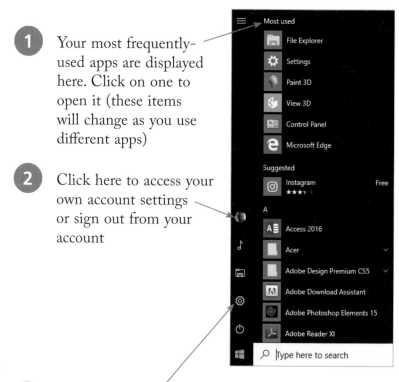

1. Your most frequently-used apps are displayed here. Click on one to open it (these items will change as you use different apps)

2. Click here to access your own account settings or sign out from your account

3. Click here to access items including the **File Explorer**, your **Documents** library within File Explorer and the Windows 10 **Settings**

4. Click on the **Power** button for options to **Sleep** your computer, **Shut down** or **Restart**

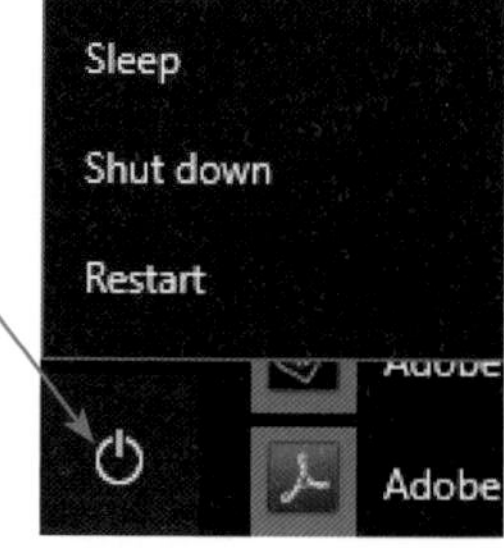

5. Use the scroll bar at the right-hand side to move through the list of apps

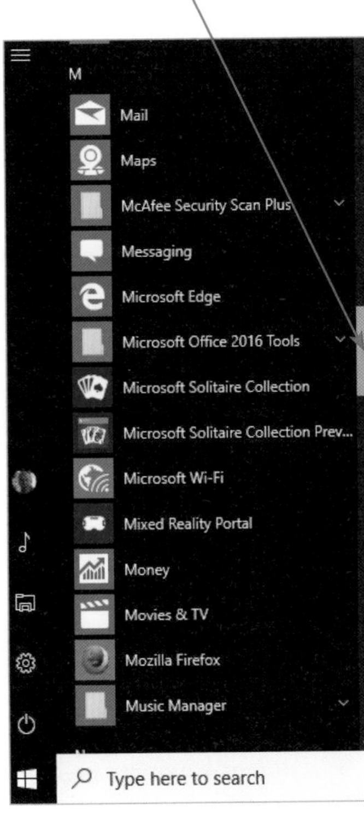

6. If there is a down-pointing arrow next to an app, this means that there are additional items that can be accessed. Click on the arrow to view these

Windows Accessories

Click on a letter at the top of a section of apps to view an alphabetic grid. Click on a letter to move to that section.

Pinning Items

In most cases, you will want to have quick access to a variety of apps on the Start menu and also the Taskbar at the bottom of the screen. To do this:

1. Click on the **Start** button

2. Right-click on an app and click on the **Pin to Start** button

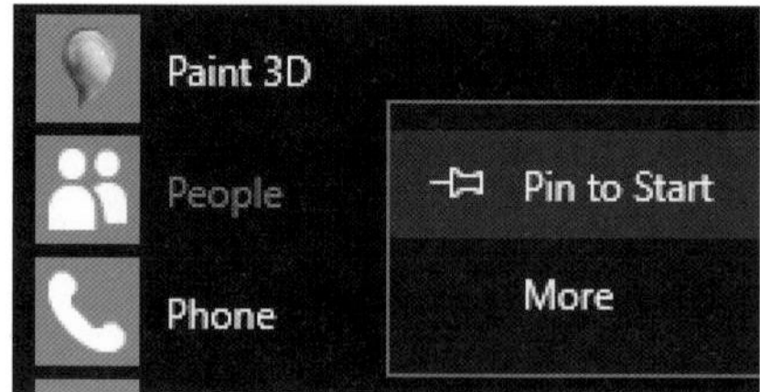

3. The apps tile is added to the **Start** menu

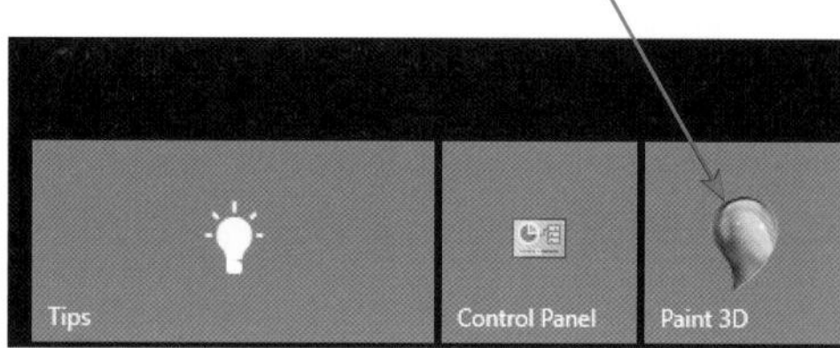

4. Right-click on an app and click on **More** > **Pin to taskbar**

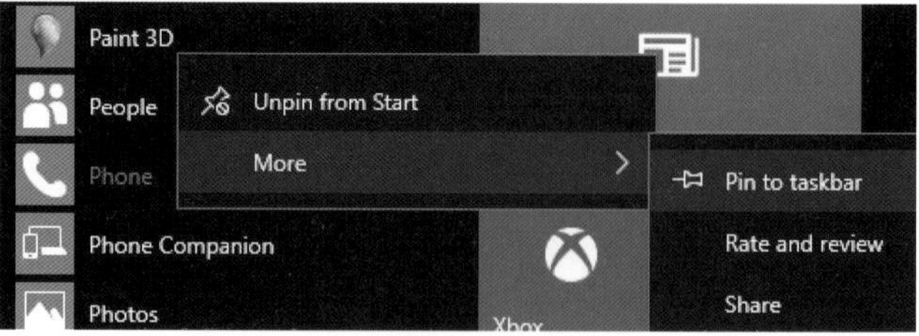

5. The app's icon is added to the Taskbar and it can be opened directly from here

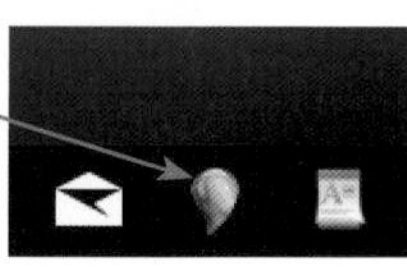

Tiles on the Start menu can be resized by right-clicking on them and clicking on the **Resize** button. The resizing options are **Small**, **Medium**, **Wide** and **Large**, although not all options can be applied to all apps.

Using Live Tiles

Before any of the Windows 10 apps have been used, some of them are depicted on the Start menu with tiles of solid color. However, once you open an app it activates the Live Tile feature (if it is supported by that app). This enables the tile to display real-time information from the app, even when it is not the app currently being used. This means that you can view information from your apps, directly from the Start menu. To use Live Tiles:

The apps with Live Tile functionality include: Mail, People, Calendar, Photos, Groove Music, News, Sport, and Money. Some of these, such as Mail, require you to first set up an account before Live Tiles can be fully activated.

1. Right-click on a tile to select it. If it has Live Tile functionality, click on the **Turn Live Tile on** button to activate this feature

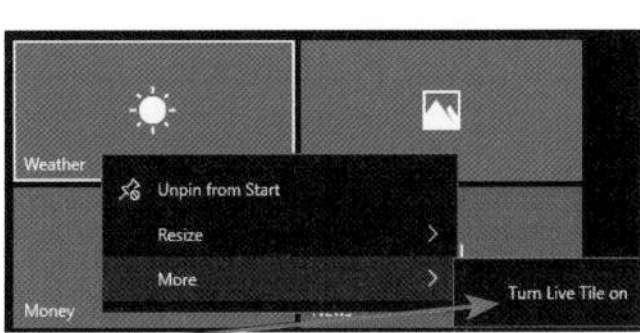

2. Live Tiles display real-time text and images from the selected apps. These are updated when there is new information available via the app

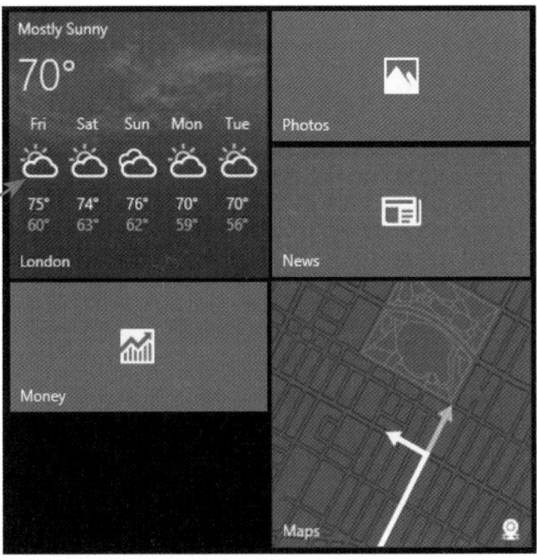

3. To turn off a Live Tile, right-click on a tile to select it, and click on the **Turn Live Tile off** button

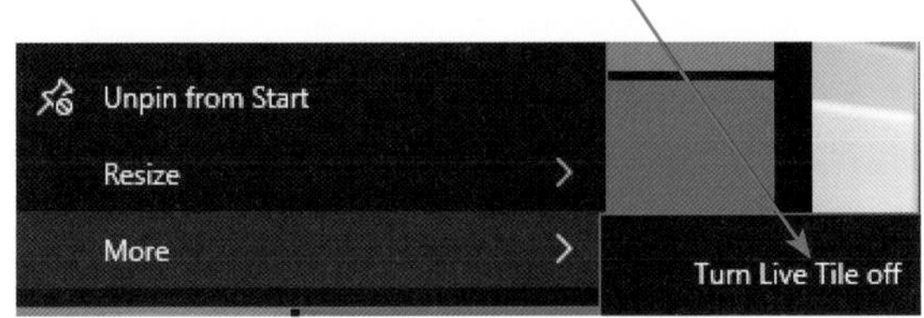

If you have too many Live Tiles activated at the same time it can become distracting and annoying, with a lot of movement on the Start menu.

Hot tip

The Desktop can also be accessed by pressing the **WinKey** + **D** or by right-clicking on the Start button and selecting **Desktop**. The WinKey can be used to access the Start menu at any time and also perform a number of tasks in conjunction with other keys.

The Desktop and Taskbar

The Windows Desktop is once again an integral part of Windows, and is visible when you turn on your laptop. This also displays the Taskbar, at the bottom of the screen.

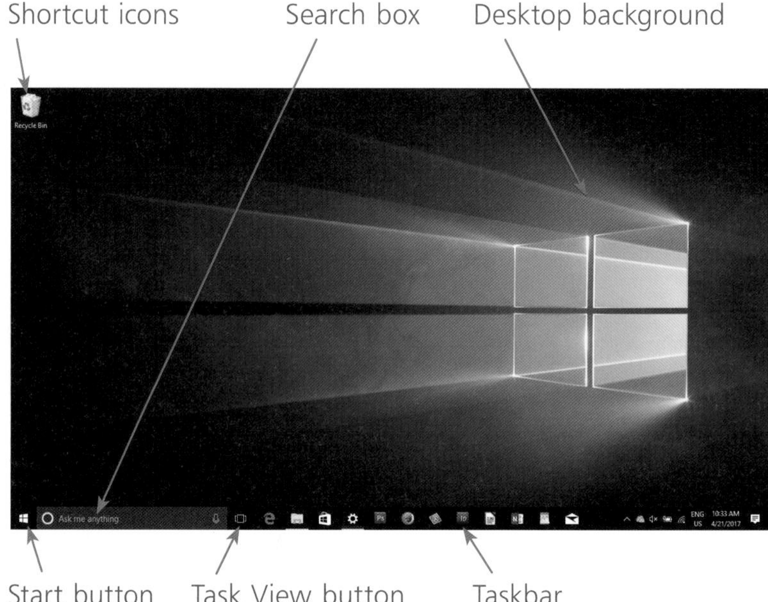

1. Click on this button on the Taskbar to access Task View, which displays minimized versions of the currently-open apps

2. To show and hide the Task View button, right-click on the button and check On or Off the **Show Task View button** option

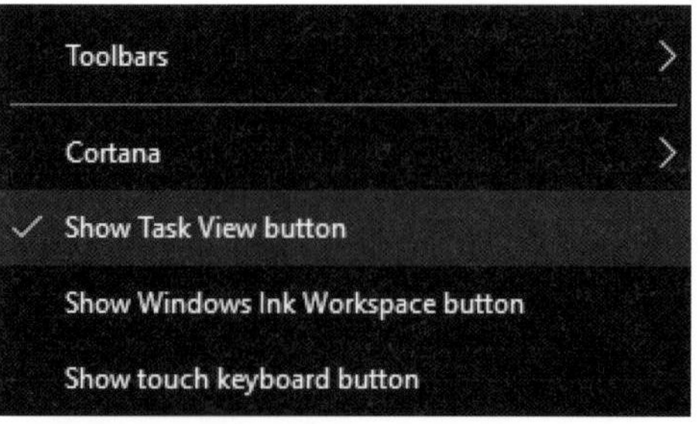

If an app has two or more windows open, each of them will be displayed when you move the cursor over the app's icon on the Taskbar.

3. The Task View displays minimized versions of the currently-open apps and windows

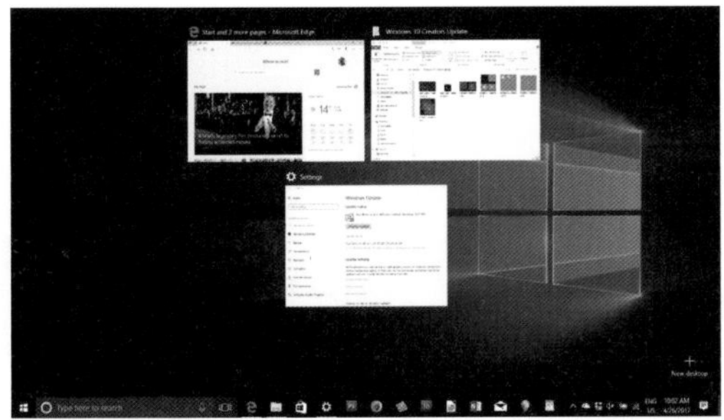

4. As more windows are opened, the format is arranged accordingly

5. If an app has more than one window open, e.g. File Manager, each window is displayed within Task View

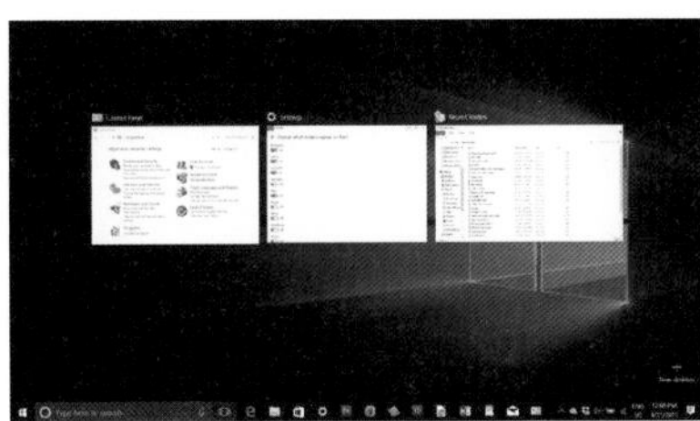

6. Click on a window in Task View to make it the active window

7. Move the cursor over items on the Taskbar to see open windows for that item. Click on a window to make that the active one

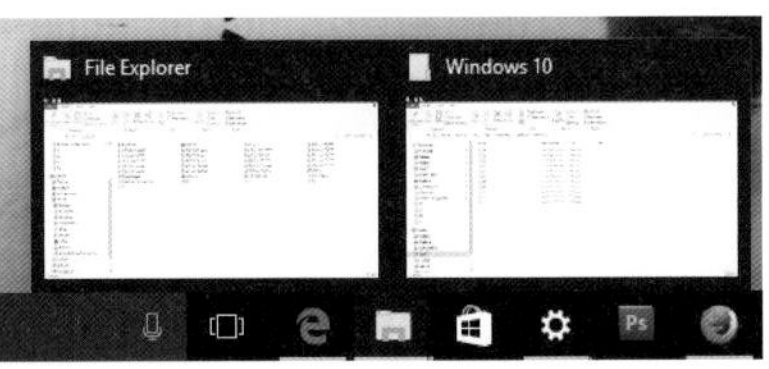

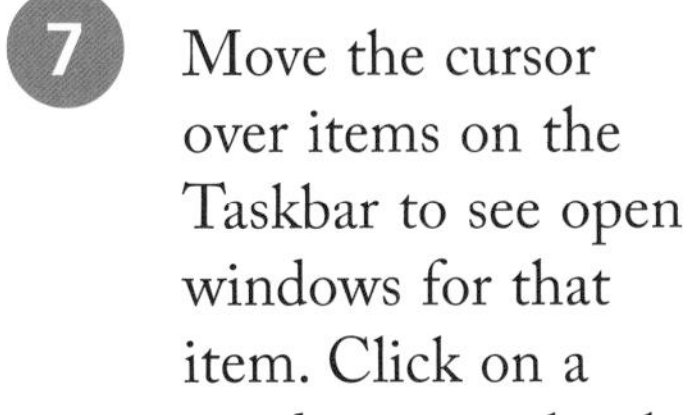

8. The Notifications area at the right-hand side of the Taskbar has speaker, network and other system tools. Click on one to see more information about each item

Apps can only be open on one desktop at a time. So if an app is open on one desktop and you try to open it on another, you will be taken to the already-open app (see page 42 for adding desktops).

...cont'd

Adding Desktops

Another function within Task View is for creating additional desktops. This can be useful if you want to separate different tasks on your computer. For instance, you may want to keep your open entertainment apps on a different desktop to your productivity ones. To create additional desktops:

1. Click on the **Task View** button on the Taskbar

2. The current desktop is displayed with the open windows

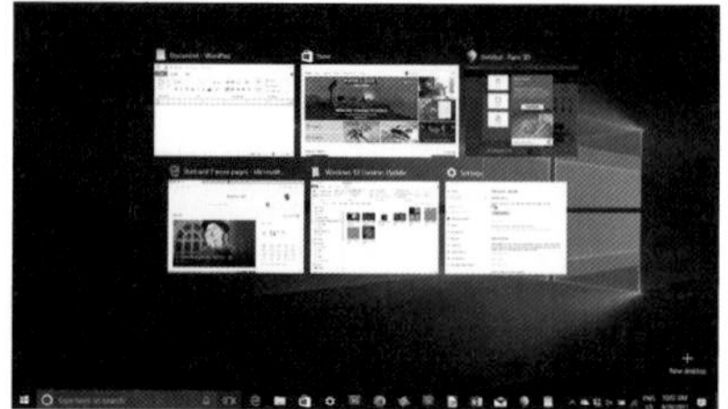

If you add too many desktops it may become confusing in terms of the content on each one.

3. Click on the **New desktop** button

4. The new desktop is displayed at the bottom of the Task View window

To delete a desktop, click on the Task View button and click on the cross that appears when you hover your mouse over the desktop you want to remove.

5. Click on the new desktop to access it. Each desktop has the same background and shortcuts

6. Open apps on the new desktop. These will be separate from the apps on any other desktop

Shutting Down

Options for shutting down Windows have been amended with some versions of the operating system. In the Windows 10 Creators Update, this functionality can be accessed from the Start menu.

Shutting down from the Start menu

1. Click on the **Start** button 

2. Right-click on the **Power** button

3. Click on either the **Sleep**, **Shut down** or **Restart** buttons; or

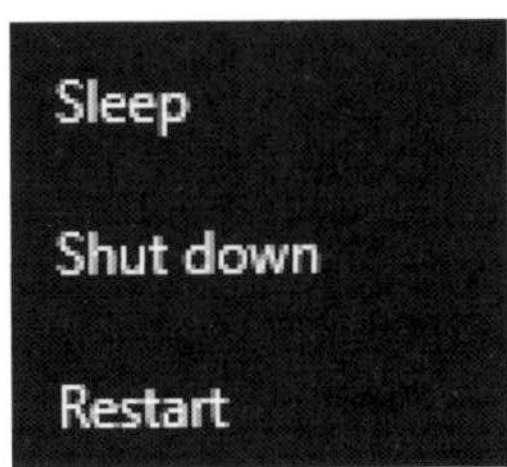

4. Right-click on the **Start** button and select either **Sign out**, **Sleep**, **Shut down** or **Restart** from the **Shut down or sign out** option

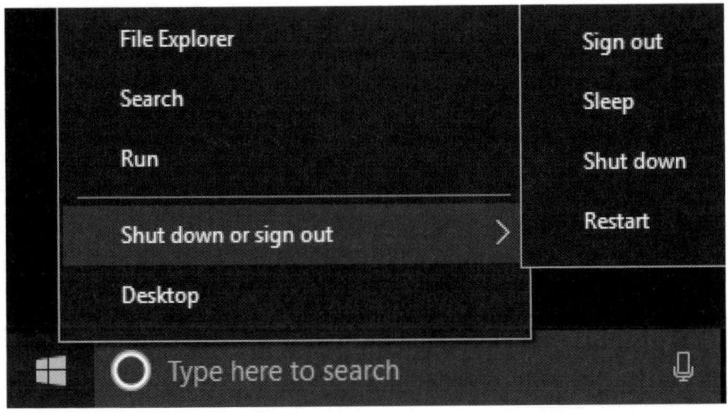

For some updates to Windows you will need to restart your computer for them to take effect.

Using a Microsoft Account

We live in a world of ever-increasing computer connectivity, where users expect to be able to access and share their content wherever they are. This is known as Cloud computing, with content being stored on online servers, from where it can be accessed by authorized users.

Without a Microsoft Account you will not be able to access the full functionality of the apps listed here.

In Windows 10, this type of connectivity is achieved with a Microsoft Account. This is a registration system (which can be set up with most email addresses and a password) that provides access to a number of services via the Windows 10 apps. These include:

- **Mail**. This is the Windows 10 email app that can be used to access and manage your different email accounts.
- **People**. This is the address book app.
- **Calendar**. This is the calendar and organizer app.
- **Windows Store**. This is the online store for previewing and downloading additional apps.
- **OneDrive**. This is the online backup and sharing service.

Creating a Microsoft Account

It is free to create a Microsoft Account – this can be done with an email address and, together with a password, provides a unique identifier for logging into your Microsoft Account and the related apps. There are several ways in which you can create and set up a Microsoft Account:

- During the initial setup process when you install Windows 10. You will be asked if you want to create a Microsoft Account at this point. If you do not, you can always do so at a later time.
- When you first open an app that requires access to a Microsoft Account. When you do this you will be prompted to create a new account.
- From the **Accounts** section of the **Settings** app (for more information about the Settings app see pages 46-53).

Whichever way you use to create a Microsoft Account, the process is similar:

1. When you are first prompted to sign in with a Microsoft Account you can enter your account details, if you have one, or

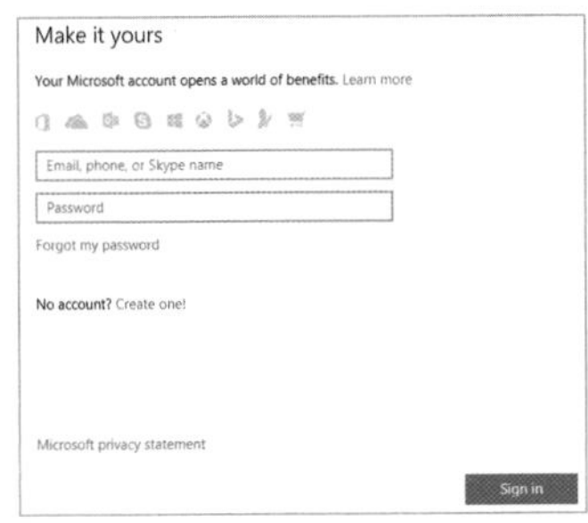

2. Click on the **No account? Create one!** link

3. Enter your name, an email address and a password for your Microsoft Account

4. Click on the **Next** button to move through the registration process

5. Enter your password again to confirm your account

6. Click on the **Finish** button in the final window to complete setting up your Microsoft Account

Microsoft Account details can also be used as your sign-in for Windows 10 (see pages 58-59).

Personalization

Customizing the look and feel of Windows 10 is a good way to feel like it is your own personal device. This can be done with some of the options in the Personalization section of the Settings app. To do this:

1. Open the **Settings** app (see page 36) and click on the **Personalization** button

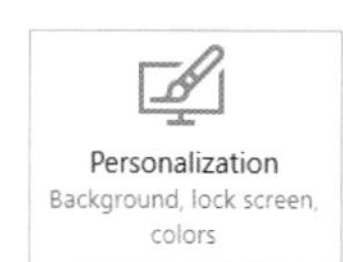

2. Click on the **Background** button to select a Desktop background. Select **Picture** in the Background box and click to select a picture, or click on the **Browse** button to select one of your own pictures

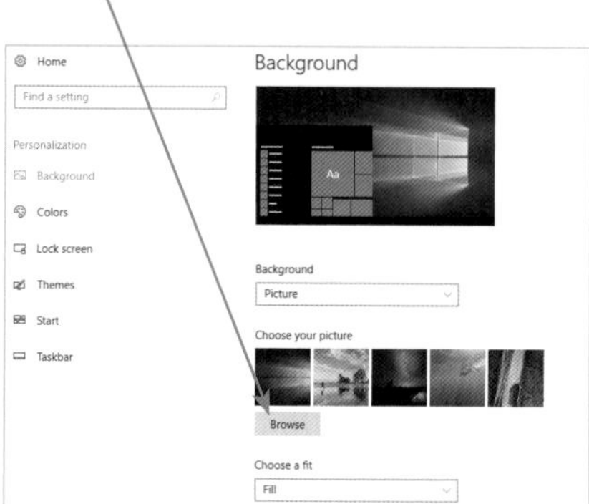

3. Click on the **Colors** button to select an accent color for the current background, Start menu and Taskbar

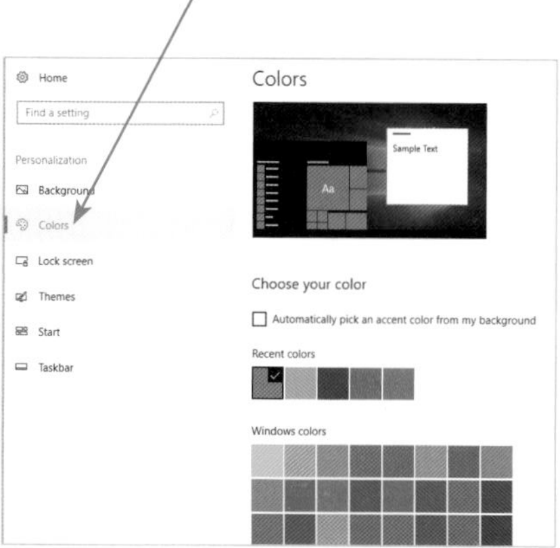

Click in the **Choose a fit** box in Step 2 to specify how the picture fills the background screen. The options are: Fill, Fit, Stretch, Tile, Center and Span.

4 Check this box **Off** to disable the automatic selection for the accent color

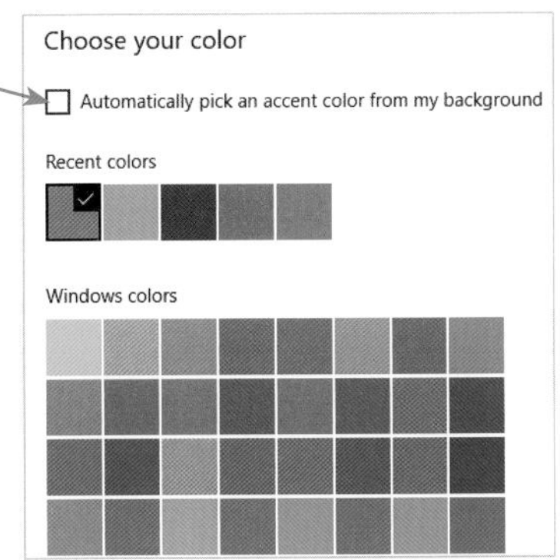

5 Click on one of the colors to select it for the accent color

6 Drag this button **On** to make the Start menu, Taskbar and Action Center transparent

More options

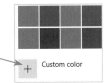

Transparency effects

On

7 Click on these buttons to use the color selected in Step 5 on the Start menu, Taskbar and Action Center and Title bars

Show accent color on the following surfaces

Start, taskbar, and action center

Title bars

8 Click on the **Custom color** button underneath the color palette

Custom color

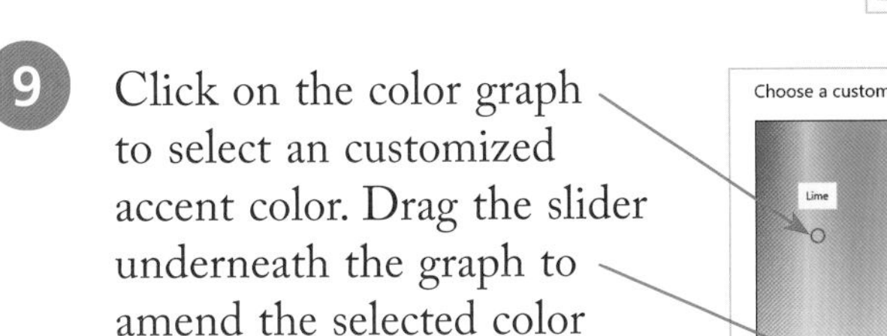

9 Click on the color graph to select an customized accent color. Drag the slider underneath the graph to amend the selected color

10 Click on the **Done** button to use the color selected in Step 9

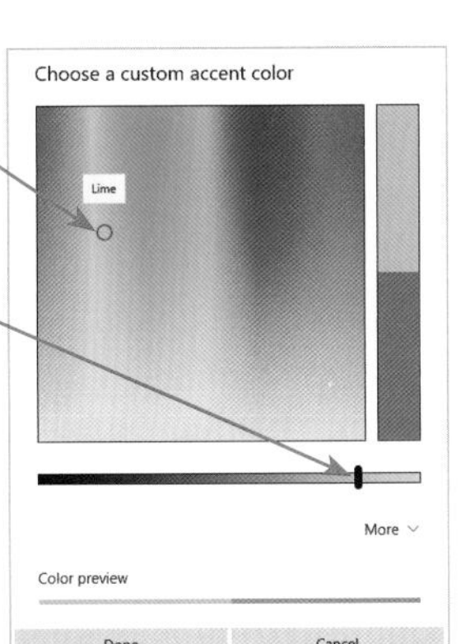

Color customization is a new feature in the Windows 10 Creators Update.

Lock Screen Settings

The Settings app enables you to set the appearance of the Lock screen, including selecting your own photo for the Lock screen background. To do this:

1. Open the **Settings** app and click on the **Personalization** button

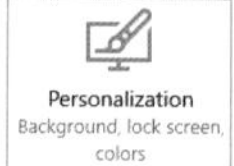

2. Click on the **Lock screen** button

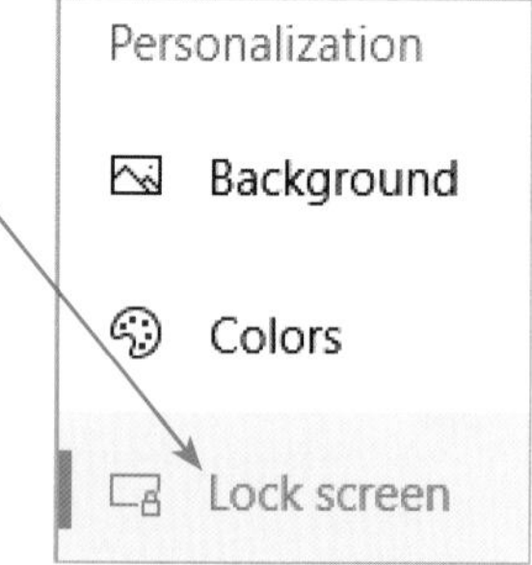

3. The current Lock screen background is shown here

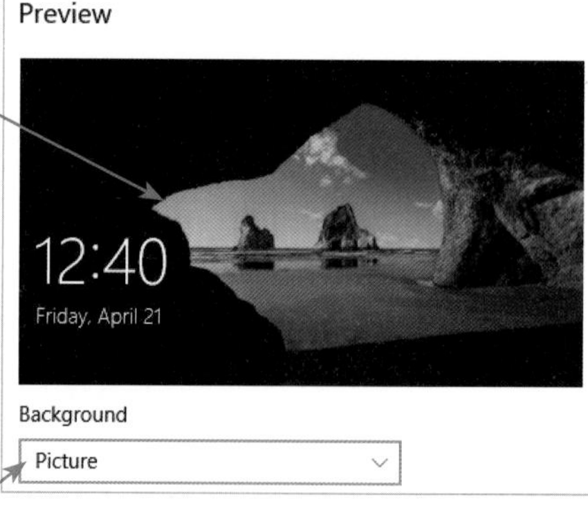

4. Click here to select options for the Lock screen background

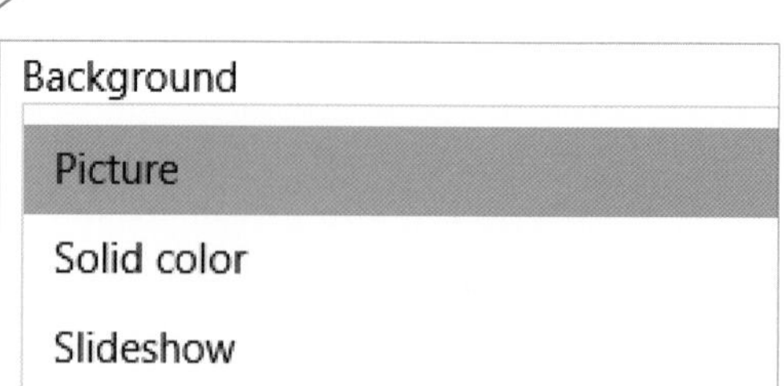

5. Select one of the Lock screen background options from **Picture, Solid color** or **Slideshow**

If **Slideshow** is selected in Step 5, you will then have the option to choose an album of photos to use as the slideshow for the Lock screen background.

6. For the Picture option, click on the **Browse** button to select your own picture

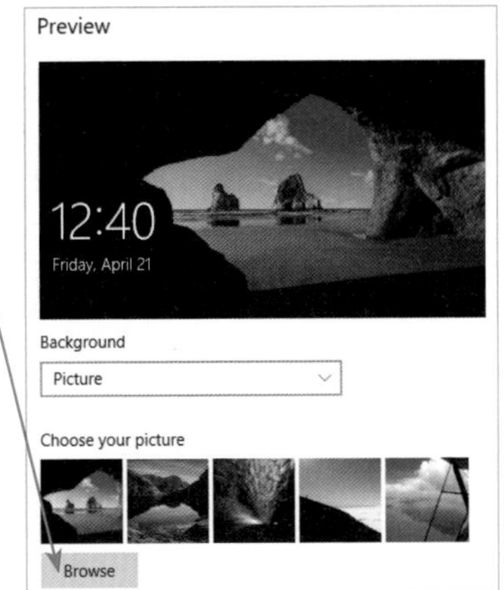

7. Select an image and click on **Choose picture** to add this to the background options for the Lock screen

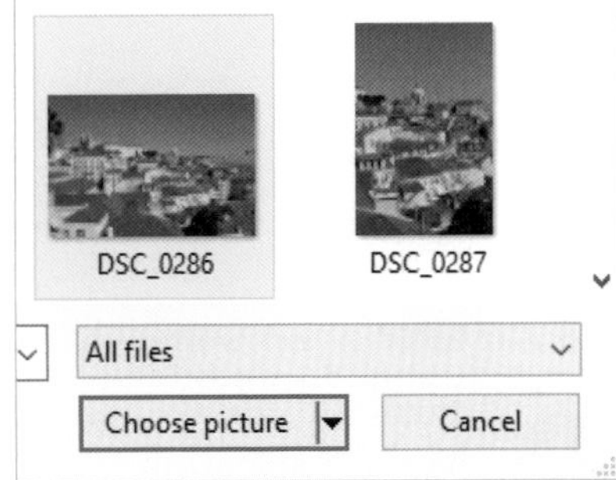

8. Other options for the Lock screen include selecting apps that display their detailed or quick status; options for screen timeout when not in use; and Screen saver settings

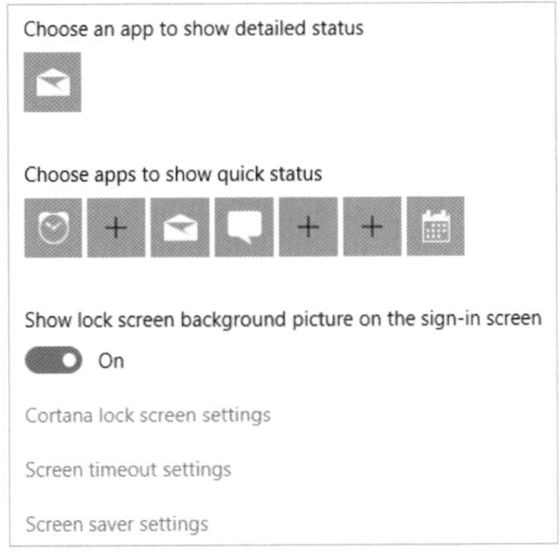

If you use your own images for the Lock screen background, these will remain available on the thumbnail row even if you switch to another image for the background.

Using Themes

Themes in the Windows 10 Creators Update can be used to customize several items for the look and feel of Windows:

NEW

Using themes has been amended in the Windows 10 Creators Update.

1. Open **Settings** and click on the **Personalization** button

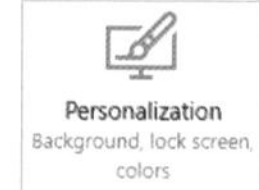

2. Click on the **Themes** button

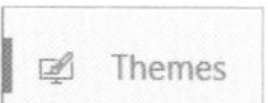

3. The current theme is displayed

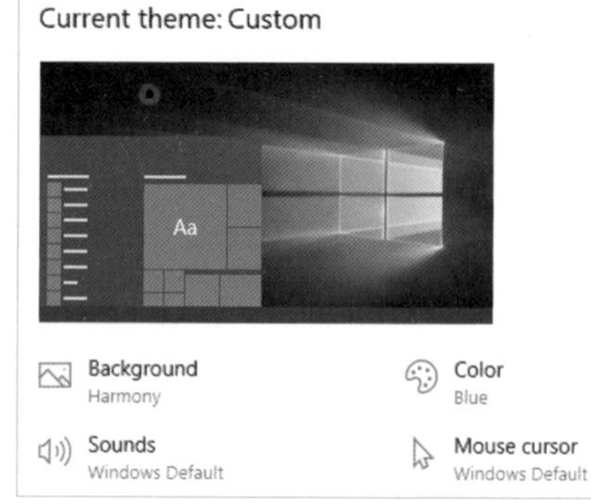

4. Make a selection for a customized theme, using **Background**, **Color**, **Sounds** and **Mouse cursor**

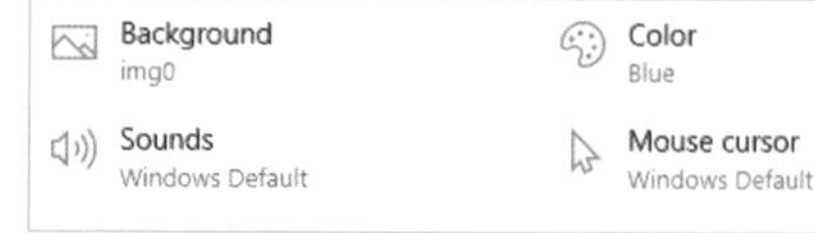

5. The selections for the customized theme are shown in the **Current theme** preview window

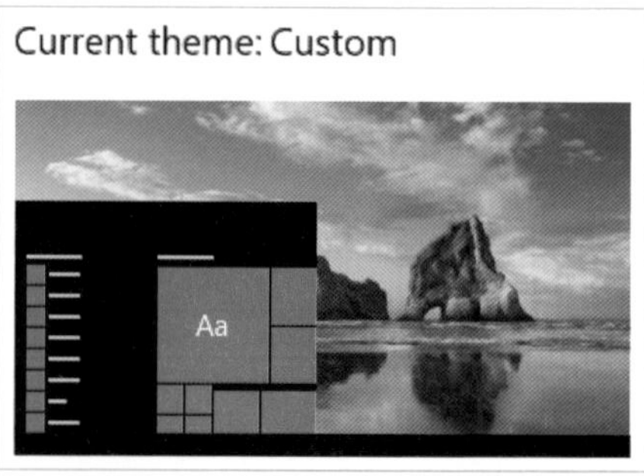

6. Click on the **Save theme** button to use it for the current theme

Save theme

7. Click on one of the preset themes to select it rather than customizing one

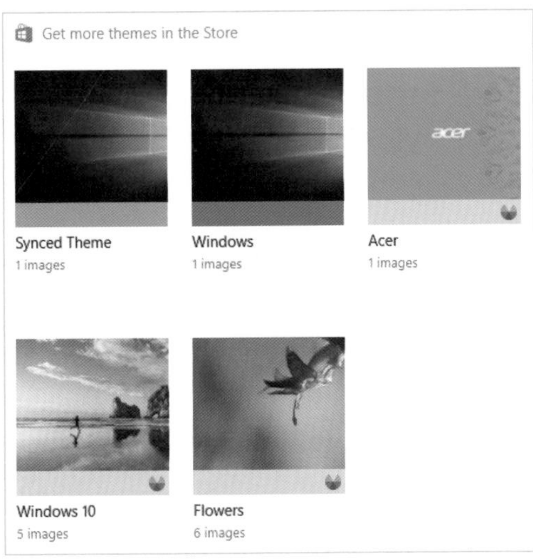

8. All of the elements of the preset theme are displayed in the preview window

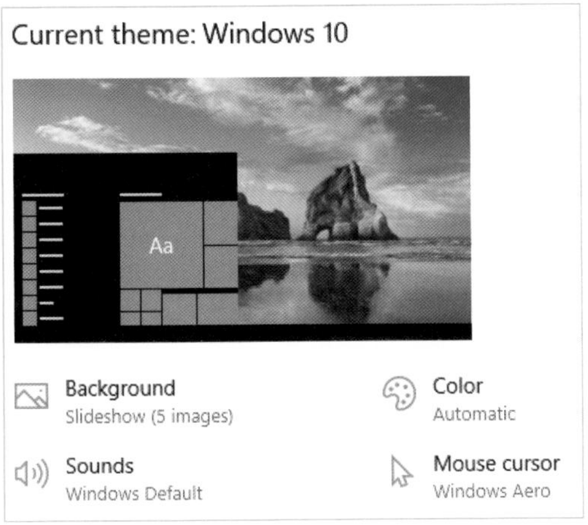

9. Click on **Get more themes in the Store** to download more themes that can be used on your PC

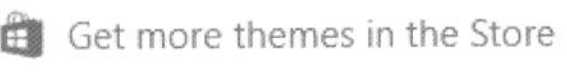

Screen Resolution

If you have a high-resolution screen, you may find that the text, as well as the icons, is too small. You can increase the effective size by reducing the screen resolution.

1. Open the **Settings** app, select **System** and then click on the **Display** button

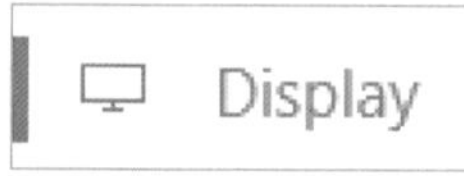

2. Drag this slider to change the overall brightness of items on your screen

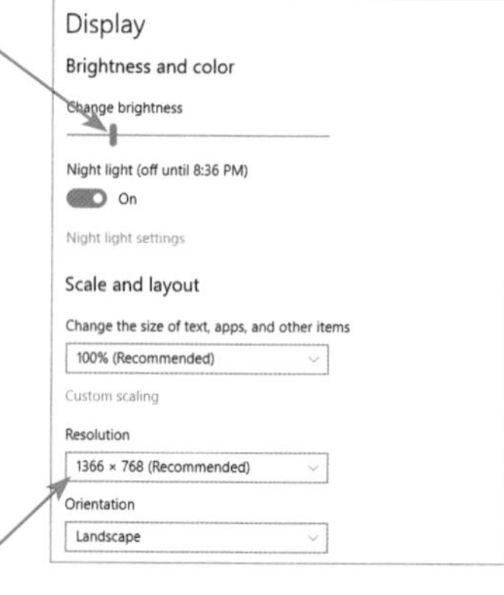

3. Click here to change the screen resolution. Select a new resolution value from the list

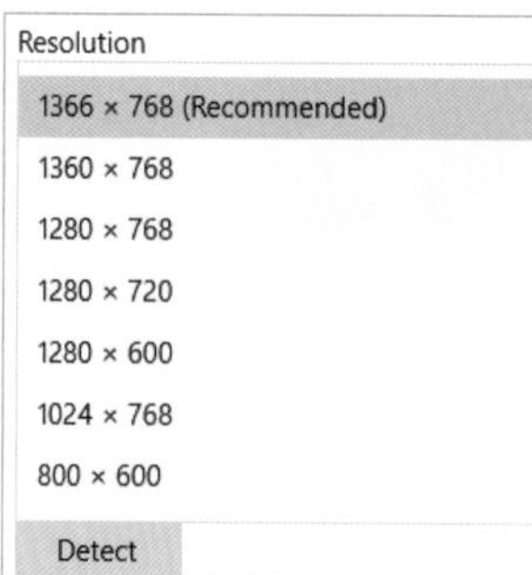

4. Click on the **Keep changes** button to change the screen resolution

Managing Storage

Computer storage is sometimes a feature that is taken for granted and left untouched. However, with the Windows 10 Creators Update there are some options for customizing how storage functions on your computer. To use these:

1. Open the **Settings** app, select **System** and then click on the **Storage** button

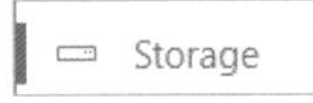

2. At the top of the window, the current storage is displayed, with the amount used shown by a colored bar

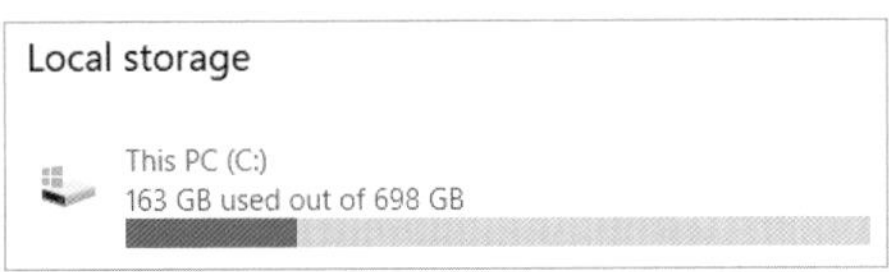

3. Drag the **Storage sense** button to **On** to enable Windows to free up storage space by deleting redundant files and items in the Recycle Bin

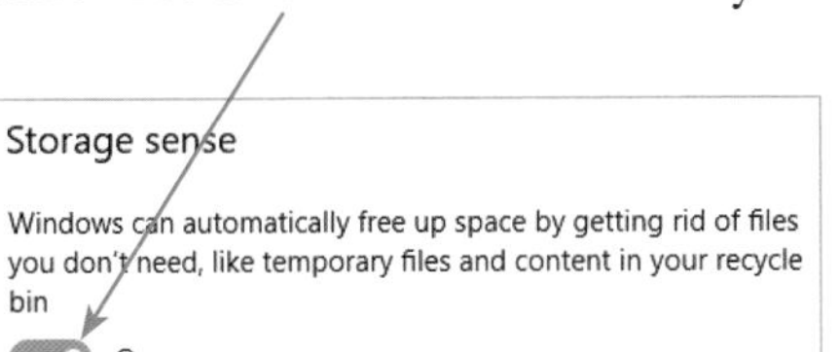

4. Under the **More storage settings** heading, click on **Change where new content is saved**

More storage settings

Change where new content is saved

5. Select options for where new items will be saved (this can be used if you are using more than one drive)

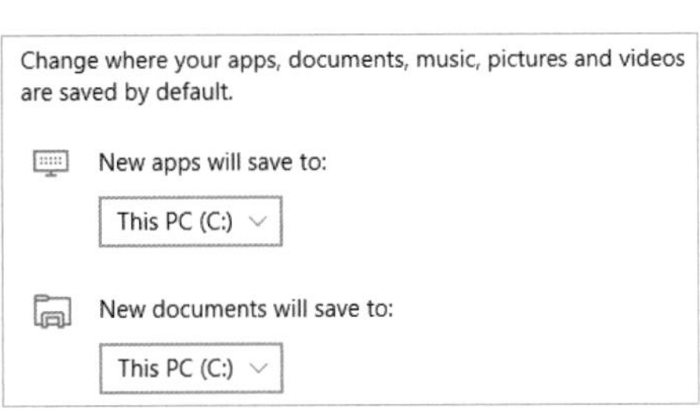

Storage sense is a new feature in the Windows 10 Creators Update.

Adjusting Volume

There are different sources of sounds on a laptop. The main two are:

- Sounds from the speakers
- Sounds from the Windows system

The volume for each of these can be adjusted independently of the other. To do this:

If you are going to be using your laptop near other people, and without headphones, make sure the volume controls are set at a reasonable level, so as not to annoy people.

1. Access the Control Panel (Start button > Windows System > Control Panel) and click on the **Hardware and Sound** link

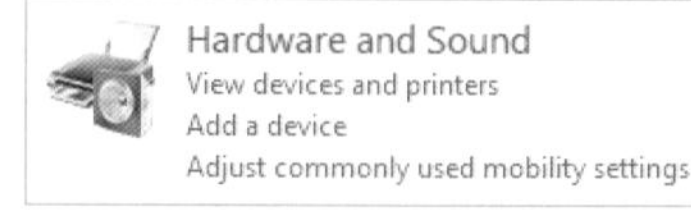

2. In the Sound section, click on the **Adjust system volume** link

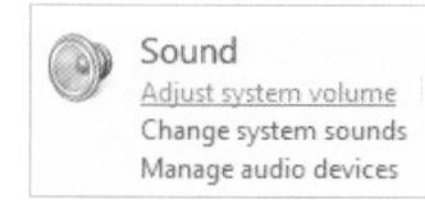

3. In the Volume Mixer window, drag the sliders to adjust the volume for a particular item

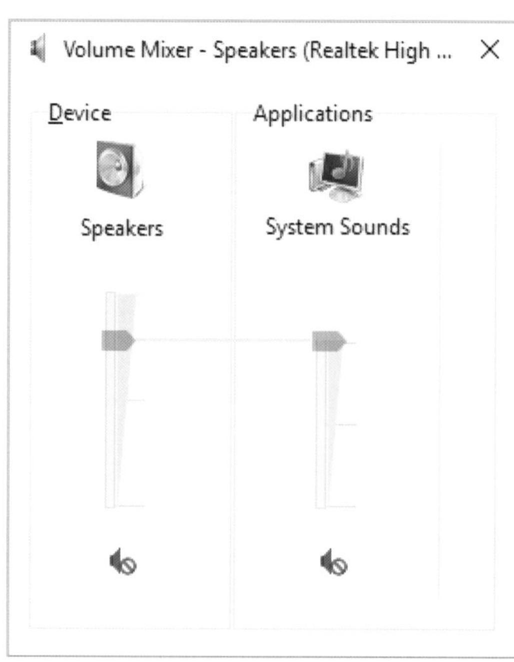

You can adjust the volume of your laptop's speakers, or mute them, by clicking on this icon in the Notifications area at the right-hand side of the Taskbar.

Loading CDs and DVDs

CDs and DVDs can be an important aspect of life with a laptop. They can be used to store information and also for playing music or movies, particularly when traveling. To load CDs or DVDs:

1. Locate the CD or DVD drive. This will be a slot that is located at the side or front of the laptop

2. Press the button on the front of the drive once, to eject the tray

3. Insert the CD or DVD into the tray and press the button again to close it, or push it in gently

Not all laptops have a CD or DVD drive, but external CD/DVD drives can be purchased and connected separately.

4. To view the location of the CD or DVD, click the **This PC** button in the File Explorer (see pages 35-36). The CD or DVD will be shown as a separate drive

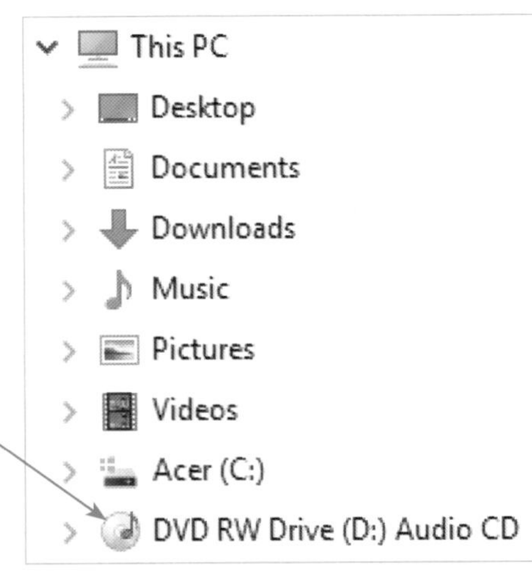

USB Flashdrives

USB flashdrives are small devices that can be used for copying files and then transferring them between computers. To connect a flashdrive to a laptop and use it:

Hot tip

Because of their size, USB flashdrives can be lost quite easily. When traveling, attach them to something like a keyring or keep them in a small pocket in your laptop case.

1. Connect the flashdrive to one of the laptop's USB ports

2. The flashdrive should be recognized automatically and the necessary software installed so that it is ready to use

3. Access the Desktop and click on the **File Explorer** button on the Taskbar

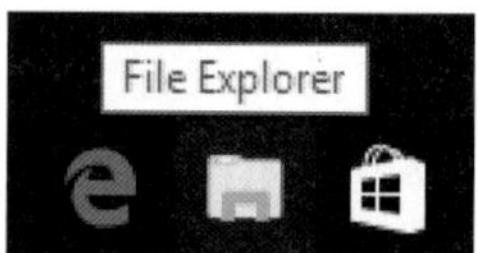

4. The flashdrive should appear as a removable drive under This PC. (Flashdrives can be renamed in File Explorer by right-clicking on the name and selecting **Rename**)

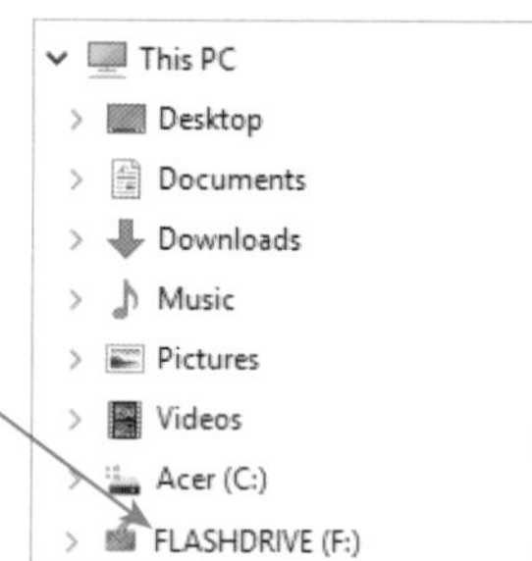

The File Explorer can also be accessed from the All Apps list on the Start screen (**Windows System** > **File Explorer**).

5. Double-click on the flashdrive to view its contents. The files can then be used in the same way as any others on your laptop

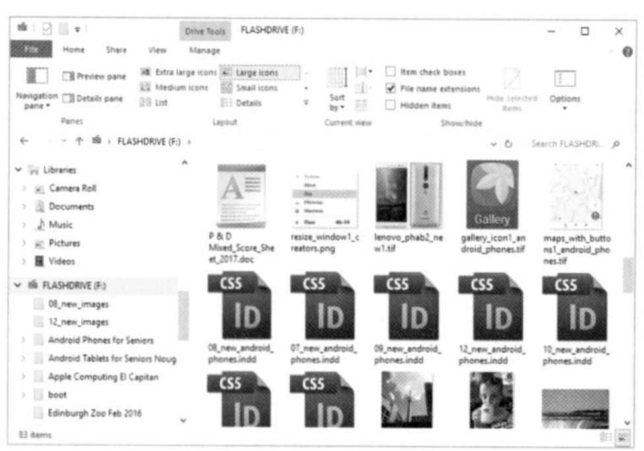

3 Getting Up and Running

This chapter looks at some of the features of Windows 10, including the settings and using the search facility, Cortana. It also shows how to access and use the File Explorer.

Sign-in Options

Each time you start up your laptop you will need to sign in. This is a security feature so that no-one else can gain unauthorized access to your account on your laptop. The sign-in process starts with the Lock screen, and then you have to enter your password.

1. When you start your laptop the **Lock screen** will be showing. This is linked to the sign-in screen

You can lock your laptop at any point by pressing the **WinKey** + **L**.

2. Click on the **Lock screen**, or press any key, to move to the **Sign-in** screen. Enter your Microsoft Account password (see page 45) and press **Enter**, or click on this arrow

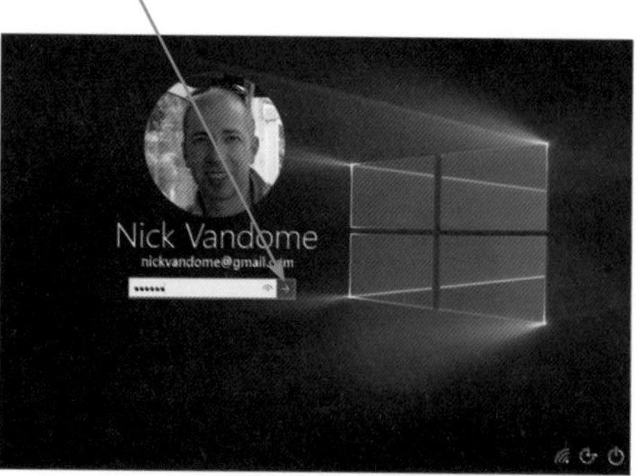

You will get an error message if you enter the wrong password, or if you simply mis-key and cause an incorrect character to be added.

3. On the sign-in screen, click on this button to select **Ease of Access** options

4. Click on this button to select **Power off** options, including Shut down and Restart

5. If there are other users with an account on the same laptop, their names will be displayed here

6. Click on another user to access their own sign-in screen

You can sign in with a Local Account or a Microsoft Account. If you sign in with the latter you will have full access to the related services, such as Mail and People. Also, you will be able to sync your settings and use them on another computer with your Microsoft Account.

Sign-in settings

Settings for how you sign in can be accessed from the Accounts section in the Settings app:

1. Access the **Settings** app and click on the **Accounts** button

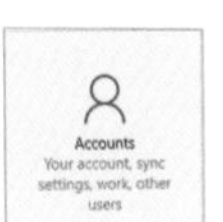

2. Under **Sign-in options**, select options to change your password, create a picture password or create a PIN instead of a password

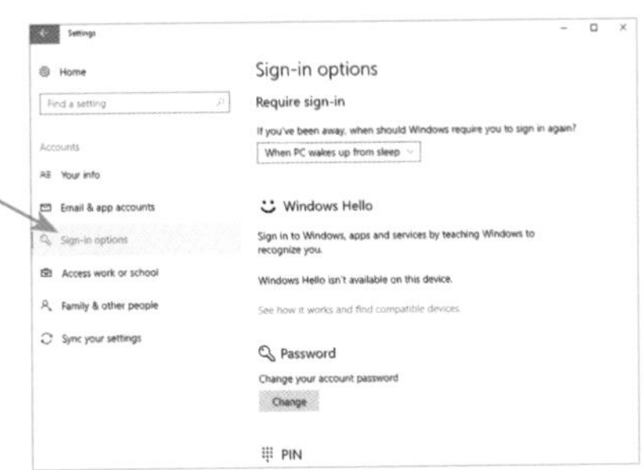

3. The picture-password option is designed primarily for touchscreen devices but can also be used with a mouse. Select a picture and draw a pattern to use as your sign-in

Windows Hello is a function that uses biometric authentication for signing in to Windows 10. This is either done by scanning your face or with a fingerprint reader. However, specialist hardware is required, and this is not available on many devices at present.

Settings

Accessing Settings

The Settings in Windows 10 provide options for how you set up your computer and how it operates. There are 11 main categories of Settings, each of which have a number of sub-categories. The Settings app can be accessed in various ways:

1. Click on the **Start** button 

2. Click on the **Settings** button on the Start menu or the **Settings** tile on the Start menu; or 

3. Click on the **Notifications** button on the Taskbar 

4. Click on the **All settings** button; or 

5. Enter **Settings** into the **Search** box and click on the **Settings** button

6. In the **Settings** app, click on one of the main categories to view the options within that category

Add the **Settings** app to the Taskbar for quick access. To do this, access it from the Start menu, right-click on it and click on **More** > **Pin to taskbar**.

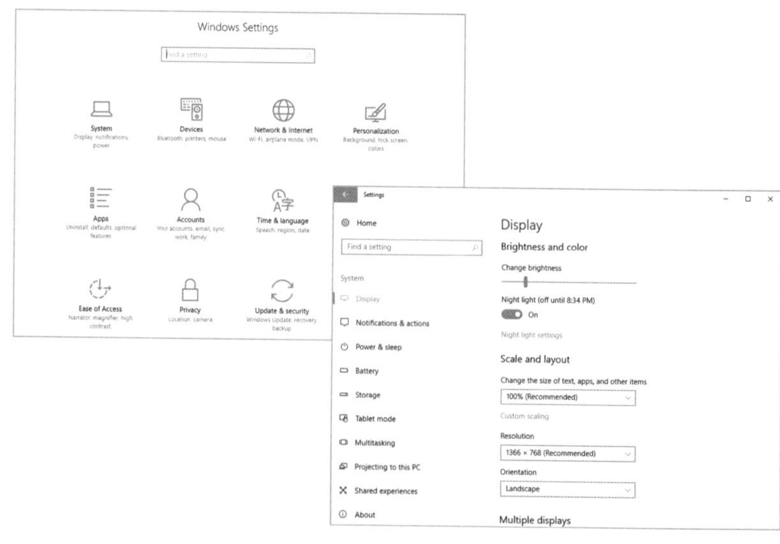

Settings categories

The categories for the Windows 10 Creators Update are:

- **System.** These are settings for how your laptop operates, including options for the display, notifications, power and sleep, battery and storage.
- **Devices.** These are settings for how devices connect to your laptop, including Bluetooth devices, printers, touchpad and USB devices.
- **Network & Internet.** These are settings for connecting to networks, including connecting to the internet, by Wi-Fi, Ethernet cable or dial-up modem.
- **Personalization.** These are settings for personalizing a range of options for your laptop, including background, colors, Lock screen, themes, Start menu and the Taskbar.
- **Apps.** These are settings for managing apps on your laptop, including viewing details about them and allocating default apps for specific tasks and file types.
- **Accounts.** These are settings for viewing and changing account settings and also setting up new accounts.
- **Time & language.** These are settings for the time, language and region used on your laptop.
- **Gaming.** These are settings for managing gamer options, including activating Game Mode and using the Game Bar.
- **Ease of Access.** These are settings for accessibility options, including the narrator for speaking items, the magnifier for magnifying areas of the screen, displaying high contrast and using closed captions (subtitles).
- **Privacy.** These are settings for general privacy options and also location settings for apps using your location.
- **Update & security.** These are settings for updating Windows, backing up your data and troubleshooting a range of options.

The separate Apps and Gaming settings are new features in the Windows 10 Creators Update.

In the Gaming settings, Game Mode ensures the best experience when playing games, and the Game bar is a control bar that opens when some types of games are played.

Searching

Searching for items and information on computers and the internet has come a long way since the first search engines on the web. Most computer operating systems now have sophisticated search facilities for finding things on your own computer as well as searching over the web. They also now have personal digital assistants, which are voice-activated search functions, which can be used instead of typing search requests.

The Cortana Search box in Step 1 can be displayed as an icon by right-clicking in it and selecting **Cortana** > **Show Cortana icon** (or **Show search box**, to revert).

Windows 10 has a search box built in to the Taskbar, which also includes the personal digital assistant, Cortana. This can also be used for a wide range of voice-activated tasks.

Using the Search box for text searching

To use the Search box for text-only searches, over either your laptop or the web:

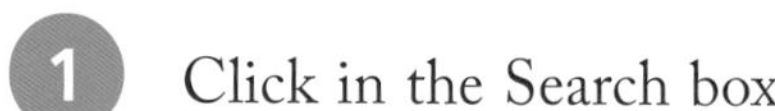

1. Click in the Search box

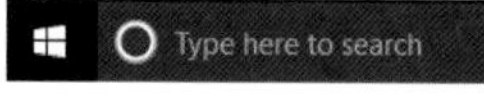

2. Enter a search term (or website address)

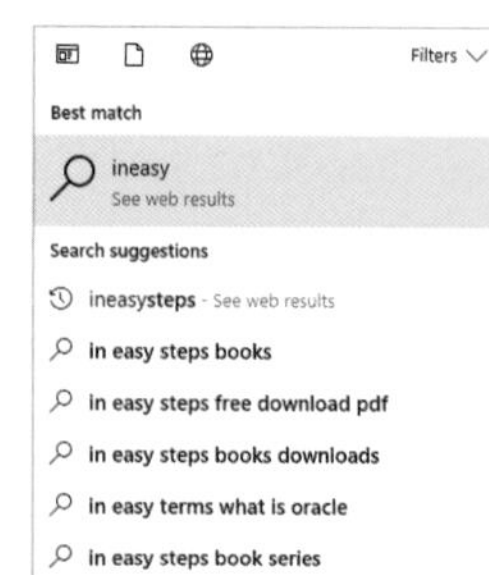

3. Click on one of the results, or on the **See web results** button, to view the search results page in the Microsoft Edge browser

The top search result is displayed at the top of the window in Step 3.

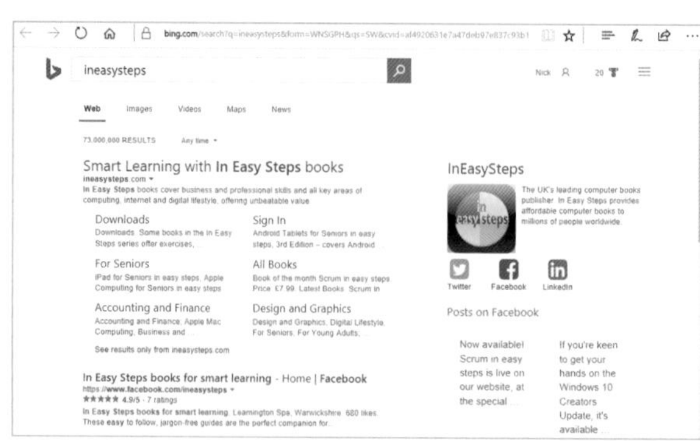

Asking a question

The Search box can also be used to ask specific questions:

1. Enter a question in the Search box

2. Click on the **See web results** button at the top of the Search box to view the results in the Microsoft Edge browser (in some instances, the answer will be displayed at the top of the Cortana Search box too)

Don't forget

The magnifying glass icon indicates that a search is going to be undertaken on the web, and this will be displayed on a search results page, as in Step 2.

Searching over your laptop

As well as searching over the web, the Search box can also be used to find items on your laptop:

1. Enter a search query into the Search box and click on one of the results to open the item on your computer

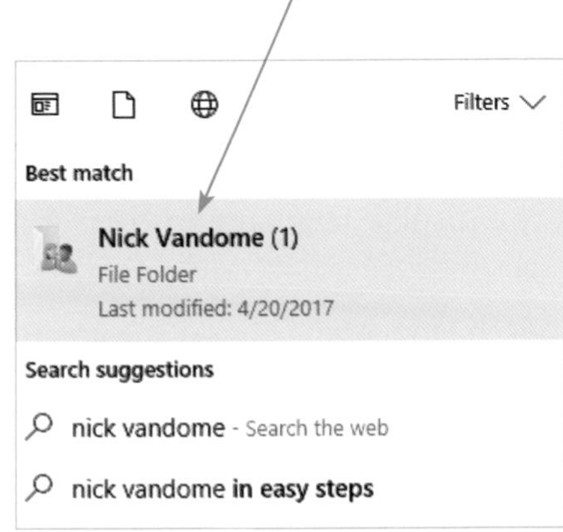

If you are searching for a keyword over files on your computer, the search will be conducted over the text in documents and folders, not just the document titles. It will also search over the online backup and storage facility, OneDrive, if you have this set up.

Setting Up Cortana

To ensure that you can use Cortana to perform voice searches and queries, the language settings on your Windows 10 laptop have to be set up correctly. To do this:

1. Open the **Settings** app and click on the **Time & language** button

2. Click on the **Region & language** button

3. Click here to select a country or region

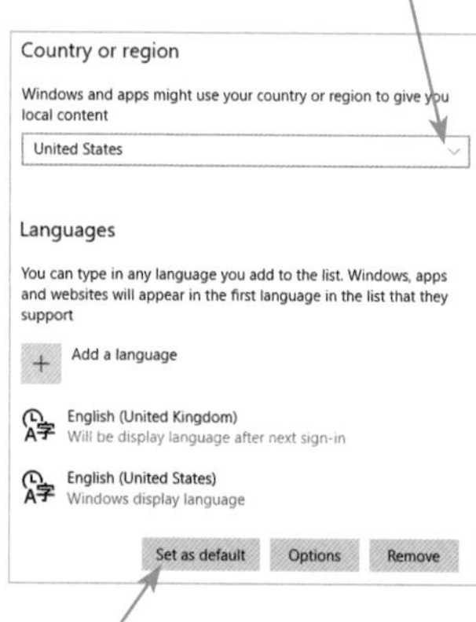

4. Click on the required display language and click on the **Set as default** button

5. Click on the **Speech** button under **Time & language**

6. Select the same **Speech language** as the one used as the display language in Step 4

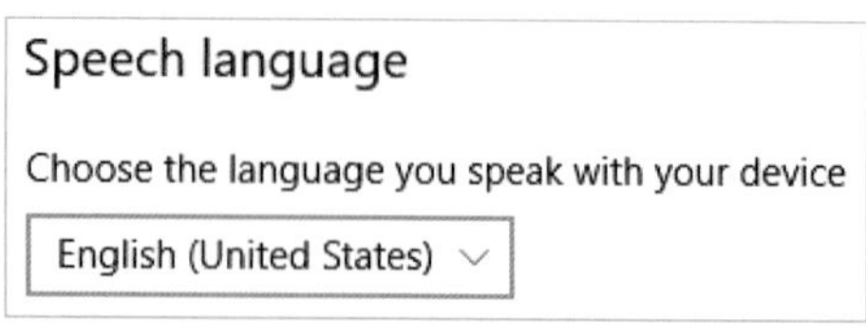

The country or region, display language and speech language should be the same in order for Cortana to work.

If the Cortana Search box is not displayed once the languages have been set, restart your computer to apply the changes.

Using Cortana

Once the correct languages have been selected for Cortana, you have to ensure that your microphone is working properly since it will be used for voice queries with Cortana.

Setting up the microphone

To set up your laptop's microphone:

1. Open the **Settings** app and click on the **Time & language** button

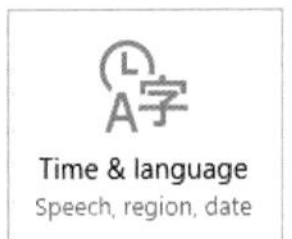

2. Click on the **Speech** button

3. Under the **Microphone** section, click on the **Get started** button

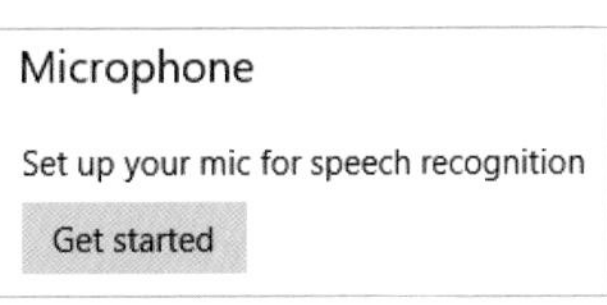

4. In the microphone wizard, click on the **Next** button

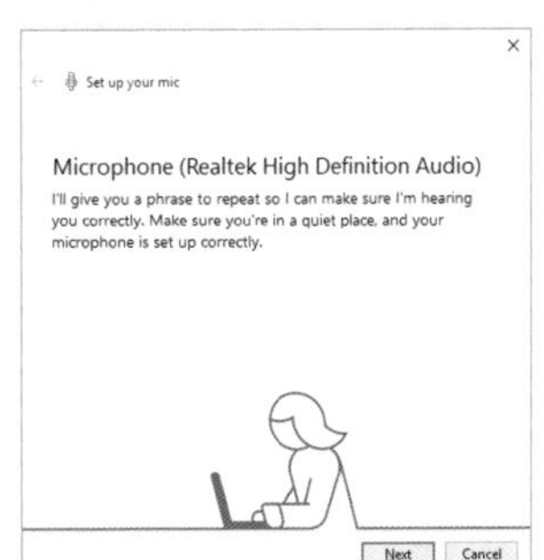

Set up your mic
Microphone (Realtek High Definition Audio)
I'll give you a phrase to repeat so I can make sure I'm hearing you correctly. Make sure you're in a quiet place, and your microphone is set up correctly.
Next
Cancel

5. Repeat the phrase in the wizard window to complete setting up your microphone. (If the setup is successful, the wizard will move to the completion page automatically)

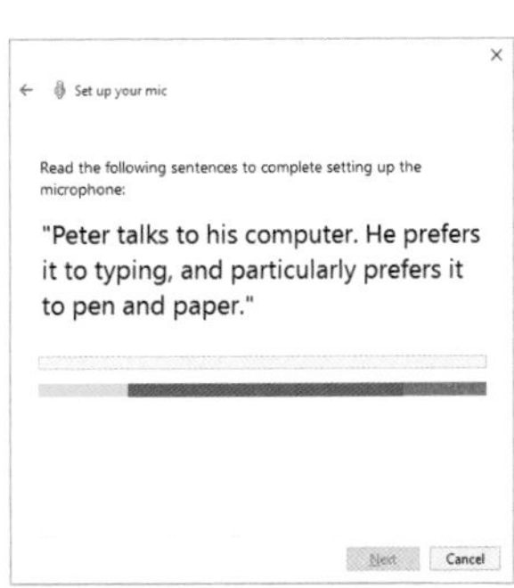

6. Click on the **Finish** button

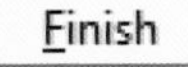

Most modern laptop computers have built-in microphones, but an external one may need to be attached to a desktop computer.

It can take Cortana a bit of time to fully recognize your voice and style of speech. Make sure that there is no loud background noise when you are using Cortana.

...cont'd

Voice searching with Cortana

As with text searches, Cortana can be used to search over various places and for different items:

1. Click on the microphone button in the Search box to begin a voice search

2. The Cortana symbol is displayed in the Search window with the word **Listening...** in the Search box. Say what you want to find

3. If Cortana cannot understand what you said, you are asked to try again

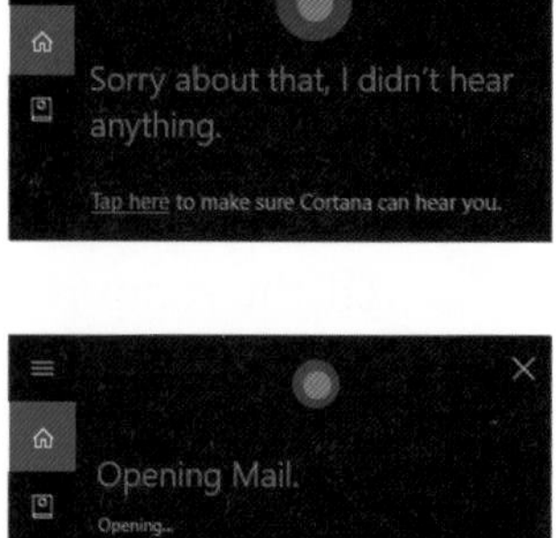

4. Cortana can be used to open specific apps, e.g. by saying **Open Mail**

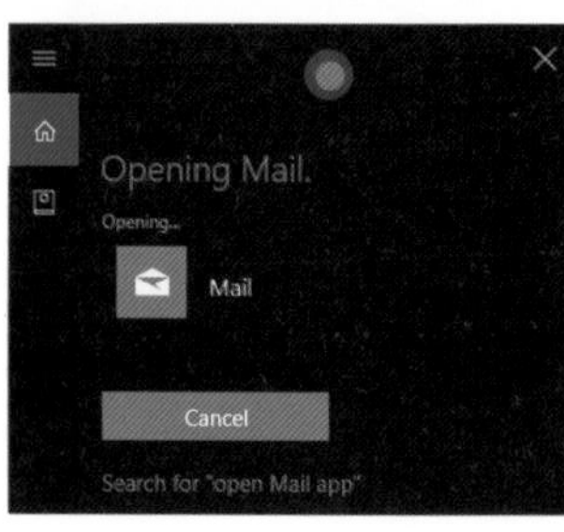

Cortana can be used directly from the Lock screen, to ask general queries such as "What is the weather in my area?" or to play a song from the Groove Music app.

5. If the query is general, e.g. **Open Microsoft**, various options will be displayed

6. For a specific request, e.g. **Open Microsoft Edge**, the required app will be opened

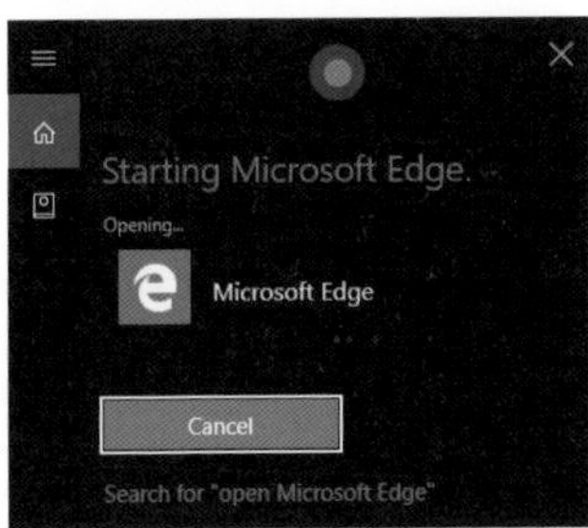

In the Windows 10 Creators Update, Cortana voice commands can be used to turn off, restart or put your PC to sleep. They can also be used to change the system volume. Also, an increasing range of apps support Cortana so can be used in conjunction with it, e.g. for playing movies with Netflix.

Text searches with Cortana

Once Cortana has been set up, text searches can be performed and a range of other information can be displayed by Cortana.

1. Click in the Search box to start a text search
2. Before a search is started, Cortana displays a range of information it thinks useful, such as the weather forecast and items from your calendar

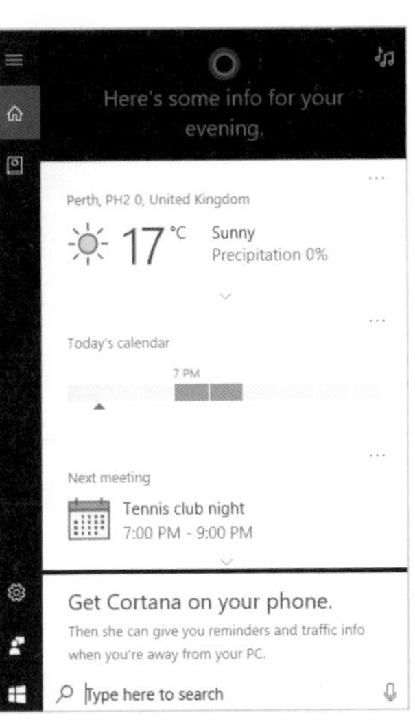

Viewing Notifications

In the modern digital world there is an increasing desire to keep updated about what is happening in our online world. With Windows 10, the Action Center (containing the Notifications panel) can be used to display information from a variety of sources, so that you never miss a notification from one of your apps. To view your notifications:

There are some enhancements in the Action Center in the Windows 10 Creators Update. Similar notifications can now be grouped together; the Quick Actions buttons have been enhanced; and some notifications (such as those for apps that are downloading) have progress bars to indicate how far through the operation they are.

Click on a notification to open it and view its full contents.

Notifications for certain apps also appear onscreen for a short period of time in a small banner, to alert you to the fact that there is a new notification.

1. Click on the **Notifications** button on the Taskbar

2. New notifications appear at the top of the panel. For selecting what appears, see next page

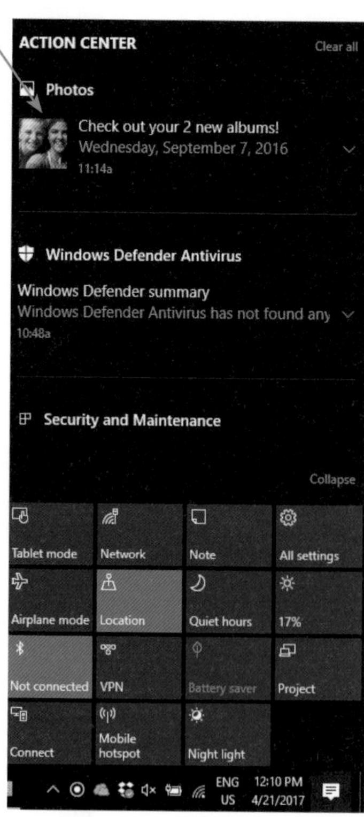

3. Quick action buttons appear at the bottom of the panel. Click on an item to activate or deactivate it (when a button is blue, the item is active)

Settings for notifications

To change settings for the Action Center:

1. Click on the **Settings** app and access **System** > **Notifications & actions**

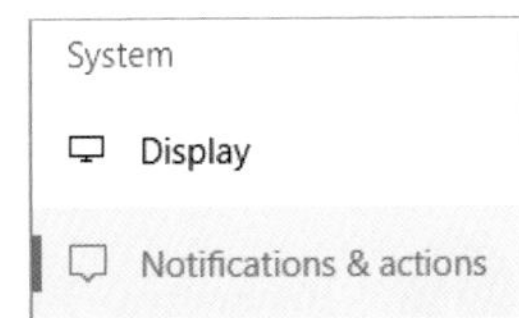

2. Under the **Quick actions** heading, click on the items and drag them into a new position to change where they appear in the Notifications panel

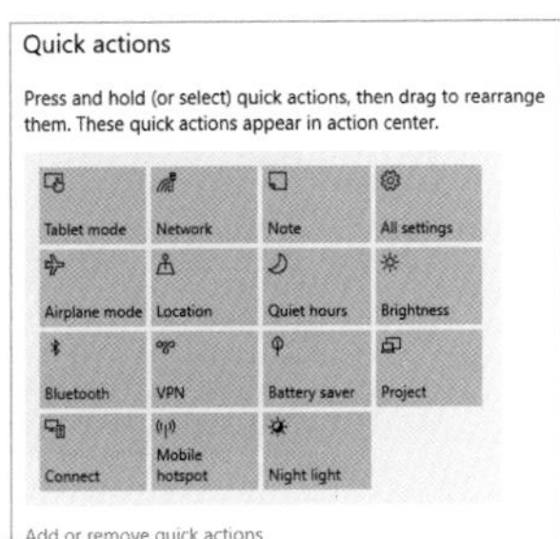

3. Click on the **Add or remove quick actions** link to turn **On** or **Off** the default items on the Taskbar

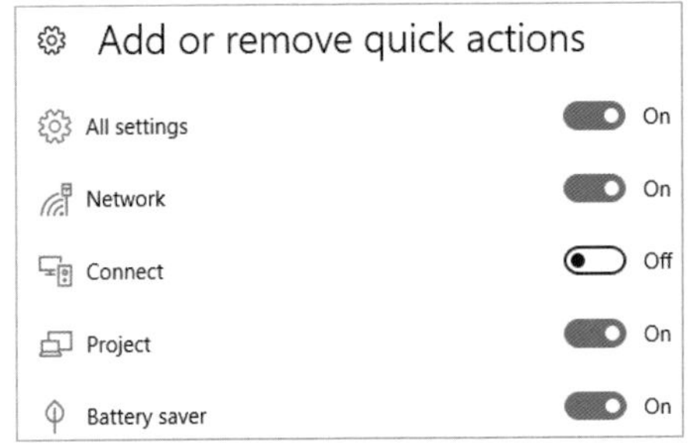

4. Under the **Get notifications from these senders** heading, drag the buttons **On** or **Off** to specify the items that appear in the Action Center. For instance, if the **Mail** button is **On**, you will be notified whenever you receive a new email

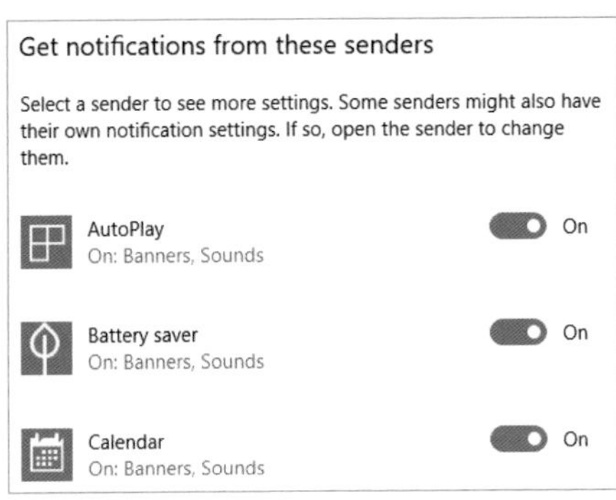

The Notifications area on the Taskbar on the previous page can be customized by right-clicking on the Taskbar and selecting **Taskbar settings** > **Select which icons appear on the taskbar**.

If notification icons are added to the Taskbar, their options can be selected by right-clicking on them.

Notifications can also be shown on the Lock screen by dragging the **Show notifications on the lock screen** button to **On** in the **Notifications & actions** settings.

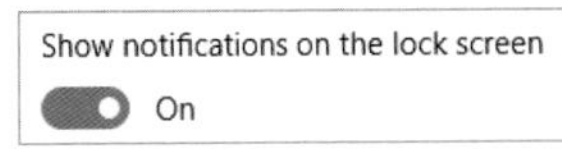

Opening File Explorer

Although File Explorer (formerly called Windows Explorer) is not necessarily one of the first apps that you will use with Windows 10, it still plays an important role in organizing your folders and files. To access File Explorer:

1. From the Desktop, click on this icon on the Taskbar, or

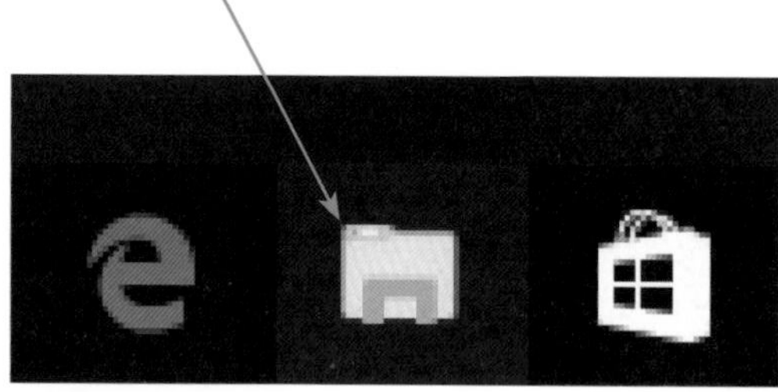

2. Press **WinKey** + **E**, and File Explorer opens at the **Quick access** folder

3. When File Explorer is opened, click on the **This PC** option to view the top-level items on your laptop, including the main folders, your hard drive and any removable devices that are connected

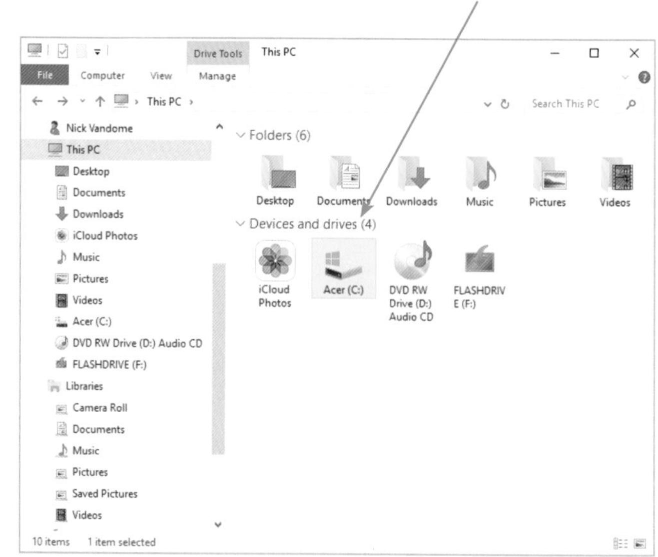

This PC displays files from different locations as a single collection, without actually moving any files.

You can click on the **Start** button and access File Explorer from here too (**Windows System** > **File Explorer**).

Quick Access in File Explorer

When working with files and folders there will probably be items which you access on a regular basis. The Quick access section of the File Explorer can be used to view the items that you have most recently accessed, and also to pin your most frequently-used and favorite items. To use the Quick access section:

1. Click on the **Quick access** button in the File Explorer Navigation pane so that the right-pointing arrow becomes downwards-pointing

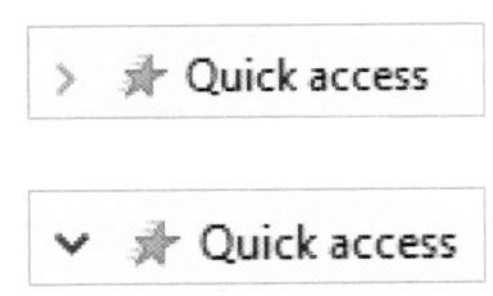

2. In the main window, your frequently-used folders and most recently-used files are displayed

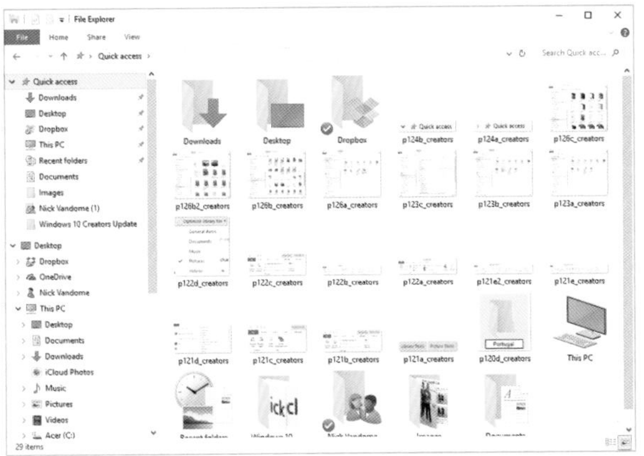

3. The folders are also listed underneath the **Quick access** button in the Navigation pane

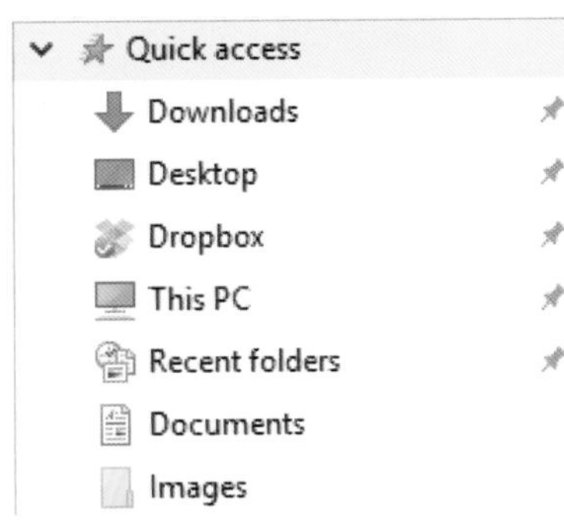

The items displayed under Quick access are not physically located here; the links are just shortcuts to the actual location within your file structure.

...cont'd

Adding items to Quick access

The folders that you access and use most frequently can be pinned to the Quick access section. This does not physically move them; it just creates a shortcut within Quick access. To do this:

1. Right-click on the folder you want to pin, and click on **Pin to Quick access**

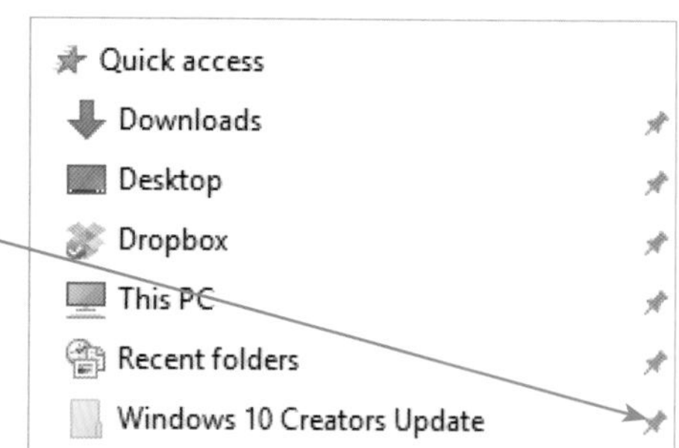

2. The folder is pinned to the Quick access section, which is denoted by the pin symbol; or

3. Drag the folder over the Quick access button until the **Pin to Quick access** option appears, and release

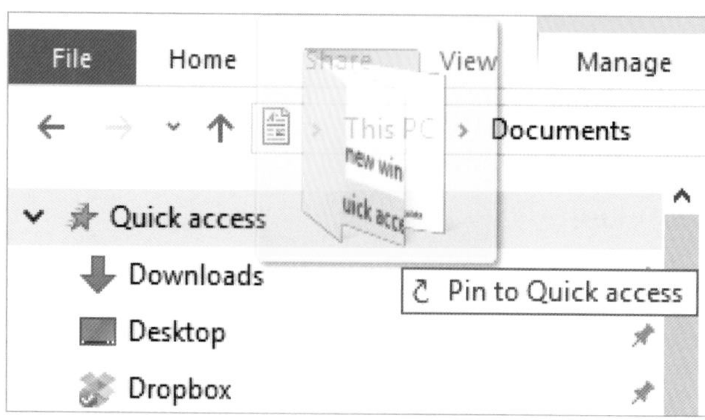

Scenic Ribbon

The navigation and functionality in the Libraries is provided by the Scenic Ribbon at the top of the window. This has options for the Library itself and also the type of content that is being viewed.

The Scenic Ribbon is also referred to as just the Ribbon.

1. Click on the tabs at the top of the Library window to view associated tools

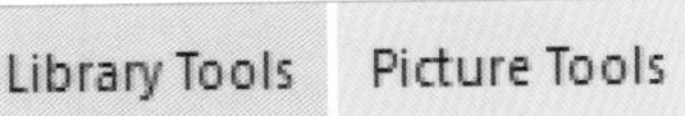

2. Click on the Library Tools tab to view the menus for the whole Library (see below)

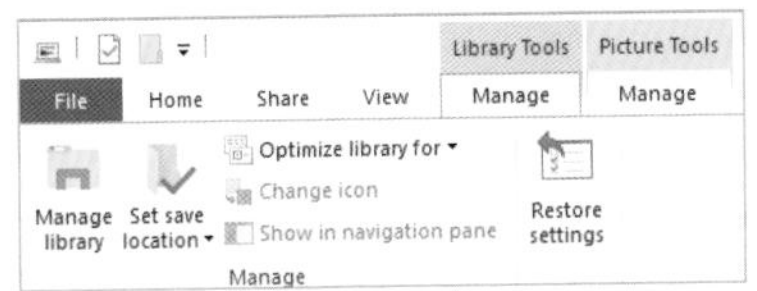

3. Click on the content tab (Picture Tools in this example) to view menus for the selected content

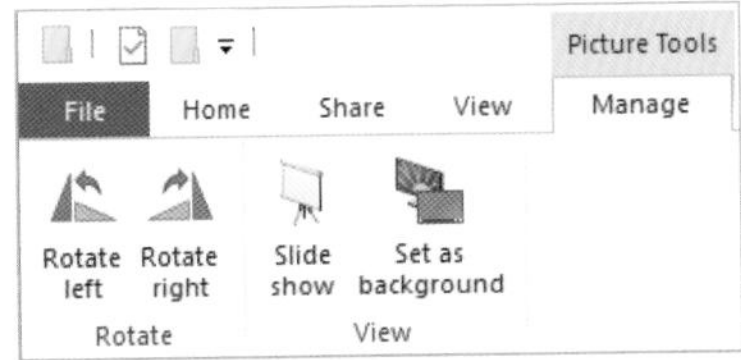

Library File menu

This contains options for opening a new window, closing the current window or moving to a frequently-visited location in the Library.

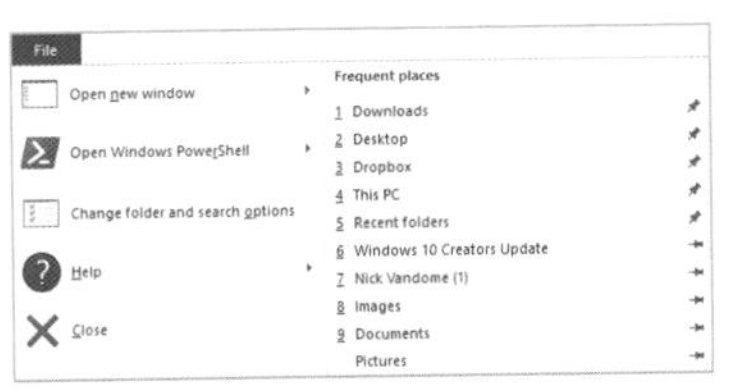

The **File** button in the Ribbon remains highlighted in blue, regardless of which other menu is accessed.

Library Home menu

This contains options for copying and pasting, moving, deleting and renaming selected items. You can also create new folders, view properties and select all items in a folder.

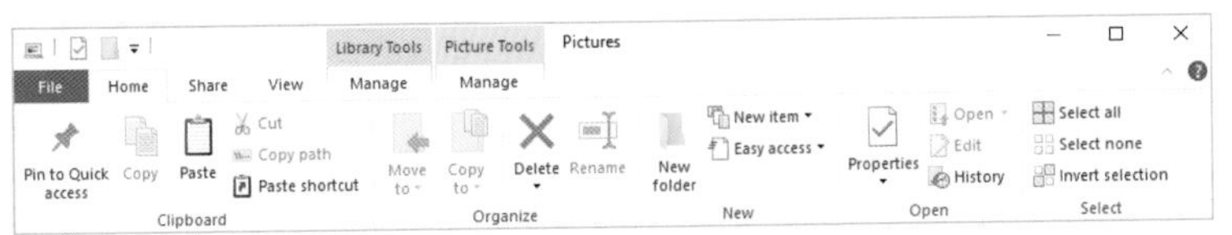

...cont'd

Library Share menu

This contains options for sharing selected items, by sending them to the HomeGroup or another user on the computer, burning them to a CD or DVD, creating a compressed Zip file or sending the items to a printer.

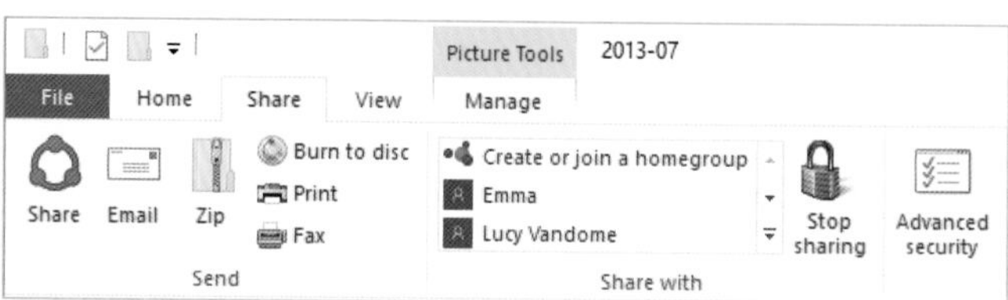

Library View menu

This contains options for how you view the items in the current active folder.

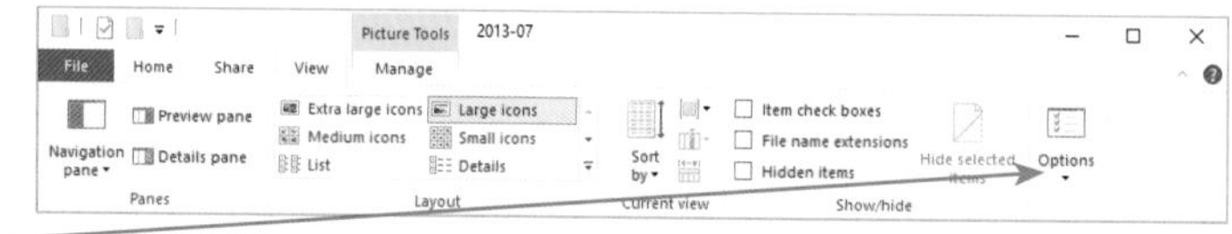

Click on the **Options** button on the View menu to set additional options for the operation of a folder and how items are displayed within it.

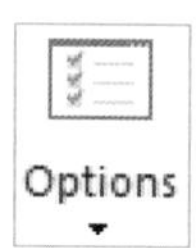

Library Manage menu

This contains options for managing specific libraries. Click on the **Manage library** button to add additional folders to the one currently being viewed.

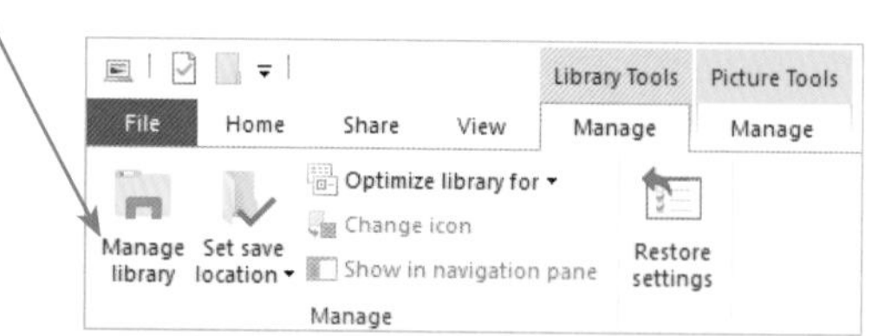

Library menu options

If there is a down-pointing arrow next to an item on a Library menu, click it to see additional options such as the **Optimize library for** button, which optimizes the folder for specific types of content.

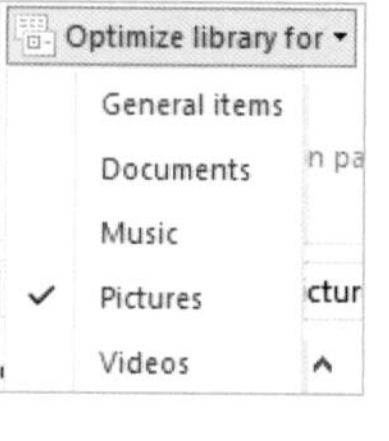

4 Working with Apps

In Windows 10, some apps are pre-installed, while hundreds more can be downloaded from the Windows Store. This chapter shows how to work with and organize apps in Windows 10.

Starting with Apps

The word "app" is now widely used to cover any computer program. So, in Windows 10 most programs are referred to as "apps", although some legacy ones may still be referred to as "programs".

There are three clear types of apps within Windows 10:

- **Windows 10 apps**. These are the built-in apps that can be accessed from the Start menu. They cover the areas of communication, entertainment and information, and several of them are linked together through the online sharing service, OneDrive. In Windows 10 they open in their own window on the Desktop, in the same way as the older-style Windows apps (see below).
- **Windows classic apps**. These are the older-style Windows apps that people may be familiar with from previous versions of Windows. These open in the Desktop environment.
- **Windows Store apps**. These are apps that can be downloaded from the online Windows Store, and cover a wide range of subjects and functionality. Some Windows Store apps are free, while others have to be paid for.

In Windows 10, all apps open directly on the Desktop and their operation is more consistent, regardless of the type of app.

Windows 10 apps

Windows 10 apps are accessed from the brightly-colored tiles on the Start menu (or listed on the left-hand side). Click on a tile to open the relevant app:

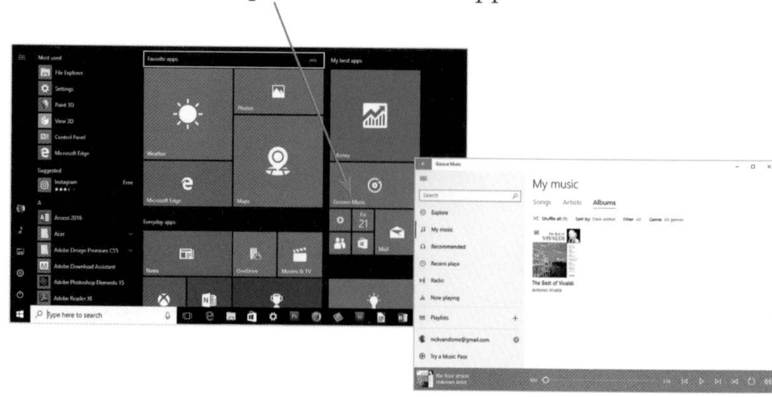

Windows classic apps

The Windows classic apps are generally the ones that appeared as default with previous versions of Windows, and would have been accessed from the Start button. The Windows classic apps can be accessed from the Start menu by using the alphabetic list, or searched for via the Taskbar Search box. Windows classic apps have the traditional Windows look and functionality, and they also open on the Desktop.

Some older Windows apps, such as Notepad and Paint, can be found in the Windows Accessories folder in the All Apps alphabetic list. Alternatively, they can be searched for using the Cortana Search box.

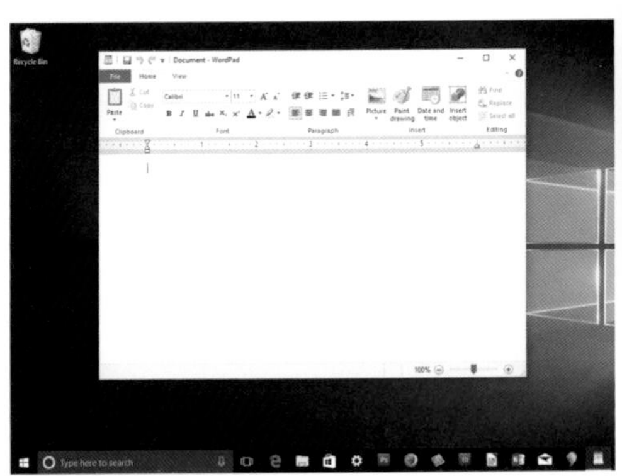

Windows Store apps

The Windows Store apps are accessed and downloaded from the online Windows Store. Apps can be browsed and searched for in the Store, and when they are downloaded they are added to the All Apps alphabetic list on the Start menu.

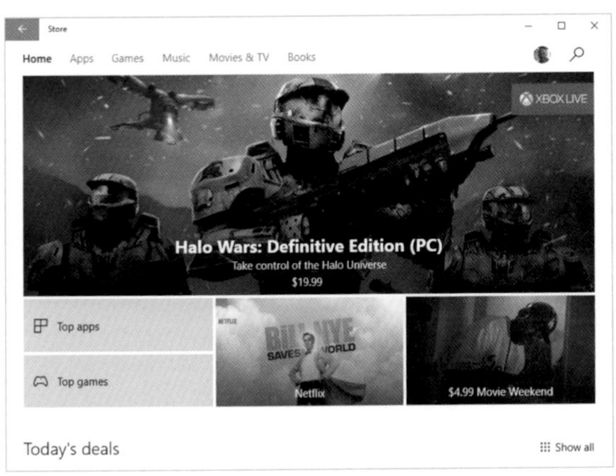

The Windows Store is accessed by clicking on the **Store** tile on the Start menu or on the Taskbar.

Windows 10 Apps

The Windows 10 apps that are accessed from the All Apps alphabetic list on the Start menu include:

Alarms & Clock. This provides alarms, clocks around the world, a timer and a stopwatch function.

Calculator. This is a standard calculator that also has an option for using it as a scientific calculator.

Calendar. This is a calendar which you can use to add appointments and important dates.

Camera. This can be used to take photos directly onto your laptop, but only if it has a built-in camera.

Connect. This can be used to connect a PC so that it can be used as a wireless projector.

Cortana. This is the personal digital assistant for Windows 10 that can be used to search for items.

Groove Music. This can be used to access the online Music Store, where music can be downloaded.

Mail. This is the online Mail facility. You can use it to connect to a selection of email accounts.

Maps. This provides online access to maps from around the world. It also shows traffic issues.

Messaging. This can be used to send text messages to other users, using a Microsoft Account.

Microsoft Edge. This is the default browser in the Windows 10 Creators Update.

Money. This is an information app that provides real-time financial news, based on your location.

Movies & TV. This is where you will see the movies and TV shows you buy in the Windows Store.

News. This is an information app that provides real-time news information, based on your location.

If some of the apps listed here are not pre-installed on your Windows 10 laptop, they can be downloaded from the Windows Store, where some of them are prefixed with MSN, e.g. MSN Money.

See pages 92-103 for more information about working with the Microsoft Edge browser.

The Movies & TV app is named Films & TV in some regions.

OneDrive. This is an online facility for storing and sharing content from your computer. This includes photos and documents.

OneNote. This is a Microsoft note-taking app; part of the Office suite of apps.

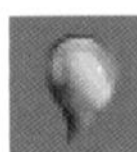

Paint 3D. This is an app that can be used to create, view and share 3D objects.

People. This is the address book app for adding contacts. Your contacts from sites such as Gmail and iCloud can also be imported into the People app.

Photos. This can be used to view and organize your photos. You can also share and print photos directly from the Photos app.

Reader. This can be used to open and view documents in different file formats, such as PDF and TIFF.

Sports. This is one of the information apps that provide real-time sports news, based on your location.

Sticky Notes. This is an app for creating short notes that can be "stuck" to the screen, so that they are readily visible.

Store. This provides access to the online Windows Store for buying and downloading apps.

View 3D. This can be used to download and view 3D objects that have been created by you or other people.

Weather. This provides real-time weather forecasts for locations around the world. By default, it will provide the nearest forecast to your location.

Xbox. This can be used to download and play games, and also play online Xbox games.

OneDrive can also be used to share your content, such as photos and documents, with other people. See pages 112-115 for details.

There is a significant focus on 3D and Mixed Reality in the Windows 10 Creators Update. The **Mixed Reality Portal** app can be used to gain an overview of this technology.

Using Windows 10 Apps

In Windows 8 and 8.1, the newer-style Windows apps had a different look and functionality. However, in Windows 10 all of the apps have been created with a more consistent appearance, although there are still some differences.

Windows 10 apps

Windows 10 apps open in their own window on the Desktop (in Windows 8 and 8.1 they only opened in full screen) and they can be moved and resized in the same way as older-style apps:

1. Click and drag on the top toolbar to move the app's window

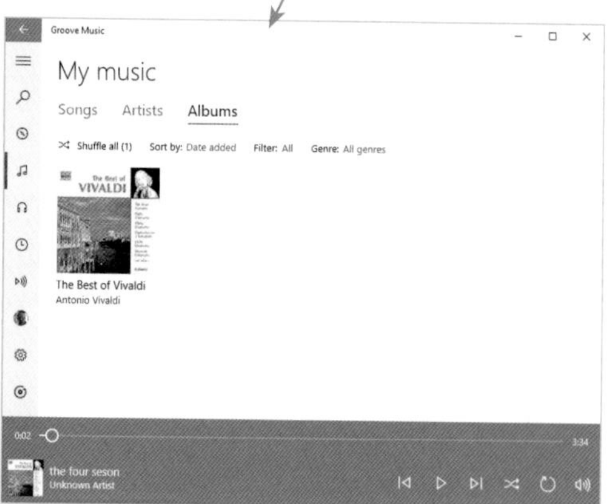

In Windows 10 there has been a conscious effort to achieve a greater consistency between the newer-style apps and the old, classic-style apps.

2. Drag on the bottom or right-hand border to resize the app's window (or the bottom right-hand corner to resize the height and width simultaneously)

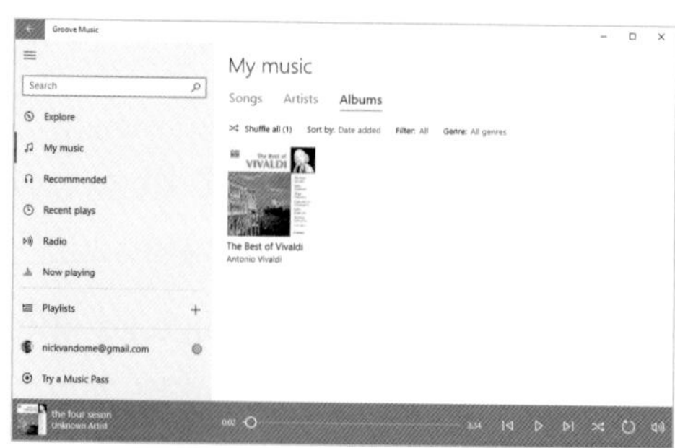

Windows 10 app menus

Some Windows 10 apps have their own menus:

1. Click on this button (if available) within the app's window to access its menu

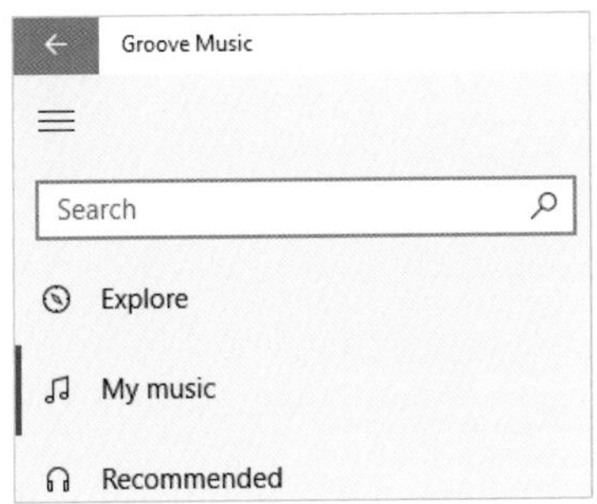

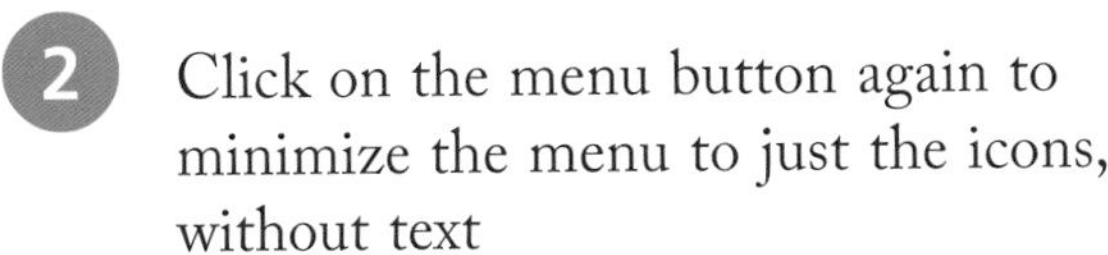

2. Click on the menu button again to minimize the menu to just the icons, without text

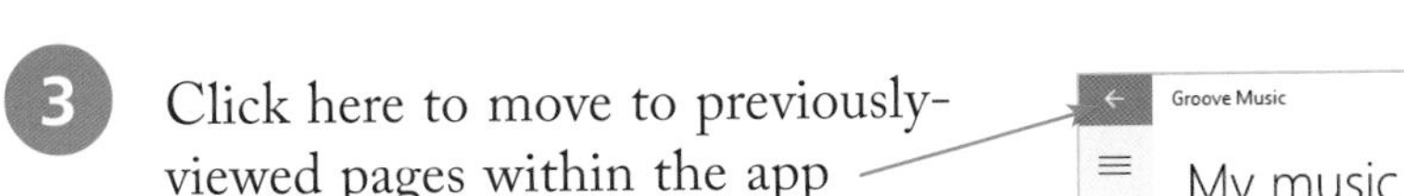

3. Click here to move to previously-viewed pages within the app

Don't forget

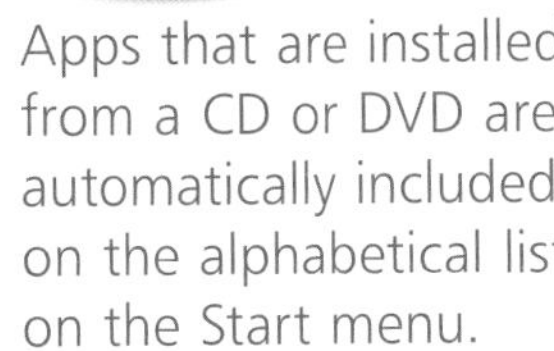

Apps that are installed from a CD or DVD are automatically included on the alphabetical list on the Start menu.

Managing an app's window

As with older-style apps, the Windows 10 apps also have the same control buttons on the top toolbar:

1. Click on this button to close the app
2. Click on this button to maximize the app's window
3. Click on this button to minimize the app's window (it will be minimized onto the Taskbar)

Closing Apps

There are several ways to close a Windows app:

- Click on the red **Close** button in the top-right of the window

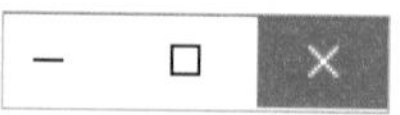

- Select **File** > **Exit** from the File menu (if available)
- Press **Alt** + **F4**

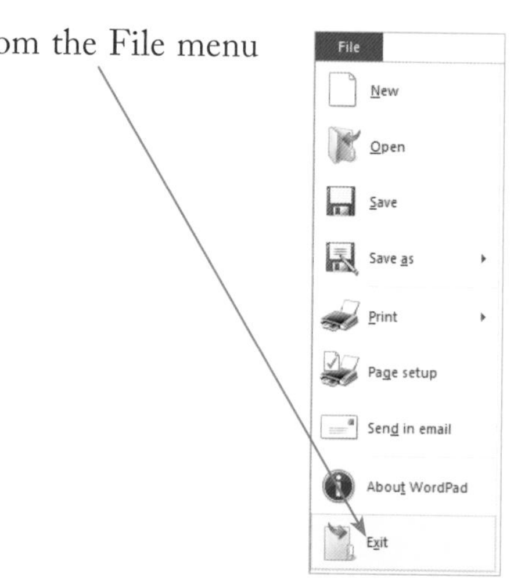

It is always worth saving a new document as soon as it is created. It should also be saved at regular intervals as you are working on it.

- Right-click on the icon on the Taskbar and select **Close window**

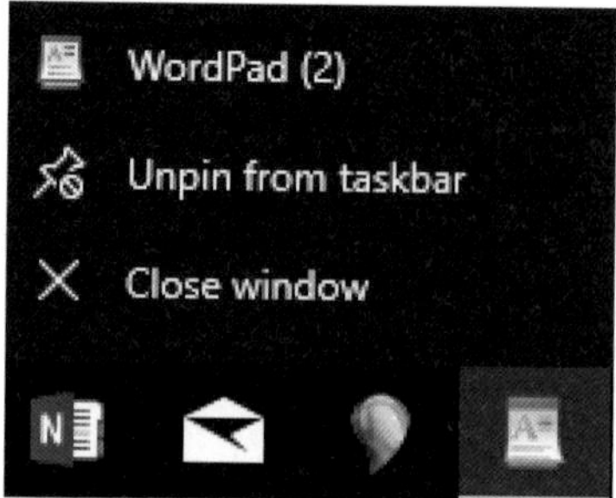

If any changes have been made to the document, you may receive a warning message advising you to save the associated file.

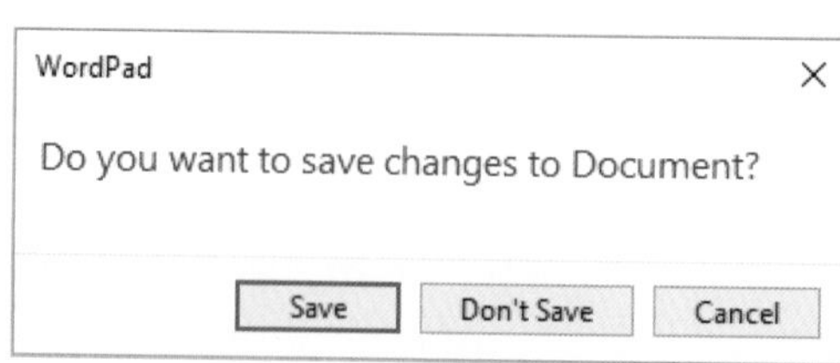

Viewing All Apps

There is a lot more to Windows 10 than the default Windows 10 apps. Most of the Windows apps that were available with previous versions of Windows are still there, and in the Windows 10 Creators Update they are all available directly from the Start button, on the Start menu. To access all of the apps:

1. Click on the **Start** button

2. All of the apps are displayed. Use the scroll bar to move through all of the apps, which are listed alphabetically

3. Click on a letter heading to view an alphabetic grid for finding apps. Click on a letter to move to that section

The All Apps list can be hidden in the Windows 10 Creators Update. This is a new feature, and can be done in **Settings** > **Personalization** > **Start**. Drag the **Show app list in Start menu** button to **Off**. The All Apps list is minimized to the side of the screen. Click on this button to maximize the list (the button above it is for viewing the tiles on the Start menu).

Searching for Apps

As you acquire more and more apps, it may become harder to find the ones you want. To help with this, you can use the Search box to search over all of the apps on your laptop. To do this:

1. Click in the Search box on the Taskbar

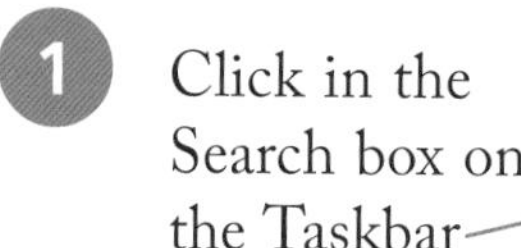

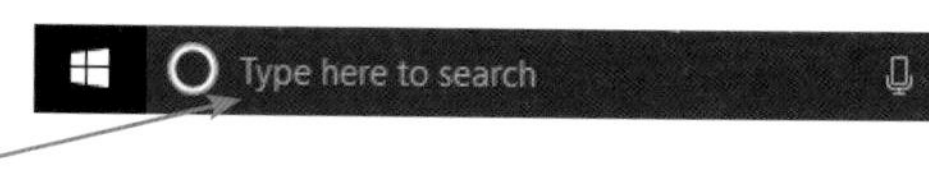

2. Enter a word in the Search box

3. As you type, relevant apps are displayed. When the one you are seeking appears, click on it to start the app

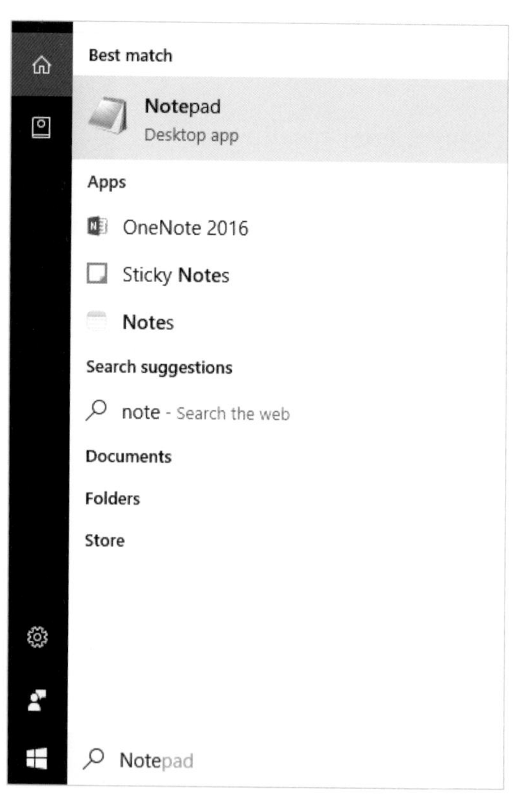

You just have to put in the first couple of letters of an app name, and the search will automatically suggest results based on this. The more that you type, the more specific the results become. Case does not matter when you are typing a search query.

Using the Windows Store

The third category of apps that can be used with Windows 10 are those that are downloaded from the Windows Store. These cover a wide range of topics and they provide an excellent way to add functionality to Windows 10. To use the Windows Store:

1. Click on the **Store** tile on the Start menu 

2. The currently-featured apps are displayed on the Home screen

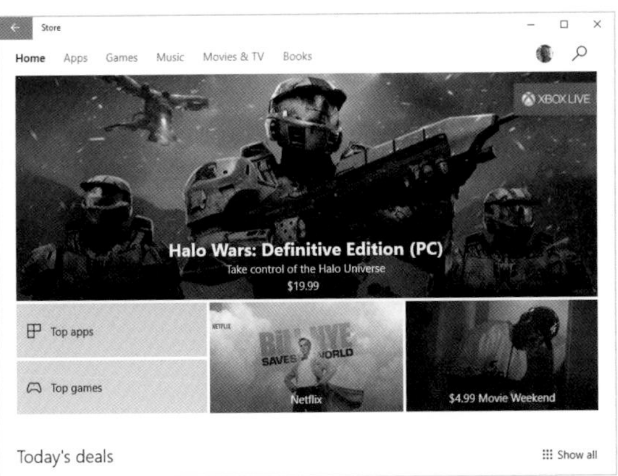

3. Scroll up and down to see additional featured apps

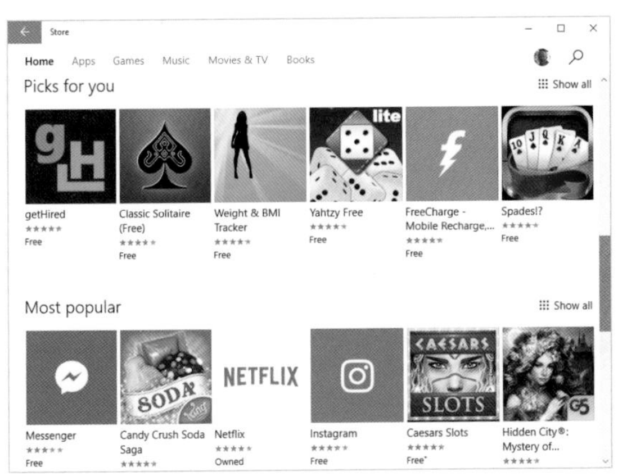

Windows 10 apps can all be downloaded from the Windows Store.

The Windows Store interface has been redesigned for the Creators Update to make it easier to find the apps that you want.

...cont'd

4. Click on the **Top apps** button on the Homepage and select apps under specific headings, e.g. **Best selling** apps

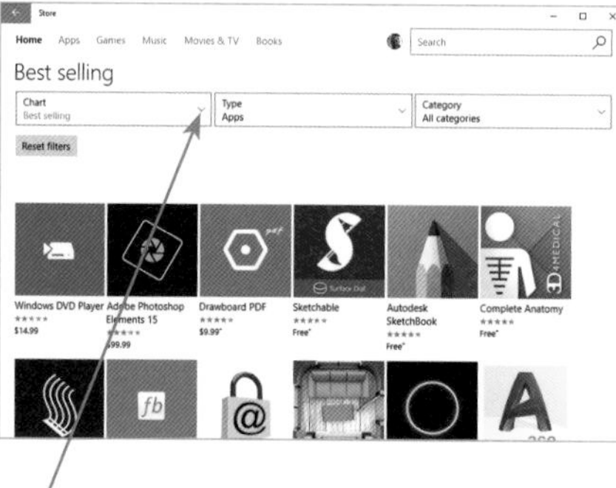

5. Click here to select options for viewing apps according to certain criteria, e.g. **Top free**

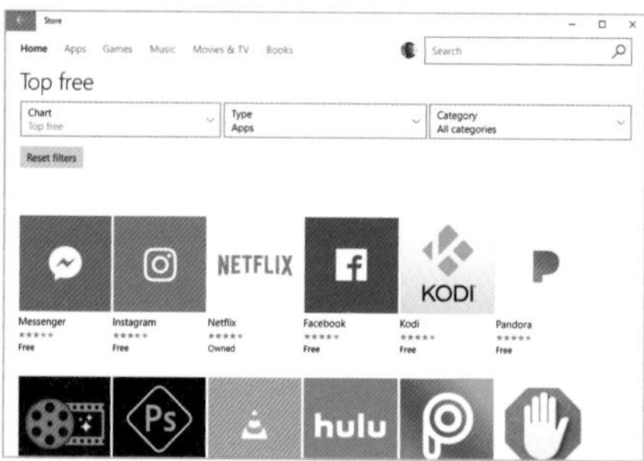

6. Click on an app to preview it, and for more details about the app

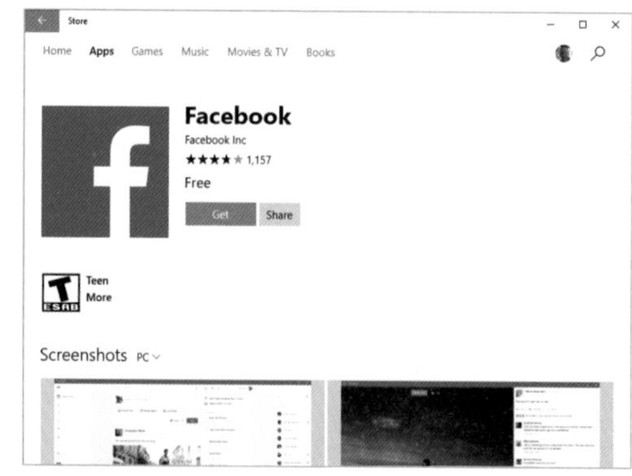

Scroll up and down in Step 6 to view ratings and reviews about the app and also any additional descriptions.

Buying Apps

When you find an app that you want to use, you can download it to your laptop. To do this:

1. Access the app and click on the **Get** (or price) button

If there is a fee for an app, this will be displayed instead of the **Get** button.

2. The app downloads from the Windows Store, and a **Downloading** message is displayed

3. The app is added to the Start menu and has a **New** tag next to it. This disappears once the app has been opened

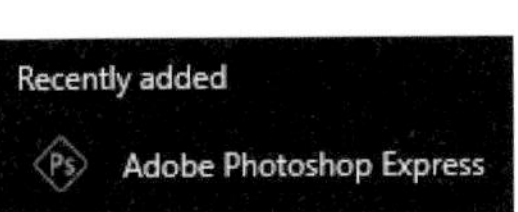

You need to have credit or debit card details registered on your Microsoft Account in order to buy paid-for apps.

4. Click on the app to open and use it (initially it will be available under the **Recently added** section of the Start menu, as well as its own alpha listing)

Recently added
Adobe Photoshop Express

Viewing Your Apps

As you download more and more apps from the Windows Store you may lose track of which ones you have obtained, and when. To help with this, you can review all of the apps you have downloaded, from within the Windows Store. To do this:

1. Open the Windows Store and click on your account picture button at the top of the screen

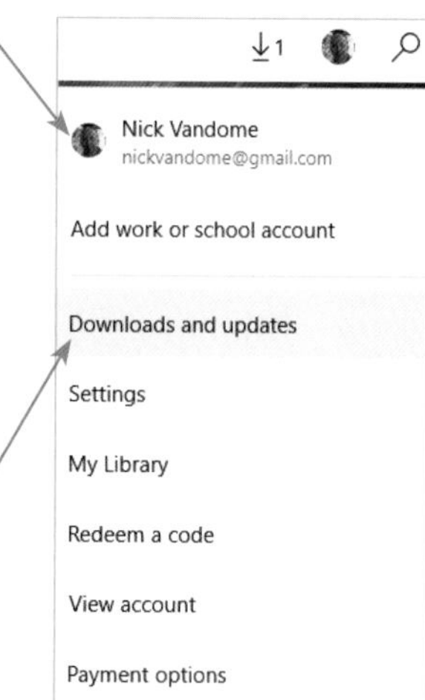

2. Click on the **Downloads and updates** button

3. All of the apps that have been downloaded are displayed. Tap on the **Check for updates** button to see if there are any updates for the listed apps

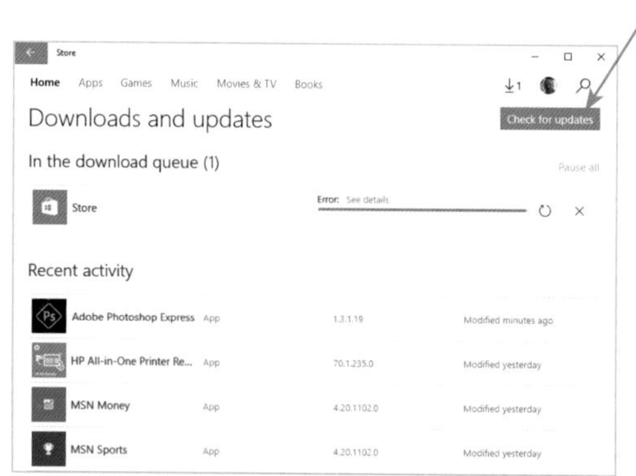

You can reinstall apps from the Downloads and updates section, even if you have previously uninstalled them. If there was a fee for an app, you will not have to pay again to reinstall it.

Installing and Uninstalling Apps

Installing apps from a CD or DVD

If the app you want to install is provided on a CD or DVD, you normally just insert the disc. The installation app starts up automatically, and you can follow the instructions to select features and complete the installation. If this does not happen automatically:

1. Insert the disc and click on this notification window

2. Double-click on the **Run Set-up.exe** file link to run it. Follow the on-screen prompts to install the app

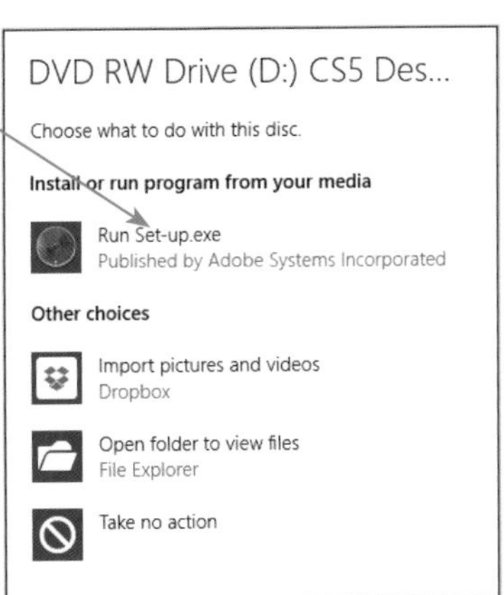

3. Apps that are installed from a CD or DVD are added to the All Apps list on the Start menu

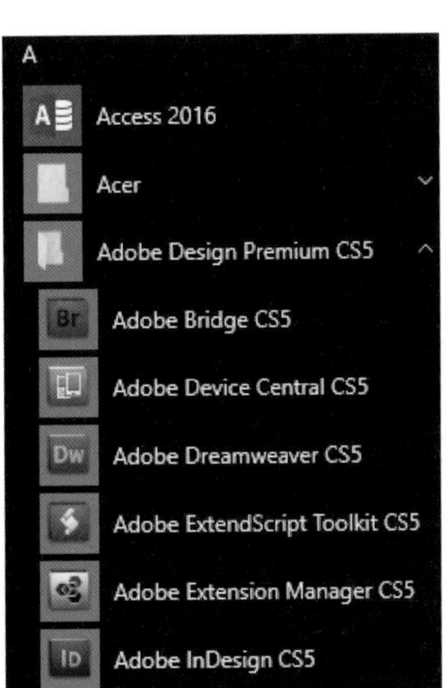

You can access the Run function in Windows 10 by right-clicking on the **Start** button and selecting **Run** from the contextual menu.

Apps can also be installed from discs from File Explorer. To do this, locate the **Set-up.exe** file and double-click on it to start the installation process in the same way as in Step 2.

...cont'd

Uninstalling apps

In some previous versions of Windows, apps were uninstalled through the Control Panel. However, in Windows 10 they can also be uninstalled directly from the Start menu. To do this:

1. Right-click on an app to access its menu

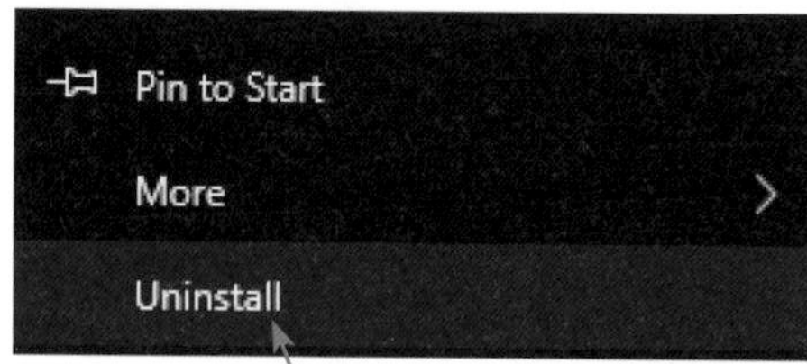

2. Click on the **Uninstall** button

3. A window alerts you to the fact that related information will be removed if the app is uninstalled. Click on the **Uninstall** button if you want to continue

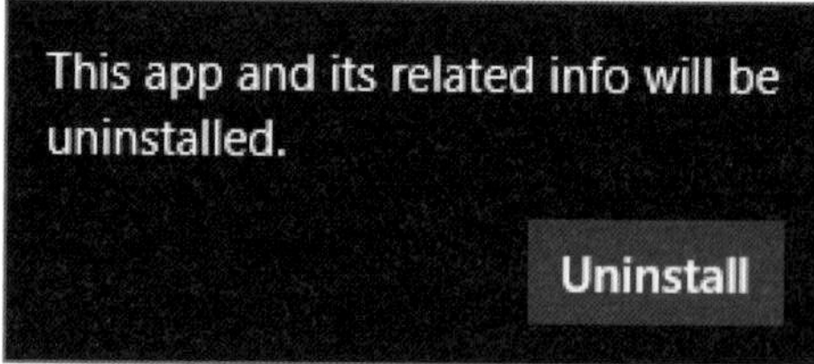

4. If the app is a new Windows 10 one, or has been pinned to the Start menu (or Taskbar), its tile will be removed from its pinned location(s). For other apps, they will no longer be available from the list of apps

Some elements of Windows 10, such as the Control Panel, still refer to apps as programs, but they are the same thing.

If apps have been installed from a CD or DVD they can still be uninstalled from within the Control Panel (**Start** > **Windows system** > **Control Panel**). To do this, select the **Programs** section and click on the **Uninstall a Program** link. The installed apps will be displayed. Select one of the apps and click on the **Uninstall/Change** link.

5 The Online World

This chapter looks at getting online so that you can make the most of the expanding online world. It covers the Microsoft Edge browser, for viewing and managing web pages; the Mail app for email; the online storage and backup facility, OneDrive; and the options for creating and viewing online address books and calendars, via your Microsoft Account.

Introducing the Edge Browser

Before you can use the internet and browse the web, your laptop needs to be set up for connection to the internet. To do this you will require an Internet Service Provider (ISP), to provide an account that gives you access to the internet, either via Wi-Fi with a router, through a cable connection using an Ethernet cable, or through a fiber-optic connection.

The web browser Internet Explorer (IE) has been synonymous with Microsoft for almost as long as the Windows operating system. Introduced in 1995, shortly after Windows 95, it has been the default browser for a generation of web users. However, as with most technologies, the relentless march of time has caught up with IE and, although it is still included and can be used with Windows 10, the preferred browser is designed specifically for the digital mobile age. It is called Microsoft Edge, and adapts easily to whichever environment it is operating in: desktop, tablet or smartphone.

The Microsoft Edge browser has a number of performance and speed enhancements compared with IE, including a function for drawing on and annotating web pages, which can then be sent to other people as screenshots.

There is also a Hub where you can store all of your favorites, downloads and pages that you have selected to read at a later date (which can be when you are offline if required).

Click on this icon from the **Taskbar** or the **Start** menu to open the Microsoft Edge browser at the default Start page.

Back/forward buttons Refresh Hub button Toolbar buttons

Menu options

Start

Where to next?

Search or enter web address

My feed

powered by MSN

Cheeky marathon runner sprays Will & Kate with water

Wonderwall

The Start page can be replaced by your own specific Homepage. See page 94 for details.

Smart Address Bar

Smart address bars are now a familiar feature in a lot of modern browsers, and Microsoft Edge is no different. These can be used to enter a specific web address, to open that page or use it to search for a word or phrase. To use the smart address bar:

1. Click anywhere in the Start page address box or in the address box at the top of a web page

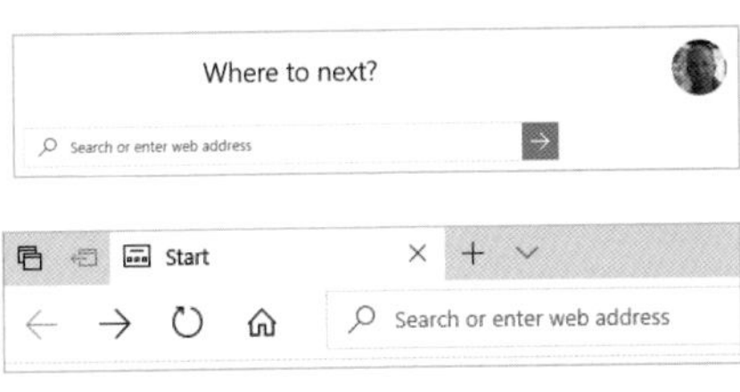

2. Start typing a word or website address. As you type, options appear below the address bar. Click on a web page address to open that website

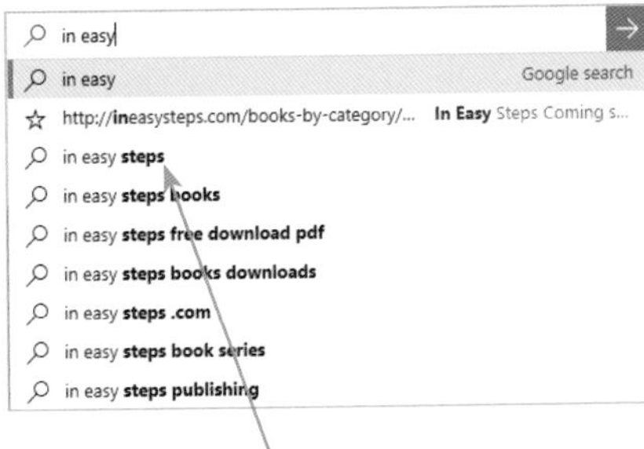

3. Click on one of the options with a magnifying glass next to it to view the search result for that item

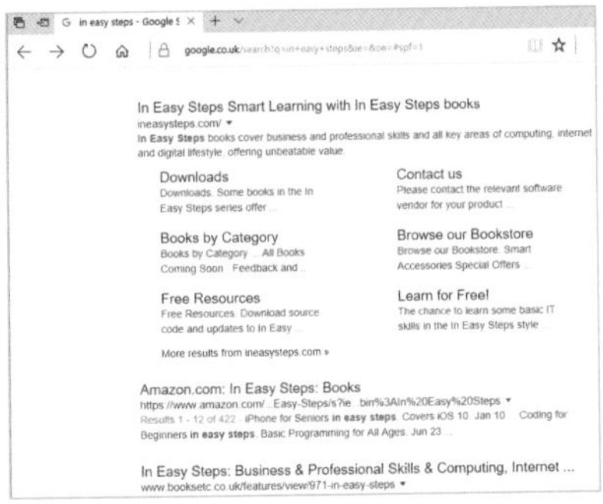

The personal digital assistant, Cortana, can also be used to open web pages, by asking it to open a specific page. The page will be opened in Microsoft Edge.

Search results are found through Microsoft's search engine, Bing. To change the default search engine, click on **... (Menu Options)** > **Settings**. Then, select the **View advanced settings** button and click on the **Change search engine** button. Select a new default search engine and click on the **Set as default** button.

Setting a Homepage

By default, Microsoft Edge opens at its own Start page. This may not be ideal for most users, who will want to set their own Homepage that appears when Microsoft Edge is launched.

Hot tip

In the Windows 10 Creators Update, the Microsoft Edge browser has a Homepage button on the top toolbar. If the Homepage button is not showing, select **Settings** as in Step 2 and select **View advanced settings** > **Show the home button**.

1. Click on this button on the top toolbar to access the menu options

2. Click on the **Settings** button

3. By default, the Start page is selected as the opening page

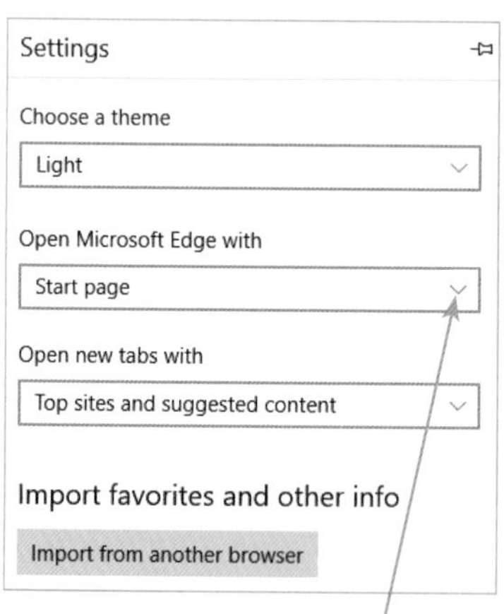

4. Click here and select **A specific page or pages**

Start page
New tab page
Previous pages
A specific page or pages

5. Enter the website address you want to use as your Homepage, and click on the **Save** button

ineasysteps.com

Within the settings for Microsoft Edge there is an option for importing favorites from another web browser. To do this, click on the **Import from another browser** button, select the required browser, and click on the **Import** button.

Using Tabs

Being able to open several web pages at the same time in different tabs is now a common feature of web browsers. To do this with Microsoft Edge:

1. Click on this button at the top of the Microsoft Edge window

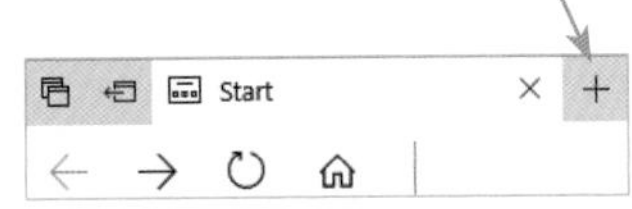

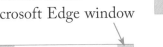

2. Pages can be opened in new tabs using the smart address bar or the list of **Top sites** that appears below it

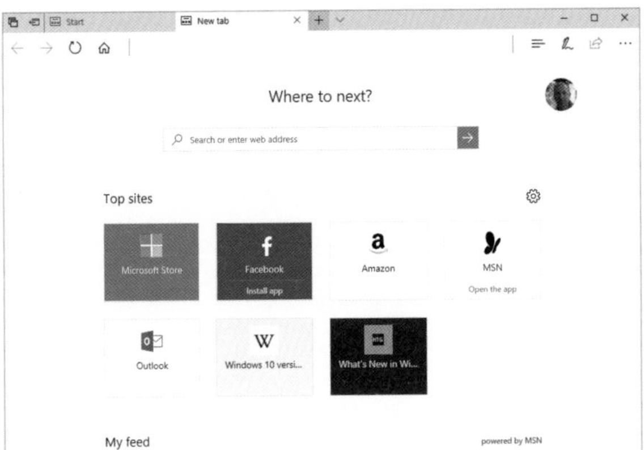

3. All open tabs are displayed at the top of the window. Click and hold on a tab to drag it into a new position

The Start page for new tabs, as displayed in Step 2, can be changed if required. To do this, open the Microsoft Edge **Settings** as shown on the previous page, and change the selection under the **Open new tabs with** heading.

...cont'd

Tab previews

If there are a large number of tabs open it can be hard to remember exactly what is in each one. This is addressed in the Edge browser through the tab previews function.

Tab previews is a new feature in the Windows 10 Creators Update.

1. All open tabs are shown at the top of the browser, with the current active tab colored light gray

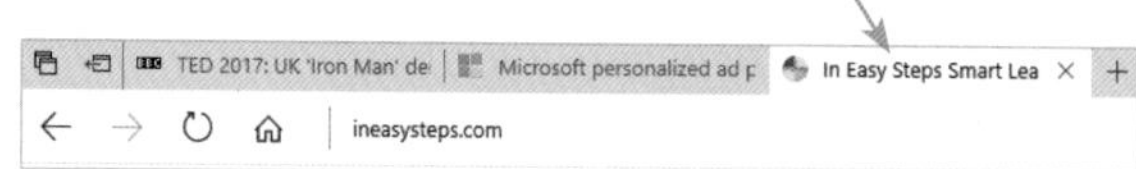

2. Move the mouse cursor over one of the inactive tabs to view a preview of the content within it

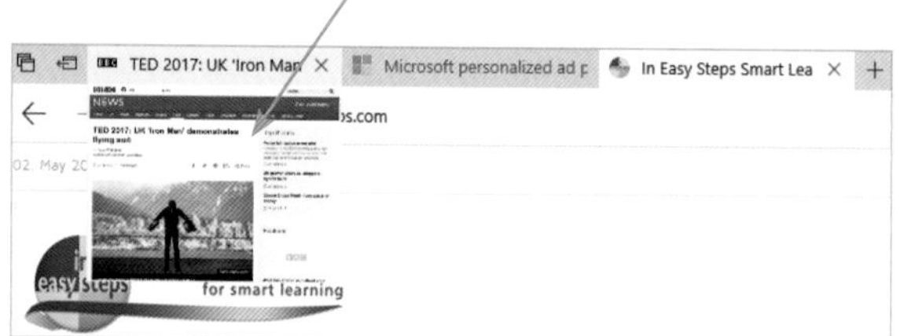

3. Click on this button next to the New Tab button to view thumbnails of the current tabs

4. Thumbnails of all of the current tabs are displayed. Click on one to view it, or click on this button to close the preview panel

Set aside tabs

To avoid the Edge browser window becoming too cluttered with open tabs at the top of it, it is possible to set aside the current tabs so that they are stored together, but not along the top of the browser window. To do this:

Set aside tabs is a new feature in the Windows 10 Creators Update.

1. All open tabs are shown at the top of the browser

2. Click on this button to set-aside the open tabs

3. The tabs are set aside, indicated by this button being colored black and only the **New tab** window showing

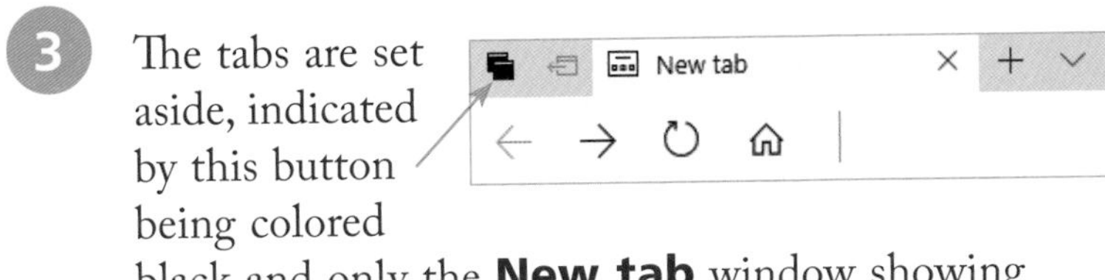

4. Click on this button to view the set-aside tabs

5. Click on one of the set-aside tabs to open it

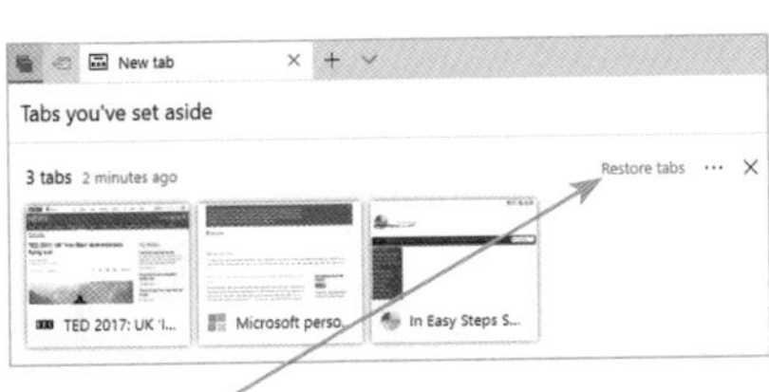

6. Click on the **Restore tabs** button to reopen all of the set-aside tabs

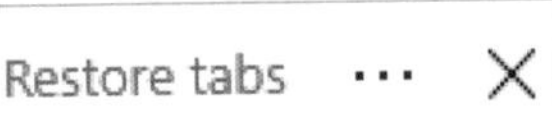

7. Click on the **Menu** button to access the options for the set-aside tabs, including adding them to your favorites or sharing them

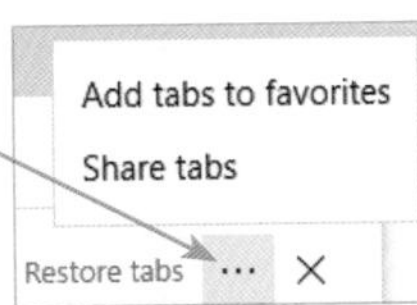

Bookmarking Web Pages

Your favorite web pages can be bookmarked so that you can access them with one click from the Hub area, rather than having to enter the web address each time. To do this:

1. Open the web page that you want to bookmark
2. Click on this button on the toolbar

The Favorites bar can be displayed underneath the Address bar by opening the Microsoft Edge **Settings** and dragging the **Show the favorites bar** button to **On**.

3. Click on the **Favorites** button
4. Enter a name for the favorite and where you want it to be saved to (click on the **Create new folder** link if you want to save it to a new location)

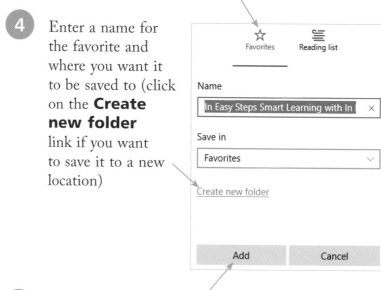

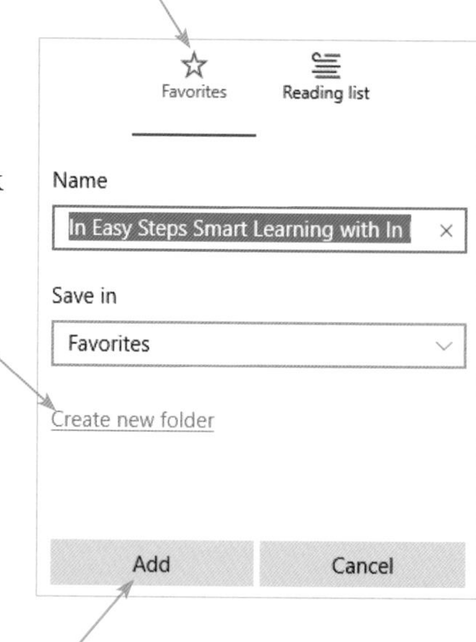

5. Click on the **Add** button
6. The star button turns yellow, indicating that the web page has been added as a Favorite

7. Click on this button to access your Favorites (see page 101)

Adding Notes to Web Pages

One of the innovations in the Microsoft Edge browser is the ability to draw on and annotate web pages. This can be useful to highlight parts of a web page or add your own comments and views, which can then be sent to other people. To add notes:

1. Open a web page to which you want to add a note or draw on, and click on this button on the toolbar of the Microsoft Edge browser

Click on this button on the Notes toolbar to create a web clipping. This is an area of a web page that is selected by dragging over it to make the selection.

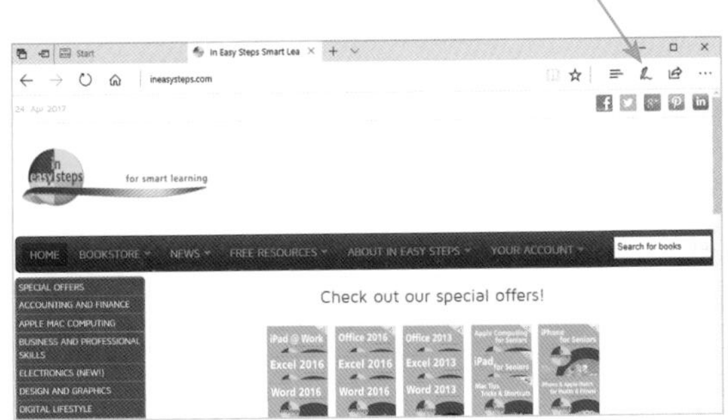

2. Click on one of the pen options

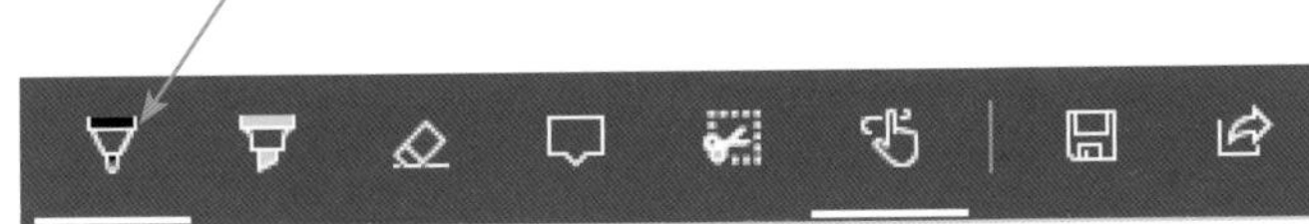

Click on this button on the Notes toolbar to save a web note or clipping. These can then be accessed from the Favorites section of Microsoft Edge (see page 101).

3. Make selections for the pen style, including color and size

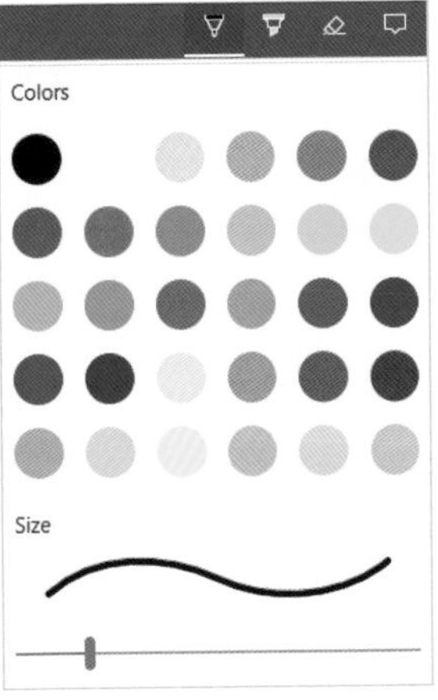

...cont'd

4. Click and drag on the web page to draw over it

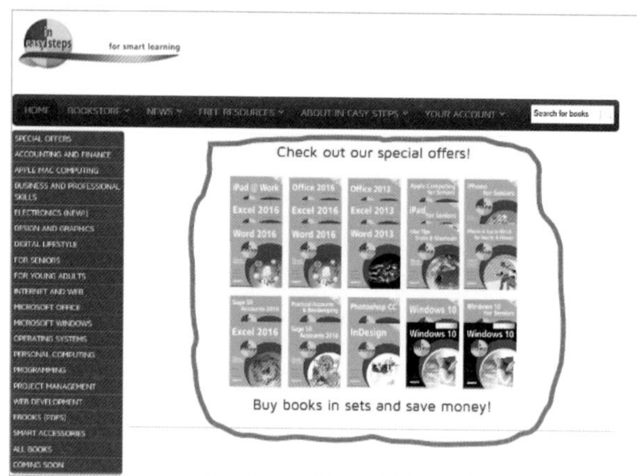

5. Click on the eraser icon and drag over any items that you have drawn to remove them, or part of them

6. Click on the text icon to add your own text

7. Drag over the web page to create a text box

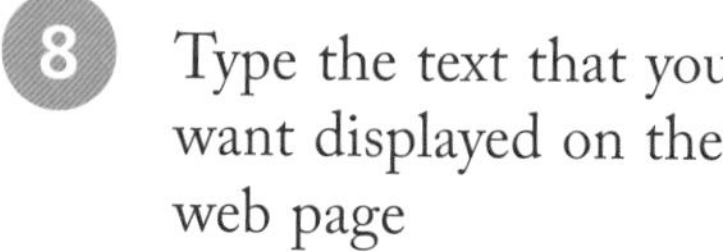

8. Type the text that you want displayed on the web page

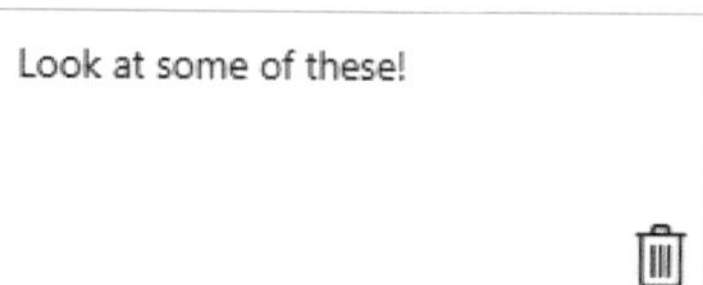

9. Click and drag here on a text box to move its position in the window

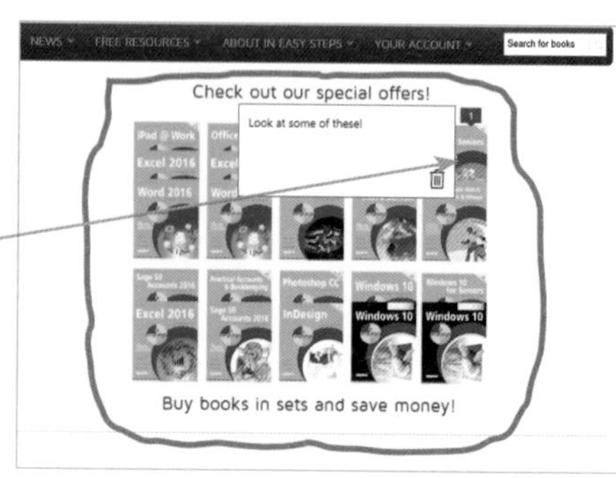

Several notes can be added to a web page, but it can begin to look a bit cluttered if there are too many.

Organizing with the Hub

The Hub is the area where you can store a variety of items, from your favorite web pages to pages that you want to read offline at a later date. To use the Hub:

The Favorites window also has an option for importing favorites from other web browsers. Click on the **Settings** button and click on **Import from another browser** link, select the required browser, and click on the **Import** button.

1. Click on this button to open the Hub

2. Click on this button to view your Favorites. Click on one to go to that page

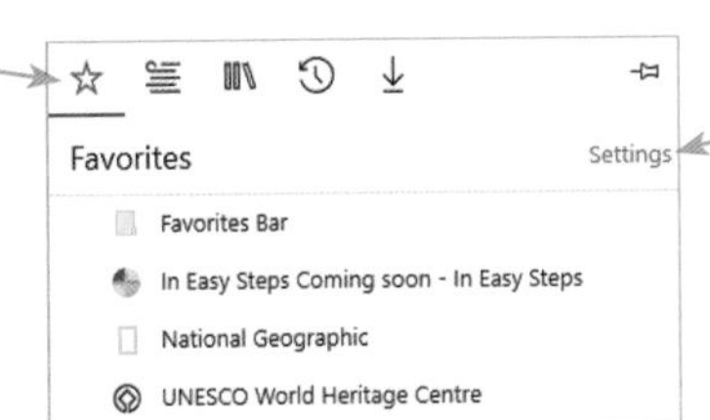

3. Click on this button to view your Reading List of pages that you have saved to read offline, or at a later date (see next page for details)

4. Click on this button to view your web browsing history

5. Click on **Clear all history** to remove the items in the history

6. Click on this button to view items that you have downloaded from the web, such as PDF documents or apps (although not those from the Windows Store)

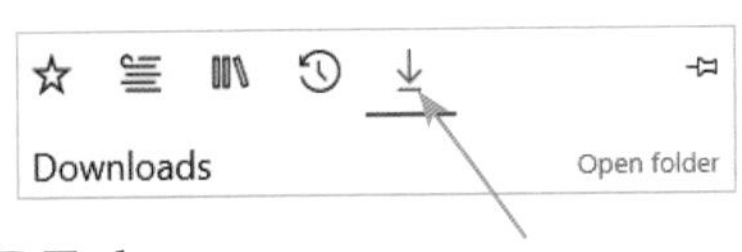

Click on the **Books** button within the Hub to view any books that have been downloaded from the Windows Store, and read them in the Edge browser.

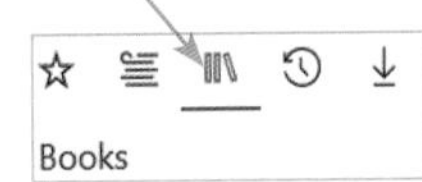

Reading List

With some web pages you may want to save the content so that you can read it at a later date. If you make the page a favorite, the content could change the next time you look at it. Instead, you can add the page to your Reading List to ensure that you can read the same content. Also, you have the advantage of being able to access the items in your Reading List when you are offline and not connected to the internet. To do this:

The Reading List is an excellent option if you are traveling and do not have internet access. You can save numerous articles in the Reading List and access them even when you are offline.

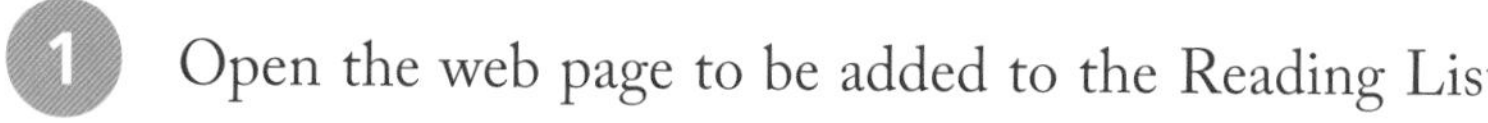

1. Open the web page to be added to the Reading List

2. Click on this button on the Edge toolbar

3. Click on the **Reading list** button

4. Enter a name for the item, and click on the **Add** button

5. Click on this button within the Hub to access and view your Reading List items

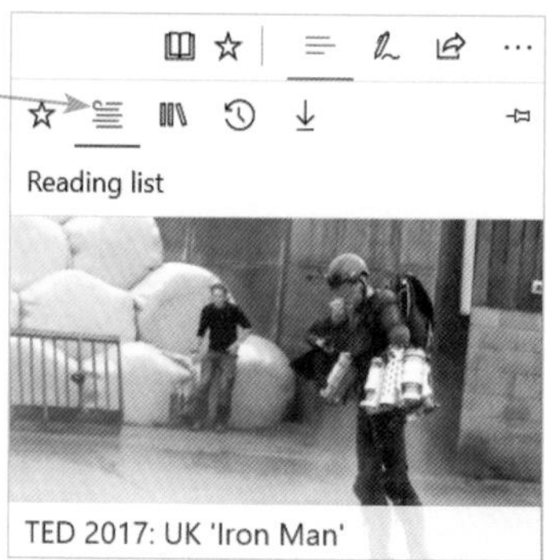

Reading View

Modern web pages contain a lot more items than just text and pictures: video clips, pop-up ads, banners, and more contribute to the multimedia effect on many web pages. At times this additional content can enhance the page, but a lot of the time it is a distraction. If you want to just concentrate on the main item on a web page, you can do this with the Reading View function:

1. Open the web page that you want to view in Reading View

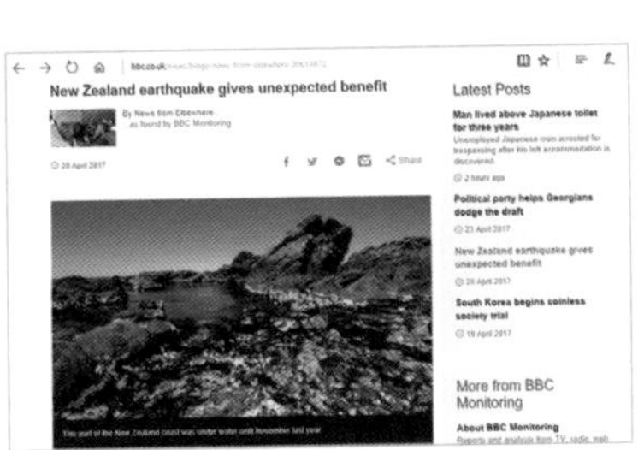

2. Click on this button on the Microsoft Edge toolbar

3. The text and pictures are presented on a new page, with any additional content removed. Click on the buttons at the bottom to move through the content

4. Click on this button again to return to the standard page view

Not all web pages support the Reading View functionality. If it is not supported, the button in Step 2 will be grayed out.

Shopping Online

Some people love physically looking around shops, while for others it is a chore. For the latter group, online shopping is one of the great innovations of the web. With a laptop, it is possible to do your shopping in the comfort of your own home, while also avoiding the crowds.

When you are shopping online there are some guidelines that you should follow, to try to ensure you are in a safe online environment and do not spend too much money:

A lot of online shopping sites list recommendations for you based on what you have already looked at or bought on the site. This is done by using "cookies", which are small programs that are downloaded from the site and then track the items that you look at on the site (see the next page for further information on cookies).

- Make a note of what you want to buy, and stick to this once you have found it. Online shopping sites are adept at displaying a lot of enticing offers, and it is a lot easier to buy something by clicking a button than it is to physically take it to a checkout.
- Never buy anything that is promoted to you via an email unless it is from a company who you have asked to send you promotional information.
- When paying for items, make sure that the online site has a secure area for accepting payment and credit card details. A lot of sites display information about this within their payment area, and another way to ascertain this is to check in the address bar of the payment page. If it is within a secure area, the address of the page will start with "https" rather than the standard "http".

Using online shopping

The majority of online shopping sites are similar in their operation:

- Goods are identified.
- Goods are placed in a shopping basket.

- Once the shopping is completed, you proceed to the checkout.
- For some sites you have to register before you can complete your purchase, while with others you do not.
- You enter your shipping details and pay for the goods, usually with a credit or debit card.

In some cases, if you are registered on a site, you can complete your shopping by using a 1-Click system. This means that all of your billing, delivery and payment details are already stored on the site, and you can buy goods simply by clicking one button without having to re-enter your details. One of the most prominent sites to use this method is Amazon.

One-click shopping is an effective way to spend money very quickly. However, you usually have a period of time in which you can cancel your purchases after you have bought them in this way.

Using cookies

A lot of online shopping sites use cookies, which are small programs that store information about your browsing habits on the site. Sites have to tell you if they are using cookies, and they can be a good way to receive targeted information about products in which you are interested. This can be done on the sites when you are logged in, or via email.

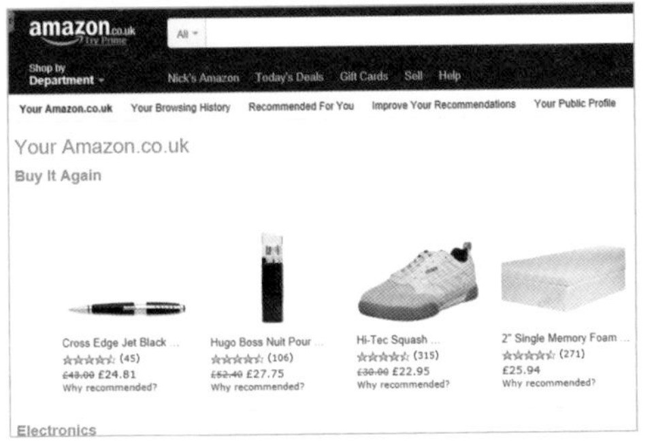

Booking a Vacation

Just as many retailers have created an online presence, the same is also true for vacation companies and travel agents. It is now possible to book almost any type of vacation on the web, from cruises to city breaks.

Several sites offer full travel services where they can deal with flights, hotels, insurance, car hire and excursions. These sites include:

- **www.expedia.com**
- **www.kayak.com**
- **www.orbitz.com**
- **www.travelocity.com**

It is always worth searching different sites to get the best possible prices. In some cases, it is cheapest to buy different elements of a vacation from different sites, e.g. flights from one and accommodation from another.

These sites usually list special offers and last-minute deals on their Homepages, or if you sign up to an email newsletter. There is also a facility for specifying your precise requirements. To do this:

1. Select your vacation requirements. This can include flight or hotel only, or a combination of both, with or without car hire options

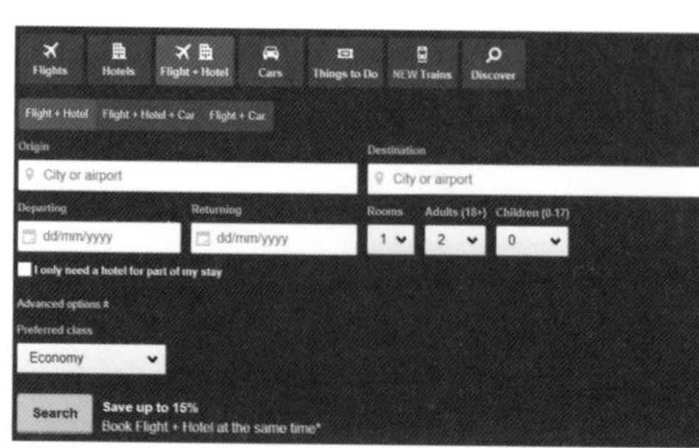

2. Enter flight details
3. Enter dates for your vacation
4. Click on the **Search** button

TripAdvisor

One of the best resources for travelers is TripAdvisor. Not only does the site provide a full range of opportunities for booking flights and hotels, it also has an extensive network of reviews from people who have visited the countries, hotels and restaurants on the site. These are independent, and usually very fair and honest. In a lot of cases, if there are issues with a hotel or restaurant, the proprietor posts a reply to explain what is being done to address any problems.

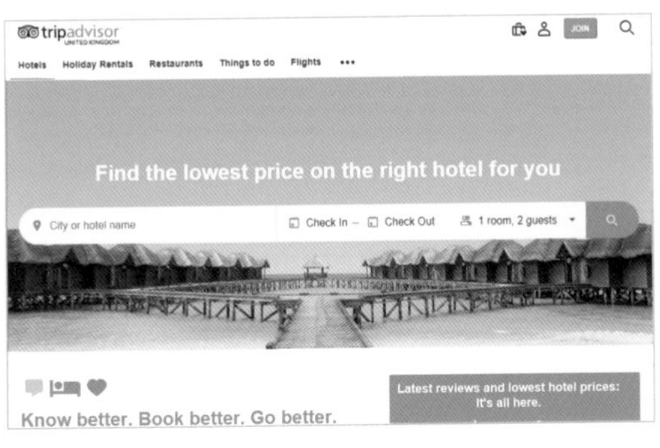

Don't forget

Vacation and hotel websites usually have versions that are specific to your geographical location.

Cruises

There are also websites dedicated specifically to cruises:

- **www.carnival.com**
- **www.cruises.com**
- **www.princess.com**

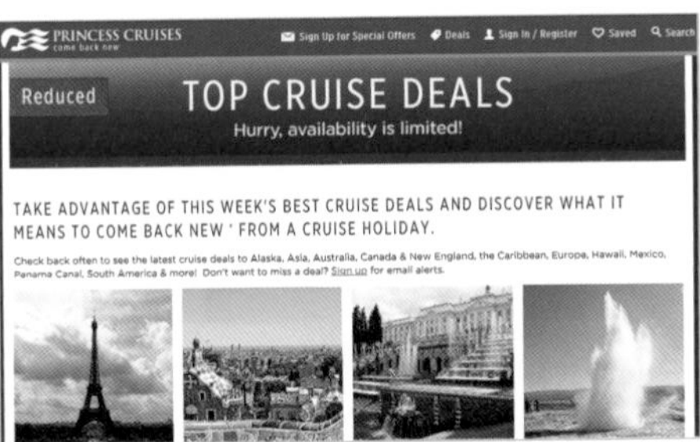

The web is also excellent for researching family history and genealogy. Some sites to try are Ancestry, Genealogy, FamilySearch and RootsWeb.Ancestry.

Hotels

There are a range of websites that specialize in hotel bookings, a lot of them at short notice to get the best price:

- **www.choicehotels.com**
- **www.hotels.com**
- **www.laterooms.com**
- **www.trivago.com**

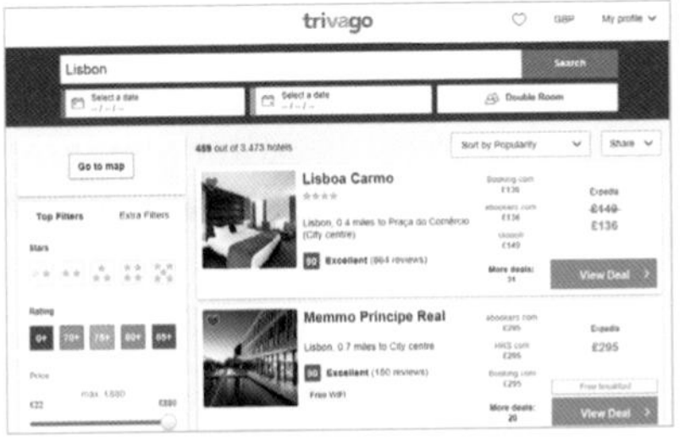

Setting Up Mail

Email has become an essential part of our online lives, both socially and for official communication. Windows 10 accommodates this with the Mail app. This can be used to link to online services such as Gmail and Outlook (the renamed version of Hotmail), and also other email accounts. To set up an email account with Mail:

The **Other account** option in Step 4 can be used to add a non-webmail account. This is usually a POP3 account and you will need your email address, username, password, and usually the incoming and outgoing email servers. If you do not know these they should be supplied by your email provider. They should also be available in the account settings of the email account you want to add to the Mail app.

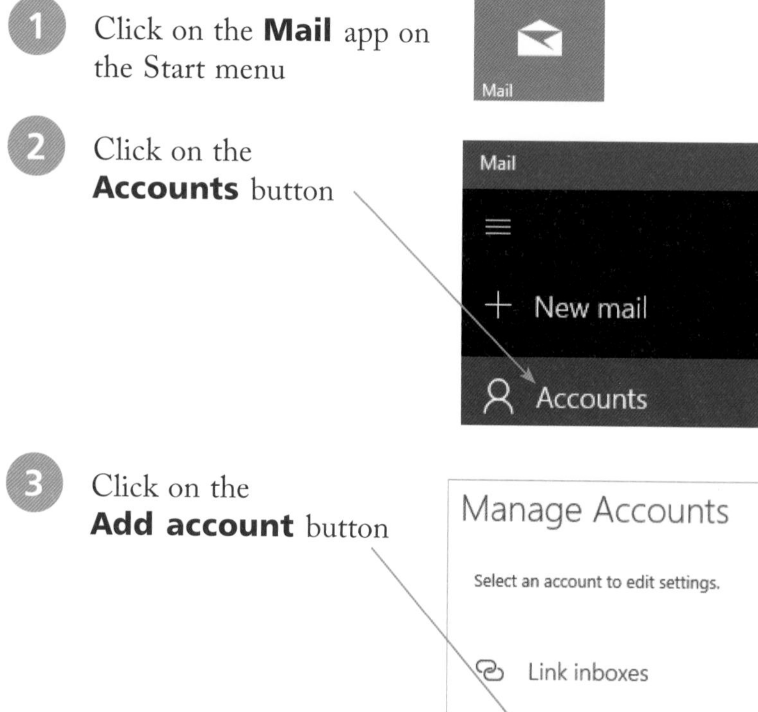

1. Click on the **Mail** app on the Start menu
2. Click on the **Accounts** button
3. Click on the **Add account** button
4. Select the type of account to which you want to link via the Mail app. This can be an online email account that you have already set up

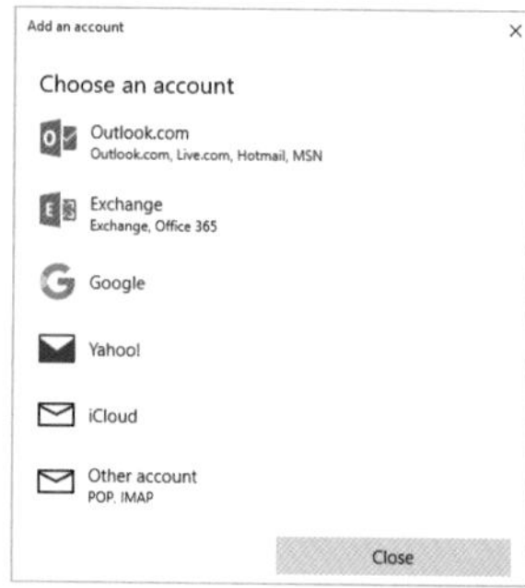

5. Enter your current sign-in details for the selected email account and click on the **Sign in** button

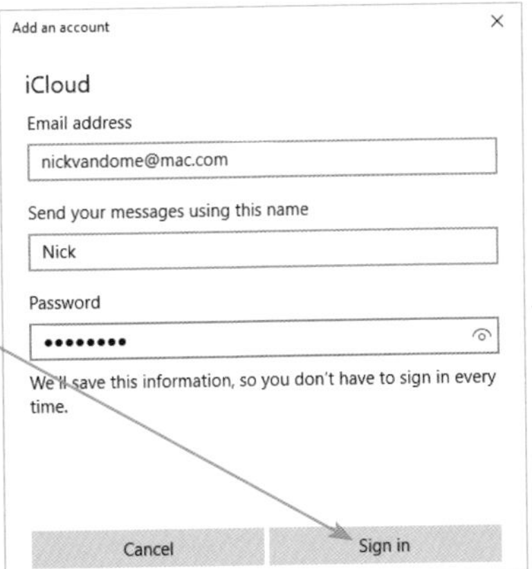

6. Once it has been connected, the details of the account are shown under the Mail heading, including the mailboxes within the account. Click on the **Inbox** to view the emails within it

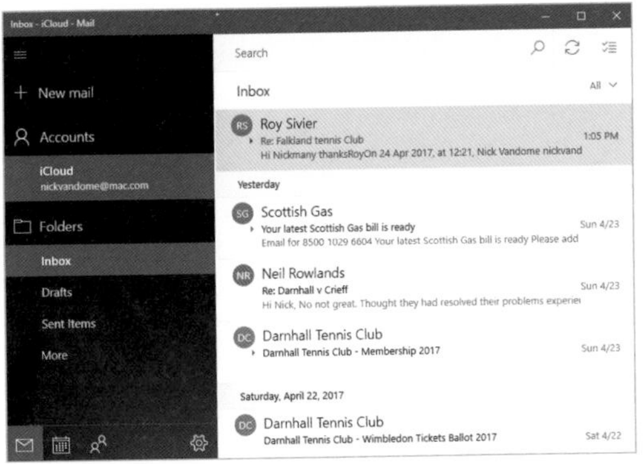

7. The list of emails appears in the main window. Double-click on an email to view it at full size

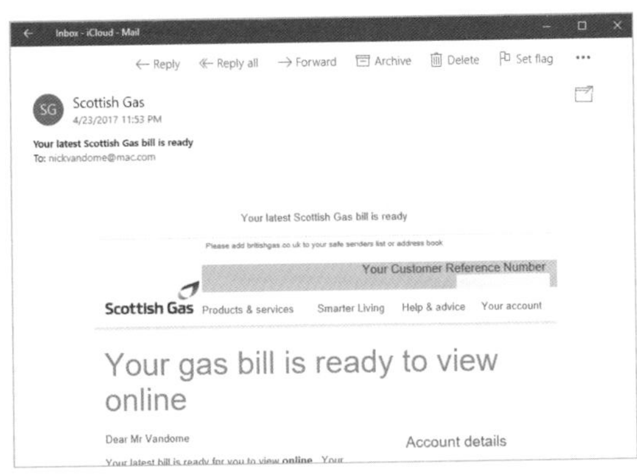

You can add more than one account to the Mail app. If you do this you will be able to select the different accounts to view within Mail.

Working with Mail

Once you have set up an account in the Mail app you can then start creating and managing your emails with it.

1. On the Inbox page, open an email and click on the **Reply**, **Reply all** or **Forward** buttons

2. Open an email and click on the **Delete** button to remove it

To compose and send an email message:

1. Click on this button to create a new message

2. Click in the **To** field and enter an email address

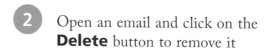

3. Click on the **Cc & Bcc** link to access options for copying and blind copying

4. The email address can either be in the format of myname@email.com or enter the name of one of your contacts from the People app and the email address will be entered automatically

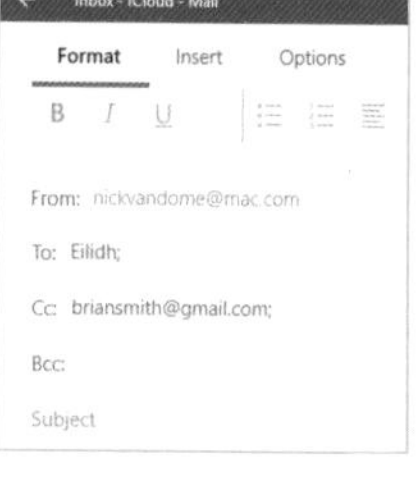

Contacts that are added automatically as email recipients are taken from the People app, providing there is an email address connected to their entry.

5. Enter a subject heading and body text to the email

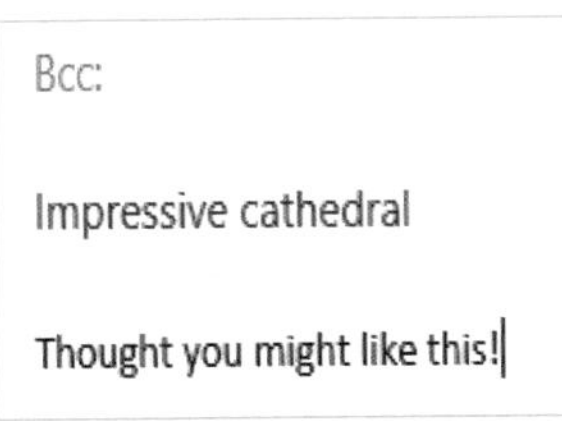

6. Click on the **Insert** button on the top toolbar in the new email window and select one of the options, such as **Pictures**

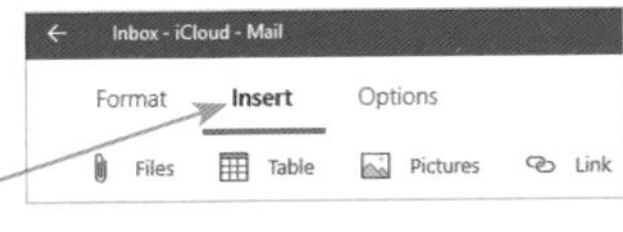

7. Click on a folder from which you want to attach the file, and click on the **Insert** button

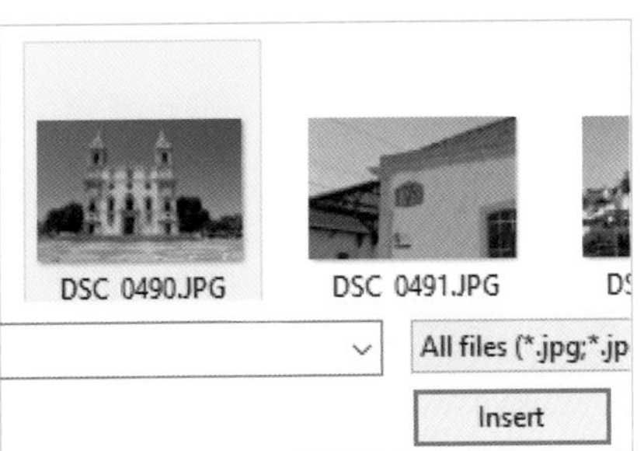

8. The file is shown in the body of the email

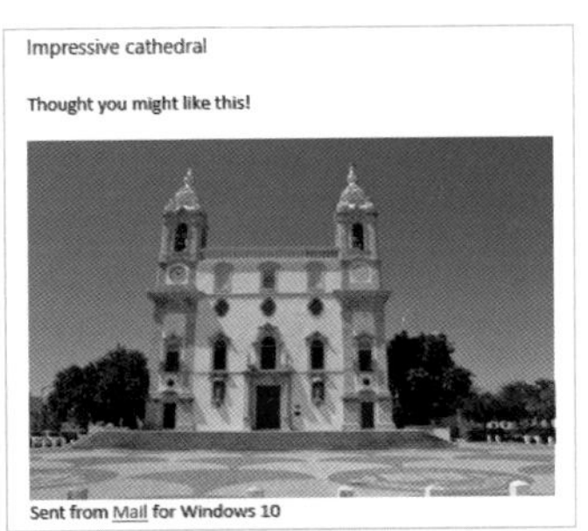

9. Select an item of text, and select the text formatting options from the top toolbar

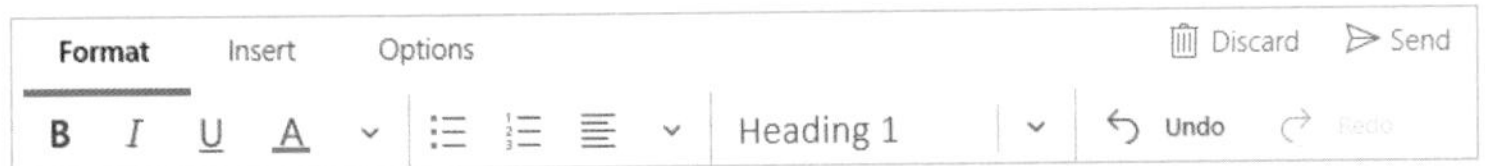

10. Click on this button to send the email

Social media is another popular way of keeping in touch with people and sharing a variety of content. Sites such as Facebook, Twitter, Snapchat, Instagram and Pinterest can be accessed through the Edge browser, and some have their own apps that can be downloaded from the Windows Store.

Using OneDrive

Cloud computing is now a mainstream part of our online experience. This involves saving content to an online server connected to the service that you are using, i.e. through your Microsoft Account. You can then access this content from any computer, using your account login details, and also share it with other people by giving them access to your Cloud service. It can also be used to back up your files, in case they get corrupted or damaged on your PC.

The Cloud service with Windows 10 is known as OneDrive, and you can use it with a Microsoft Account.

Click on these buttons on the right-hand side of the OneDrive toolbar in Step 3 to, from left to right: sort the content; display it as a list, tiles or photo; and view the details about the current folder or file.

Click on these buttons on the left-hand side of the OneDrive toolbar in Step 3 to, from left to right: create new folders in the file structure, and upload files from other locations.

1. Click on the **OneDrive** app on the Start Menu and follow the wizard to sign in to OneDrive

2. Open File Explorer and click on the **OneDrive** folder to view its contents

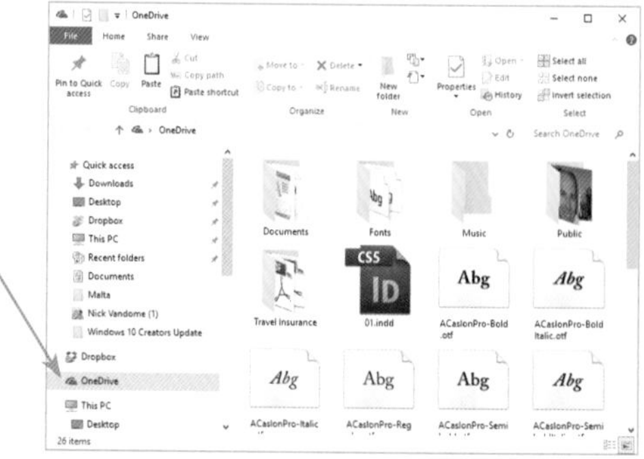

3. To view the contents of OneDrive online, go to the website at **onedrive.live.com** and sign in with your Microsoft Account details. Your OneDrive content is the same as in your OneDrive folder on your computer. Click on items to open, view and edit them

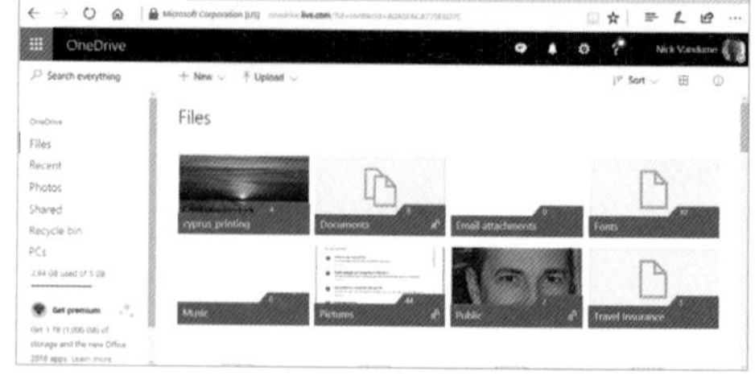

OneDrive Settings

A range of settings can be applied to OneDrive, including adding and syncing folders. To do this:

1. Right-click on the OneDrive icon on the Notifications area of the Taskbar and click on **Settings**

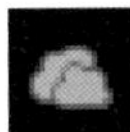

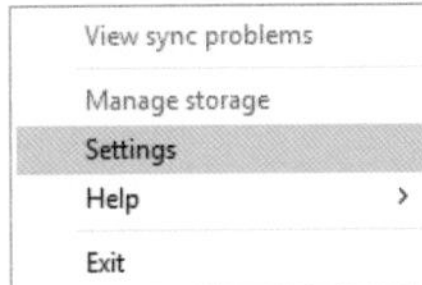

2. Click on the **Settings** tab for options for starting OneDrive when you sign in, and for unlinking your OneDrive so that it does not sync with the online function

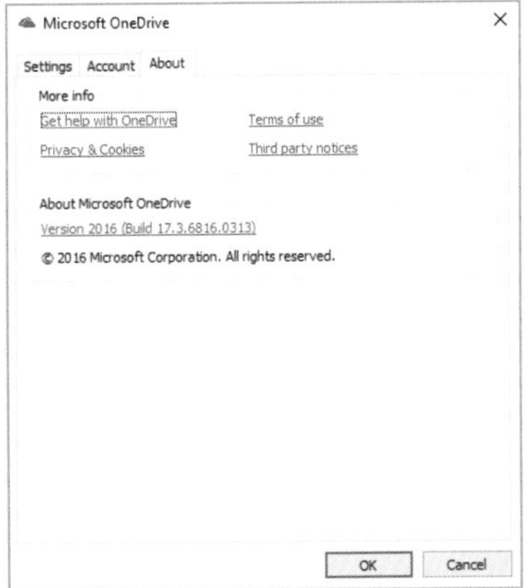

3. Click on the **Account** tab and click on the **Choose folders** button to select the folder from your computer that you want to sync with your OneDrive account

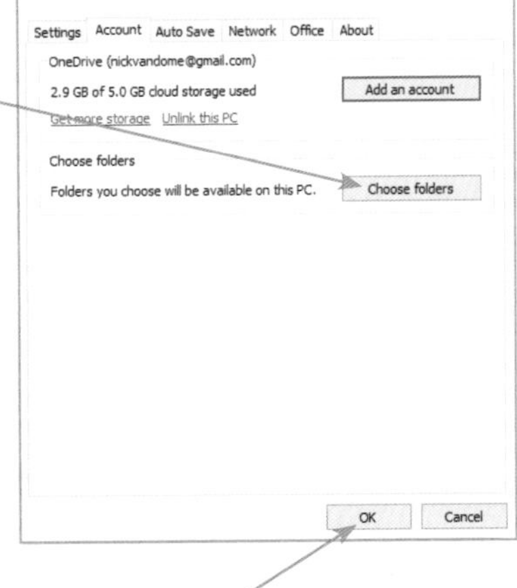

4. Click on the **OK** button to apply any changes to the OneDrive settings

Adding Files to OneDrive

OneDrive is built into the file structure of Windows 10 and as well as adding files from OneDrive itself, it is also possible to add them to the OneDrive folder from your computer. Once this has been done, the files can be accessed from your OneDrive folder from your laptop, online or any compatible device, using your Microsoft Account login details.

Your OneDrive folder can be pinned to the Quick access section in File Explorer. To do this, right-click on the OneDrive icon in File Explorer and click on **Pin to Quick access**.

Adding from File Explorer

To add files from File Explorer:

1. In File Explorer, the OneDrive folder is located underneath Quick access (and any other folders that have been added)

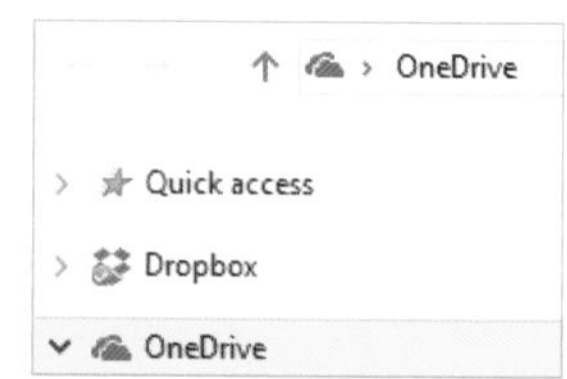

2. Click on the OneDrive folder to view its contents

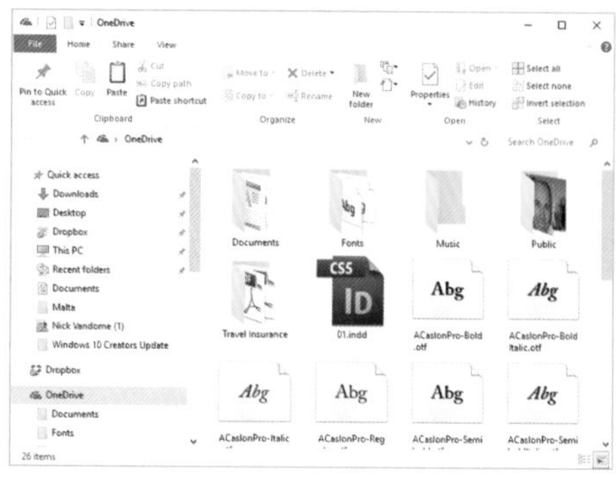

3. Add files to the OneDrive folder by dragging and dropping them from another folder, or by using Copy and Paste

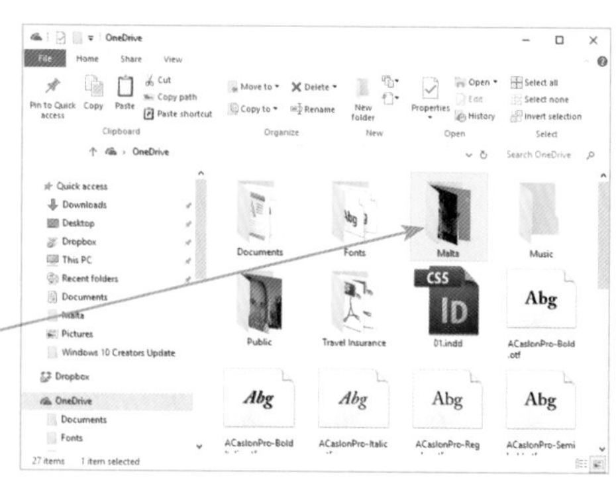

By default, you get 5GB of free OneDrive storage space with Windows 10 (the free allowance was reduced from 15GB in July 2016). This is an excellent way to back up your important documents, since they are stored away from your computer. For up-to-date information on plan allowances and pricing, visit **https://onedrive.live.com/about/plans/**

4 The new content is available from the OneDrive app and also online from your OneDrive account

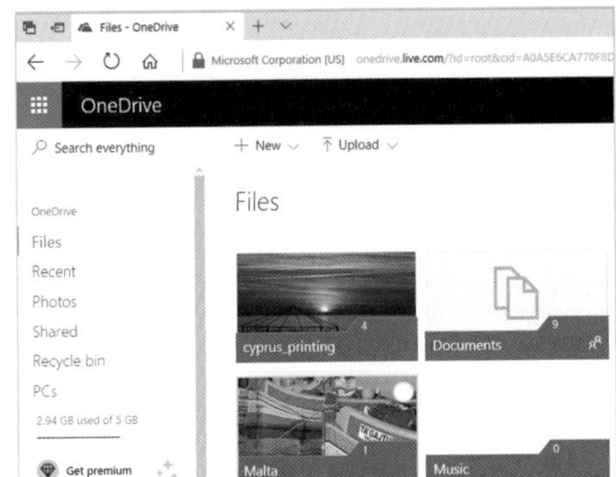

You can share your **Public** folder from your online OneDrive account by opening it, and clicking or tapping on the **Share** button. You can then email the link to the Public folder to selected recipients.

Saving files to OneDrive

Files can also be saved directly to OneDrive when they are created. To do this:

1 Open a new file in any app and create the required content

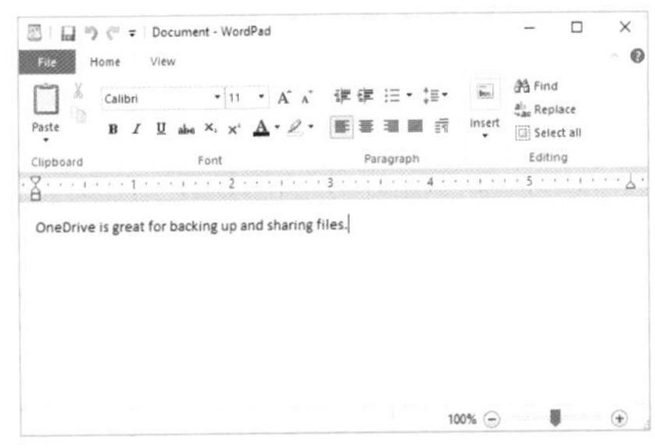

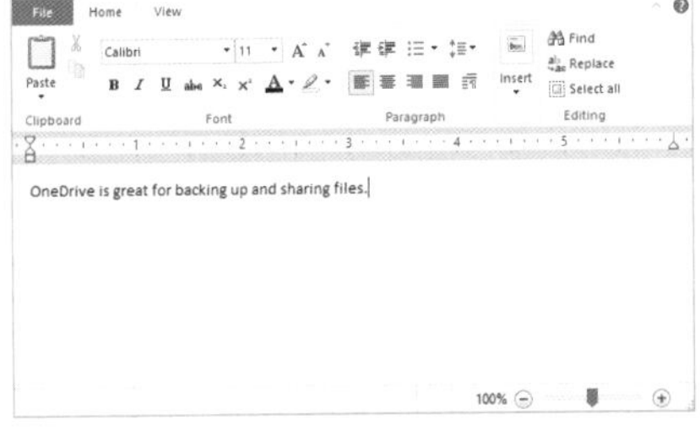

2 Select **File** > **Save** from the menu bar and select a OneDrive folder into which you want to save the file

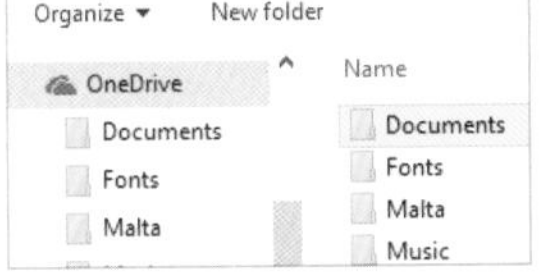

3 Click on the **Save** button

4 The file is saved into the OneDrive folder and will be available from the OneDrive app, and also online from your OneDrive account

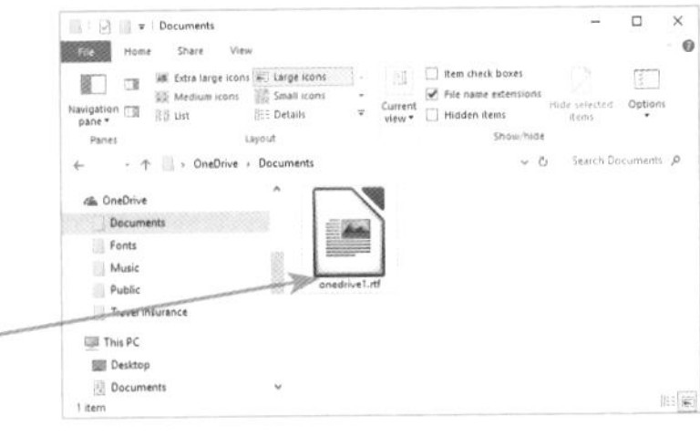

Finding People

An electronic address book is always a good feature to have on a computer, and with Windows 10 this function is provided by the People app. This can be used with a Microsoft Account so that your address book can be viewed online from any internet-enabled computer. You can also link to any of your online accounts, such as Gmail or iCloud, and import the contacts that you have there.

You can also select accounts to add to the People app from the Homepage when you first open it.

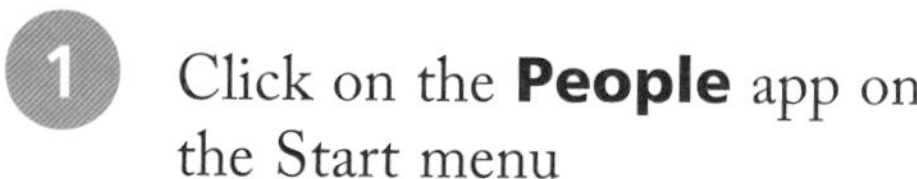

1. Click on the **People** app on the Start menu

2. The current contacts are displayed. By default, these will be linked to your Microsoft Account, if you have created one

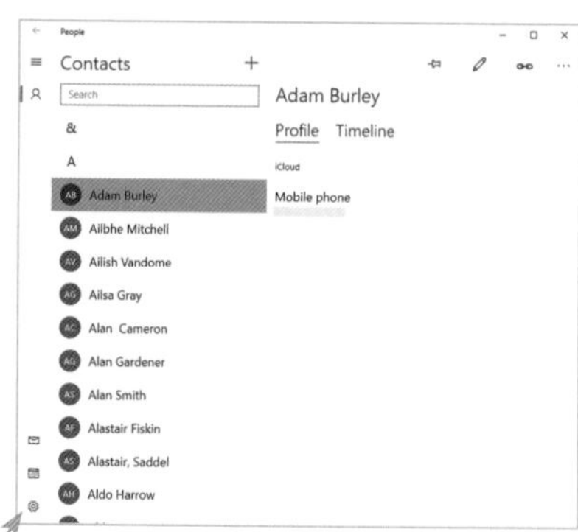

3. Click on the **Settings** button to add new accounts from which you want to import contacts, such as a Google or an iCloud account (in the same way as setting up a new email account). Click on the **Add an account** button to add the required account: the contacts from the linked account are imported to the People app

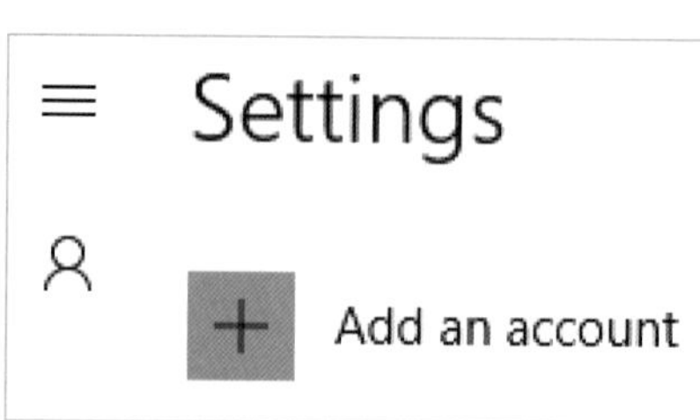

Adding contacts manually

As well as importing contacts, it is also possible to enter them manually into the People app:

1. Click on this button at the top of the **People** app

2. Enter details for the new contact, including name, email address and phone number

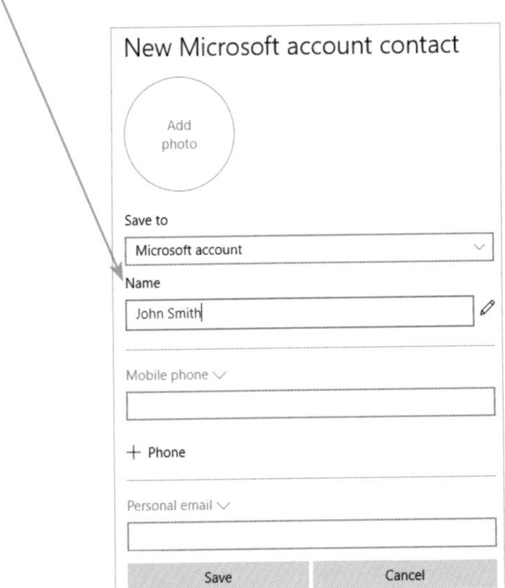

3. Click on the down arrow next to a field to access additional options for that item

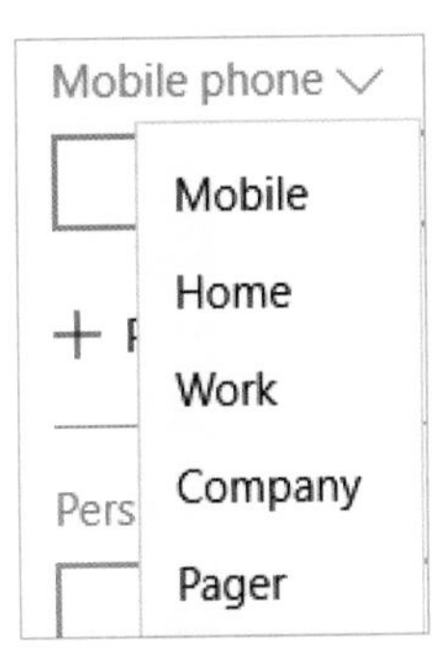

4. Click on the **Save** button at the top of the window to create the new contact

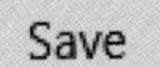

To delete a contact, right-click on their name in the Contacts list and click on the **Delete** button to remove it.

Once a contact has been added, select it as in Step 2 on the previous page and click on this button to edit the contact's details.

Using the Calendar

The Calendar app can be used to record important events and reminders. As with the People app, it can be connected to your Microsoft Account so that it can be viewed online from any internet-enabled computer. It can also be linked to other online account, so that you can import details from these. To use the calendar:

Don't forget

Accounts can be added to the Calendar app in the same way as for the Mail and People apps.

1. Click on the **Calendar** app on the Start menu, or access it from the All Apps list

2. Click on the **Settings** button

3. Click on the **Manage Accounts** button to add or delete a calendar account

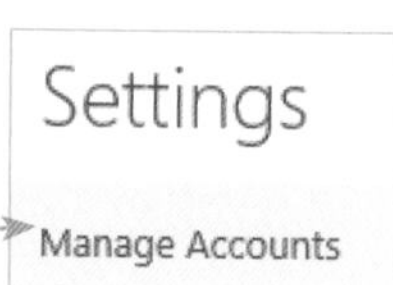

4. Click on the **Add account** button to add contacts from other online accounts, such as Google or iCloud

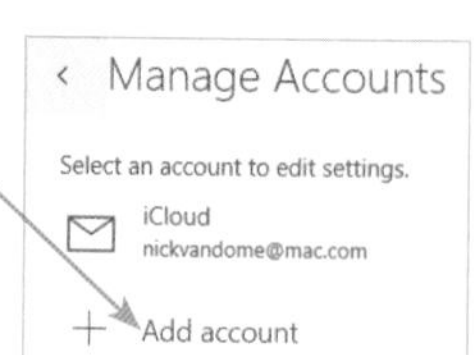

5. The calendar is displayed in the main window

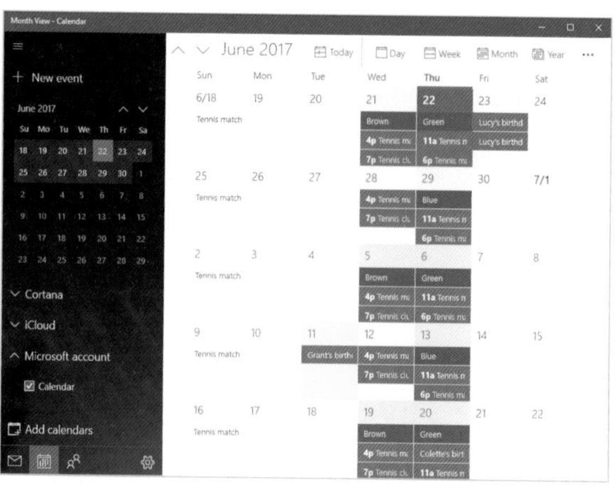

6. Click on these buttons at the top of the window to view the calendar in **Today**, **Day**, **Week**, **Month** or **Year** view

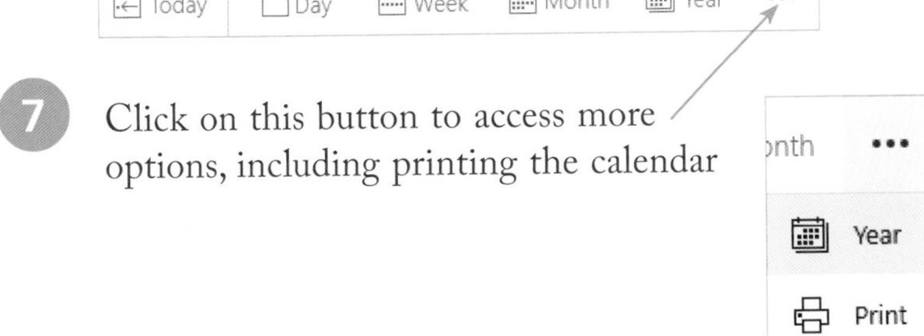

7. Click on this button to access more options, including printing the calendar

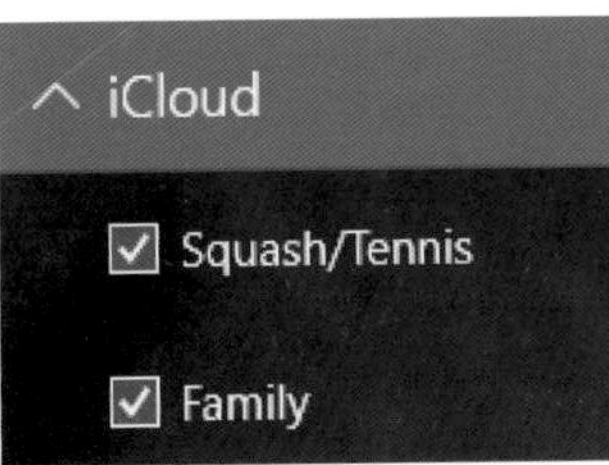

8. If other accounts have been added they will be displayed in the left-hand panel. Click on one to display the items within it. Check items On or Off to show or hide them on the calendar

9. Click on these buttons to move between months (or swipe left or right on a touch pad)

10. Click on these buttons to move to **Mail** (left) or **People** (right)

Adding events

Events can be added to the calendar and various settings can be applied to them, such as recurrence and reminders.

1. Click on a date to create a new event or click on the **New event** button

2. Enter an **Event name** and a **Location** at the top of the window

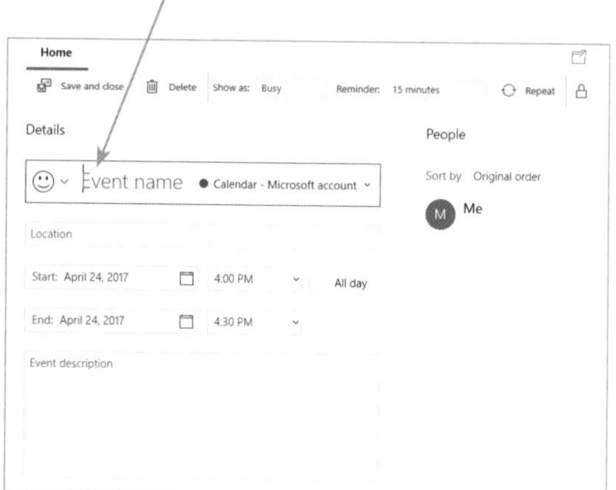

3. Click on the **Start** field, and enter a date and time for the event

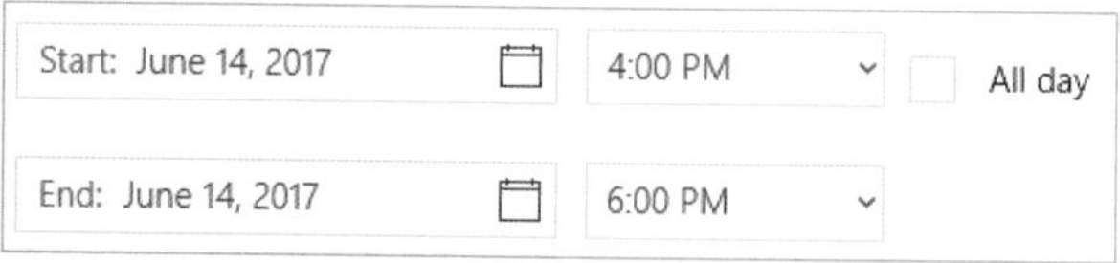

4. If **All day** is selected, the time in the **Start** and **End** fields will be grayed out

Reminders can be set for calendar events, and these appear in the **Notifications** section. Click on this box on the top toolbar to set a time period for a reminder.

6 A Digital Lifestyle

This chapter shows how to work with a range of apps that can be used for entertainment options, so you can fully immerse yourself in the digital world.

Viewing Photos

The Photos app can be used to manage and edit your photos, including those stored in your **Pictures** Library. To do this:

The **Photos** app interface has been updated in the Windows 10 Creators Update.

1. Click on the **Photos** app on the **Start** menu

2. The main categories are at the left-hand side of the top toolbar

Collection Albums Folders

3. Other options are at the right-hand side of the toolbar, including refresh the current item, select an item(s), play the current photos in a slideshow and import photos

4. Click on the **Collection** button to view all of the photos in the Photos app, arranged by date. Scroll up and down to view the photos

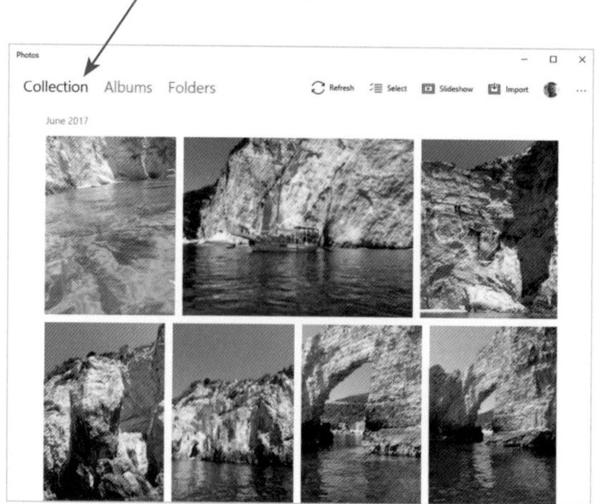

Hot tip

To import photos into the Photos app, click on this button on the top toolbar and select the location from where you want to import the photos. This can be a folder on your own computer; a camera or flash drive attached with a USB cable; or a memory card from a camera inserted into a card reader.

5. Click on the **Albums** button to view photos from specific albums. This includes the Camera roll

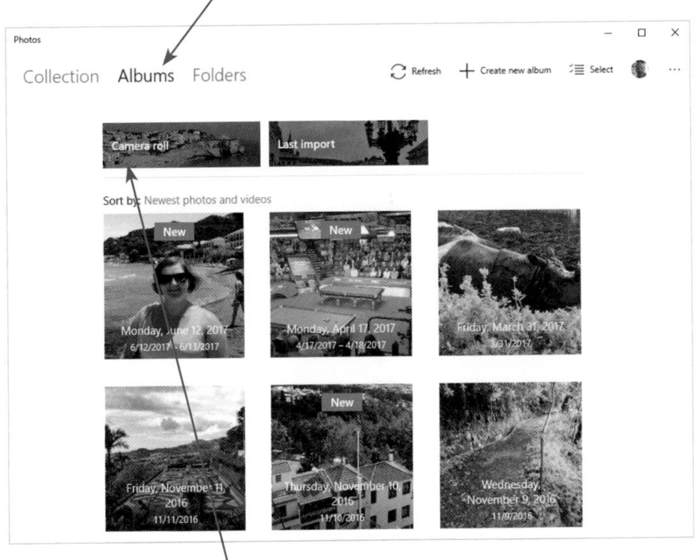

The albums displayed are taken from those stored in the specific folders in File Explorer (by default, the Pictures library). However, the Photos app displays what it thinks are the best photos in the folder, thus creating its own albums.

6. Click on the **Camera roll** album to view photos that have been taken with your computer's camera (or copied into this folder from another location)

...cont'd

Albums can include photos and videos.

7 Within the Albums section, double-click on an album to view its contents. The first photo is also displayed as a banner at the top of the album

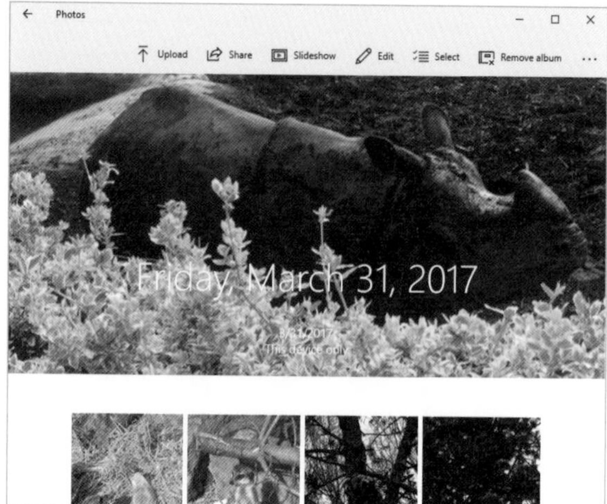

8 Double-click on a photo within an album, or collection, to view it at full size. Move the cursor over the photo and click on the left and right arrows (if available) to move through an album or collection

9 Click here to view the photo in full-screen mode

Sharing photos

Photos within either a collection or an album in the Photos app can be selected and then shared with other people in various ways, or deleted. To do this:

1. In Collections, or an open album, click on the **Select** button on the top toolbar

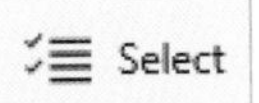

2. Click here to select a photo or photos

3. Click on the **Share** button to share the selected photo(s)

4. Click on one of the options for sharing the selected photo(s)

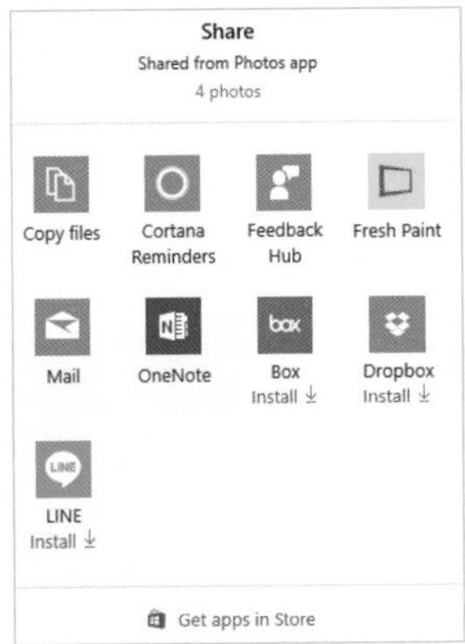

5. Alternatively, click on the **Copy** button on the top toolbar so that the select image(s) can be pasted into another app

The **Share menu** has been updated throughout the Windows 10 Creators Update and has the same appearance as in Step 4.

Editing Photos

In Windows 10, the Photos app has a range of editing functions so that you can improve and enhance your photos. To use these:

1. Open a photo at full size

2. Click on the **Edit** button on the top toolbar (or click on the **Menu** button first if the Edit button is not showing) to access additional editing options. Scroll up and down the right-hand panel to view the editing options

Rotate ...
Slideshow
Edit

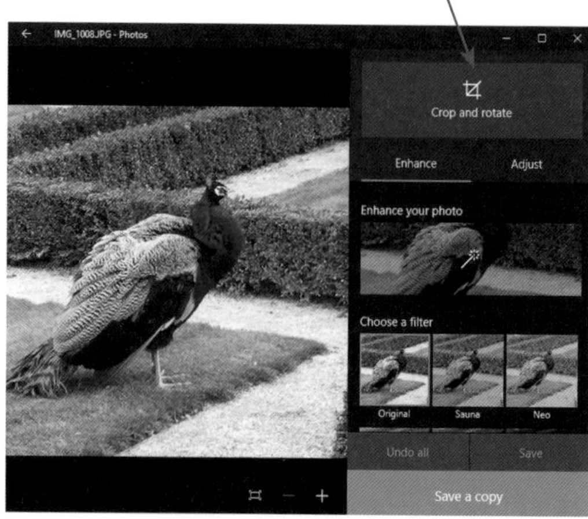

The editing functions of the Photos app have been updated in the Windows 10 Creators Update.

The **Draw** option (below) is a new feature in the Windows 10 Creators Update.

Draw

Also on the top toolbar is the **Draw** button. Click on this to access pen options for drawing directly on an image. Click on the **Save** button to save a copy of the image, or click on the cross to discard changes.

3. Click on the **Crop and rotate** button in Step 2 to crop the current photo or rotate it in a variety of ways, such as flipping horizontally or vertically or by a specific amount, by dragging here

Most photos benefit from some degree of cropping, so that the main subject is given greater prominence by removing unwanted items in the background.

4. Click on the **Enhance** button in Step 2 to apply filter effects. Click on the **Adjust** button to adjust elements in the photos by dragging on these bars for each element

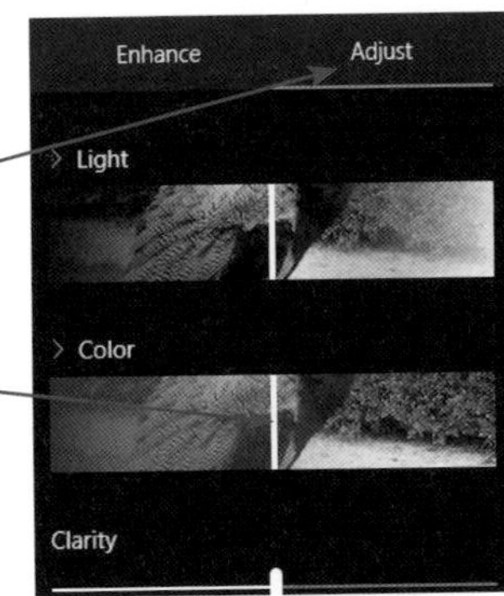

5. As the bar moves, so the elements of the photos are amended

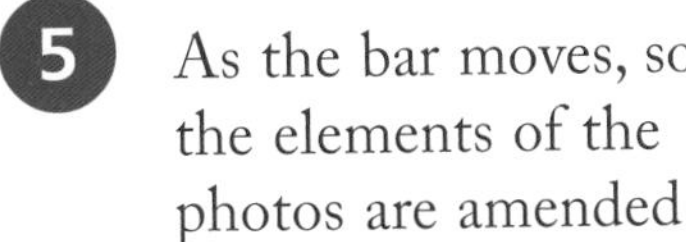

6. Click here next to one of the editing functions to view additional items

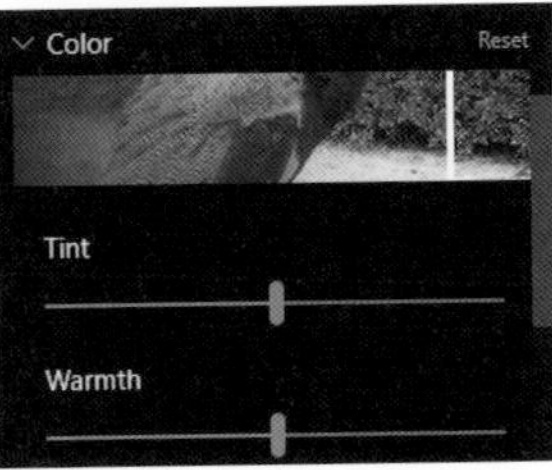

7. Click on the **Save** button to save the changes to the original photo, or **Save a copy** to create a new image

Groove Music App

The Groove Music app is used to access music that you have added to your laptop, and also the Music section of the Windows Store where you can preview, buy and download more music.

1. Click on the **Groove Music** app on the **Start** menu

2. Click on the **Menu** button to expand the menu so that the titles are visible, not just the icons

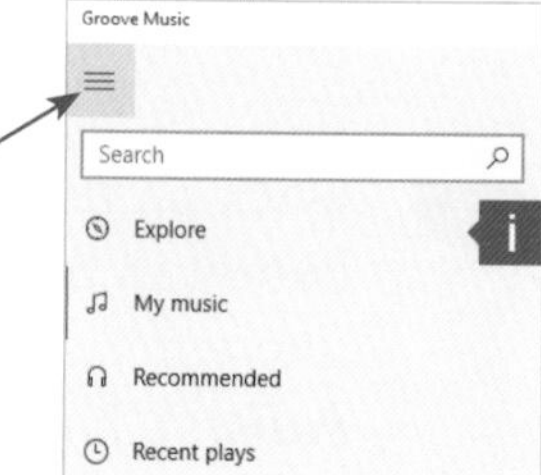

Scroll up and down to view the rest of the available content in the Music section of the Windows Store.

3. Click on a category to view those items

4. Click on the **Explore** button to access the Music section of the Windows Store

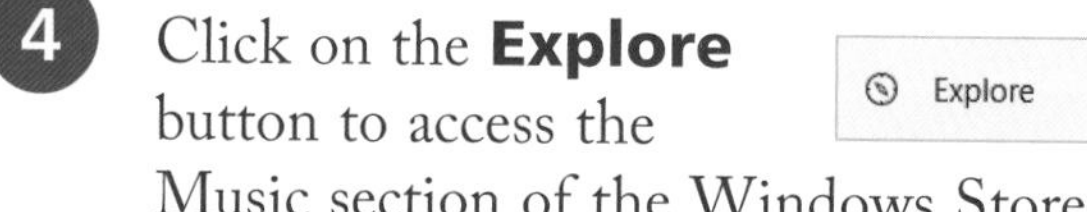

Music that has been bought in the Music section of the Windows Store is then available to be played within the Groove Music app.

5. Browse through the store using the categories in the main window. Click on an item to view details about it

Playing Music

Playing your own music

Music that has been added to your laptop can be played through the Groove Music app. To do this:

1. Open the Groove Music app and click on the **My music** button

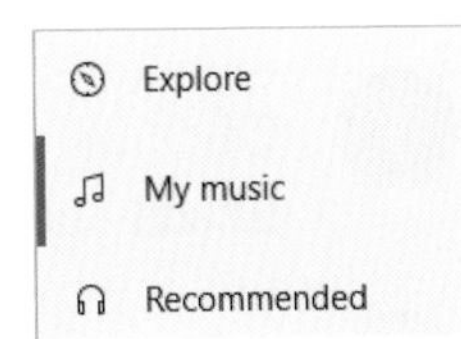

2. Click on the buttons at the top of the My music window to view your music according to Songs, Artists or Albums

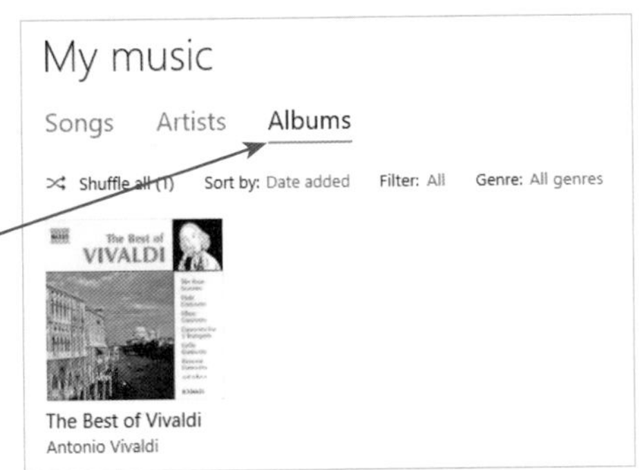

3. Click on an item to access it

4. Click on a track or album to start playing it

5. Use these buttons above to, from left to right: go to the start of a track; pause/play a track; go to the end of a track; shuffle the available tracks; repeat a track; or change or mute the volume

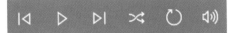

You can also add music to the Groove Music app from the Library that you have stored in your OneDrive folder.

When a folder is added to the Music library, any music that is copied here will be displayed by the Groove Music app.

Do not copy music and use it for commercial purposes as this will infringe the copyright of the artist.

Viewing Movies and TV

For movie and TV lovers, the Movies & TV app performs a similar function to the Groove Music app. It connects to the Windows Store, from where you can preview and buy your favorite movies and TV shows.

Don't forget

The Movies & TV app is named Films & TV in some regions.

1. Click on the **Movies & TV** app on the **Start** menu

2. The Windows Store opens at the Movies & TV section. Click on these buttons to view the items in the **Movies & TV** section and items you have bought

3. Click on the **Movies** button to view the available items (or **TV** for TV shows)

4. Click on an item to see more information, view a preview clip, buy, or rent, and download the movie

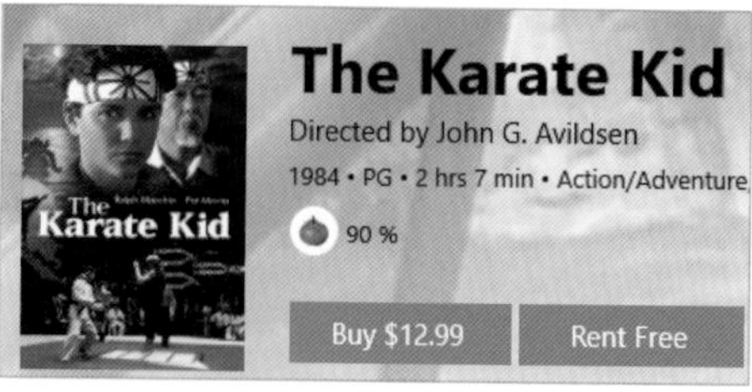

Don't forget

Movies and TV shows can be streamed (viewed from the computer server where the item is stored, rather than downloading it) if you have a fast internet connection. They can also be downloaded to a single device so that they can be viewed while you are offline.

Books in Windows 10

Windows 10 now caters for eBooks that can be downloaded from the Windows Store and read on your Windows 10 laptop:

Books in the Windows Store is a new feature in the Windows 10 Creators Update.

1. Open the **Windows Store** and click on the **Books** button on the top toolbar

Books

2. The range of books is displayed and can be navigated around in a similar way as for music, or movies and TV

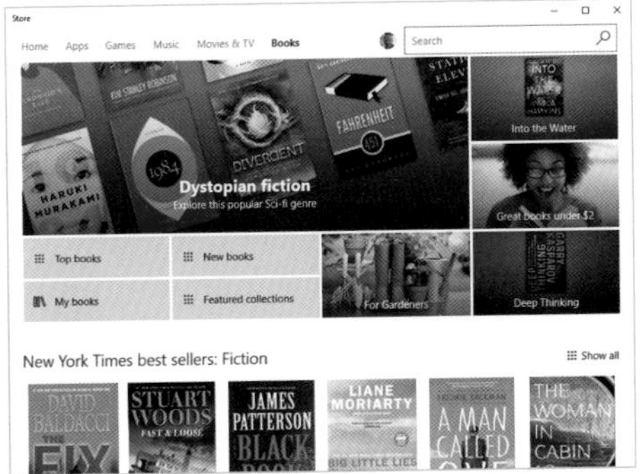

3. Tap on a book to see details about it. Tap on the **Buy** button to download the full text, or the **Preview** button to view a free sample

4. Books from the Windows Store are displayed within the Edge browser. Tap the spacebar to move forwards through the pages, or click on the left- and right-hand sides of the screen to move in those directions

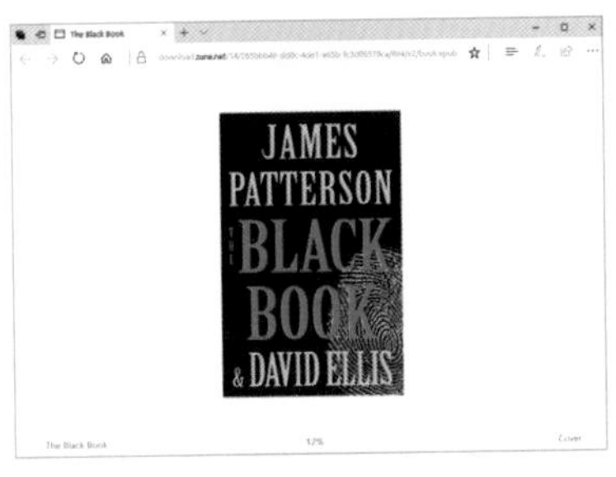

Hot tip

In the Edge browser, click on the **Hub** button and click on the **Books** button to view books that you have downloaded, and also get more from the Windows Store.

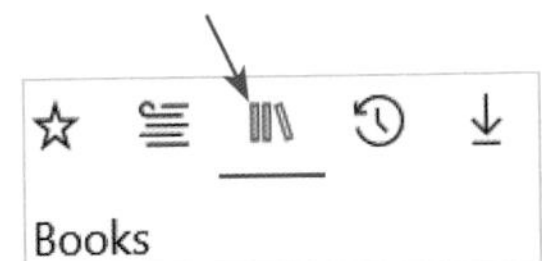

Using Paint 3D

Paint 3D is a new feature in the Windows 10 Creators Update.

The Windows 10 Creators Update caters for a wide range of 3D use, and one of the most significant is the Paint 3D app that can be used to create your own 3D pictures and also import ones from other places.

In some ways, Paint 3D is an extension of the Windows Paint app. However, it has a much greater array of features and brings the creation of 3D pictures within reach of anyone. To get started with creating 3D pictures:

Click on this button to access the main toolbar, containing the options on the following page. (If the Paint 3D window is maximized, the toolbar will be displayed at the top of the screen.)

Click on this button in the top left-hand corner of the window to access the Paint 3D menu options.

1. Click on the **Paint 3D** app

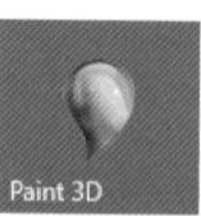

2. The Home screen displays a range of options, including creating a new project, opening an existing one, pasting a copied 3D object, and introductory help videos

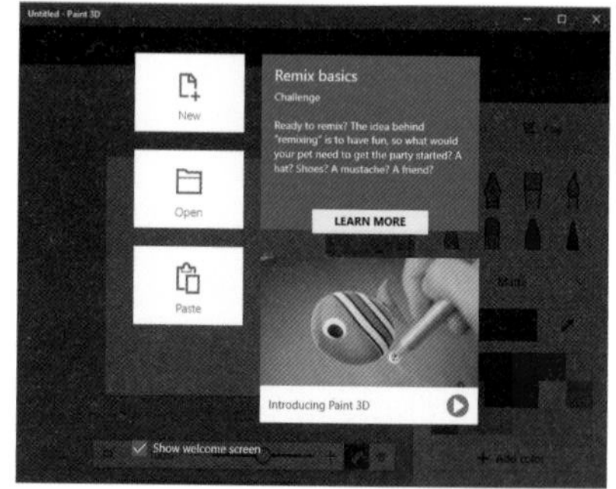

3. Click on the **New** button to create a new, blank, project

4. The Paint 3D workspace includes the canvas (the white square in the middle), the background, the tools for creating content, and the tools palette (at the right-hand side). Select a tool and a color from the palette to draw 2D shapes on the canvas

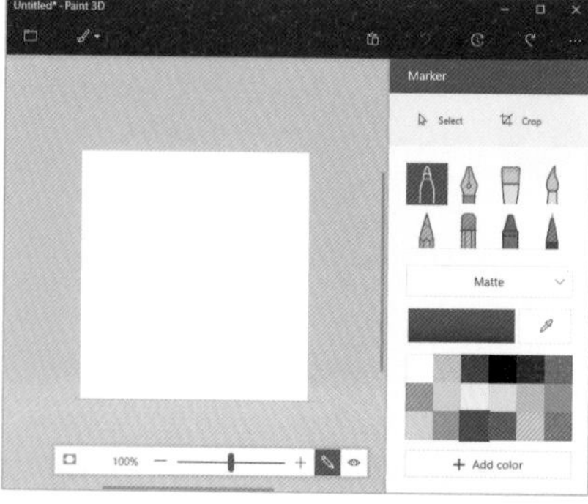

Adding 3D content

Paint 3D really comes into its own when you start adding, and editing, 3D shapes, stickers and text. To do this:

1. Click on the **3D objects** button on the top toolbar

2. Click on one of the 3D objects to select it. Select a color for it in the same way as for one of the drawing tools. Click on the canvas to add the object. Drag the controls around the object to display the 3D effect

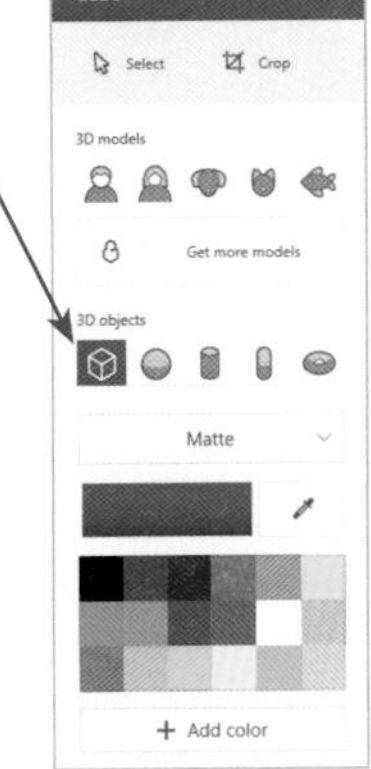

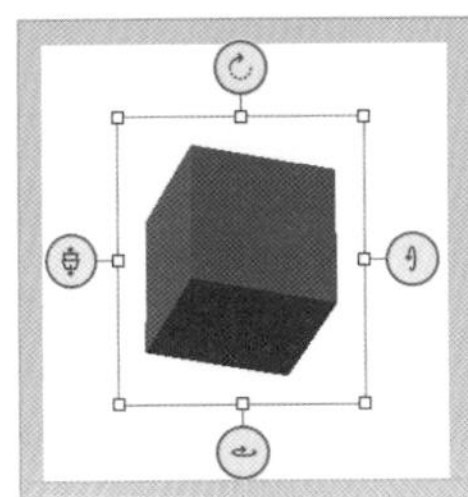

3. Click on the **Stickers** button on the top toolbar to select a sticker. Click on an object on the canvas to add the sticker to it. The object will take on the properties of the sticker (the sticker can also be added on its own on the canvas, in which case it initially appears in 2D)

4. Click on the **Text** button on the top toolbar, make formatting selections in the palette, and click on the canvas to add 3D text

5. Click on the **Effects** button on the top toolbar, and select a background effect. Click on the image to add the effect. This is added to the canvas and the background behind it

Click on these buttons on the top toolbar to, from left to right: select the canvas to manage its properties; and access Remix 3D, which is an online facility for sharing 3D images with other online users and downloading those that other people have created. This is done within the Xbox Live environment.

When one of the top toolbar options is selected, these buttons at the right-hand side of the window can be used to, from left to right: paste content that has been copied; undo actions; view the history of the actions performed on the current image; and redo actions that have been undone.

Gaming with Windows 10

The gaming experience has been enhanced in the Windows 10 Creators Update, with an overhaul of the Xbox app interface, for playing games and interacting with other gamers. To play games with the Windows 10 Creators Update:

NEW

The Xbox app has been updated for the Windows 10 Creators Update.

1. Click on the **Start** button and click on the **Xbox** app

2. Click on the **Home** button to view the Xbox Homepage. This contains the **Toolbar** (down the left-hand side), the **Activity feed** (in the left-hand panel) and the options for joining clubs and connecting with other gamers (in the right-hand panel)

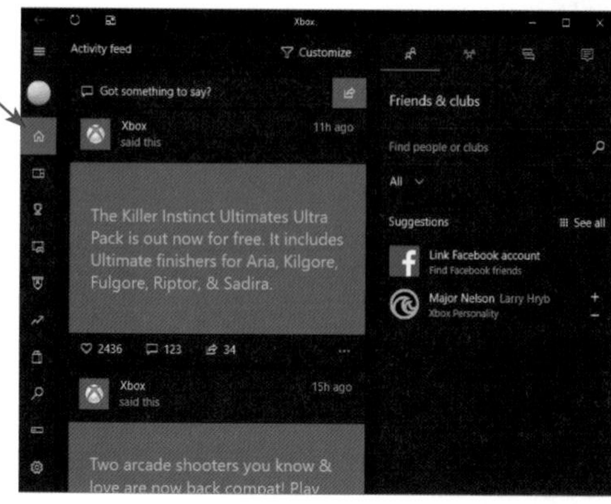

You have to be signed in with your Microsoft Account in order to use the Xbox app and all of its features.

3. Click on the **My games** button to view system games or those that you have downloaded from the Windows Store

4. Click on the **Achievements** button to view your scores from games you have played, and compare them with other gamers

5. Click on the **Clubs** button to view details of online game-playing clubs. This is where you can join up with other players, to compare scores and also play online games against other players (multiplayer games)

7 On Vacation

Due to their portability, laptops are ideal for taking on vacation. This chapter looks at the issues of taking your laptop with you and keeping it safe.

Transporting Your Laptop

When you are going on vacation, your laptop can be a valuable companion. It can be used to download vacation photographs from a digital camera, download home movies from a digital video camera, keep a diary of your vacation, and keep a record of your itinerary and important documents. In many parts of the world, it can access the internet via wireless hotspots so that you can view the web and send emails. However, when you are traveling with your laptop it is sensible to transport this valuable asset as safely and securely as possible. Some of the options include:

A backpack for carrying a laptop can be more comfortable than a shoulder bag as it distributes the weight more evenly.

Laptop case

A standard laptop case is a good option for when you are on vacation; it is compact, lightweight and designed to accommodate your laptop and its accessories.

Metal case

If you are concerned that your laptop may be in danger of physical damage on your vacation, you may want to consider a more robust metal case. These are similar to those used by photographers and, depending on its size and design, you may also be able to include your photographic equipment.

Backpacks

A serious option for transporting your laptop on vacation is a small backpack. This can either be a standard backpack or a backpack specifically designed for a laptop. The latter is clearly a better option as the laptop will fit more securely, and there are also pockets designed for accessories:

Keeping Your Laptop Safe

By most measures, laptops are valuable items. However, in a lot of countries around the world their relative value can be a lot more than it is to their owners: in some countries the value of a laptop could easily equate to a month's, or even a year's, wages. Even in countries where their relative value is not so high, they can still be seen as a lucrative opportunity for thieves. Therefore, it is important to try to keep your laptop as safe as possible when you are on vacation. Some points to consider in relation to this are:

- If possible, try to keep your laptop with you at all times, i.e. transport it in a piece of luggage that you can carry rather than having to put it into a large case.
- Never hand over your laptop, or any other items of your belongings, to any local who promises to look after them.
- If you do have to detach yourself from your laptop, try to put it somewhere secure, such as a hotel safe.
- When you are traveling, try to keep your laptop as unobtrusive as possible. This is where a backpack carrying case can prove useful, as it is not immediately apparent that you are carrying a laptop.
- Do not use your laptop in areas where you think it may attract undue interest from the locals, particularly in obviously poor areas. For instance, if you are in a local café, the appearance of a laptop may create unwanted attention for you. If in doubt, wait until you get back to your hotel.
- If you are accosted by criminals who demand your laptop, then hand it over. No piece of equipment is worth suffering physical injury for.
- Make sure your laptop is covered by your vacation insurance. If not, get separate insurance for it.
- Trust your instincts with your laptop. If something doesn't feel right, then don't do it.

Save your important documents, such as vacation photos, onto a flashdrive on a daily basis when on vacation, and keep this away from your laptop. This way, you will still have these items if your laptop is lost or stolen.

Temperature Extremes

Traveling includes seeing different places and cultures, but it also invariably involves different extremes of temperature: a visit to the pyramids of Egypt can see the mercury in the upper reaches of the thermometer, while a cruise to Alaska would present much colder conditions. Whether it is hot or cold, looking after your laptop is an important consideration in extremes of temperature.

If a laptop gets too hot it could buckle the plastic casing, making it difficult to close.

Heat

When traveling in hot countries, the best way of avoiding damage to your laptop is to prevent it from getting too hot in the first place:

- Do not place your laptop in direct sunlight.
- Keep your laptop insulated from the heat.
- Do not leave your laptop in an enclosed space, such as a car. Not only can this get very hot, but the sun's power can be increased by the vehicle's glass.

Try wrapping your laptop in something white, such as a t-shirt or a towel, to insulate it against the heat.

Cold

Again, it is best to try to avoid your laptop getting too cold in the first place, and this can be done by following similar precautions as for heat. However, if your laptop does suffer from extremes of cold, allow it to warm up to normal room temperature again before you try to use it. This may take a couple of hours but it will be worth the wait, rather than risking damaging the delicate computing elements inside.

Laptops at Sea

Water is the greatest enemy of any electrical device, and laptops are no different. This is of particular relevance to anyone who is taking their laptop on vacation near water, such as on a cruise. This not only has the obvious element of water in the sea, but also the proliferation of swimming pools that are a feature of cruise ships. If you are going on vacation near water, then bear in mind the following:

- **Avoid water**. The best way to keep your laptop dry is to keep it away from water whenever possible. For instance, if you want to update your diary or download some photographs, then it would be best to do this in an indoor environment, rather than when sitting around the pool.
- **Keeping dry**. If you think you will be transporting your laptop near water then it is a good precaution to protect it with some form of waterproof bag. There is a range of "dry-bags" that are excellent for this type of occasion, as they remain waterproof even if fully immersed in water. These can be bought from a number of outdoor suppliers.

- **Drying out**. If the worst does occur and your laptop does get a good soaking, then all is not lost. However, you will have to ensure that it is fully dried out before you try to use it again.

Power Sockets

Different countries and regions around the world use different types of power sockets, and this is an issue when you are on vacation with your laptop. Wherever you are going in the world, it is vital to have an adapter that will fit the sockets in the countries you intend to visit, otherwise you will not be able to charge your laptop.

There are over a dozen different types of plugs and sockets used around the world, with the four most popular being:

Hot tip

Power adapters can be bought for all regions around the world. There are also kits that provide all of the adapters together. These provide connections for anywhere, worldwide.

North America, Japan

This is a two-point plug and socket. The pins on the plug are flat and parallel.

Continental Europe

This is a two-point plug and socket. The pins are rounded.

Hot tip

Check before you travel which type of power socket your ship has, and get the right adapter.

Australasia, China, Argentina

This is a three-point socket that can accommodate either a two- or a three-pin plug. In a two-pin plug, the pins are angled in a V shape.

UK

This is a three-point plug. The pins are rectangular.

Airport Security

Because of the increased global security following terrorist attacks, levels of airport security have been greatly increased around the world. This has implications for all travelers, and if you are traveling with a laptop this will add to the security scrutiny you will face. When dealing with airport security when traveling with a laptop, there are some issues that you should always keep in mind:

- Keep your laptop with you at all times. Unguarded baggage at airports immediately raises suspicion and it can make life very easy for thieves.
- Carry your laptop in a small bag so that you can take it on board as hand luggage. On no account should it be put in with your luggage that goes in the hold.
- X-ray machines at airports will not harm your laptop. However, if anyone tries to scan it with a metal detector, ask them if they can inspect it by hand instead.
- Keep a careful eye on your laptop when it goes through the X-ray conveyor belt and try to be there at the other side as soon as it emerges. There have been some stories of people causing a commotion at the security gate just after someone has placed their laptop on the conveyor belt. While everyone's attention (including yours) is distracted, an accomplice takes the laptop from the conveyor belt. If you are worried about this, you can ask for the security guard to hand-check your laptop rather than putting it on the conveyor belt.
- Make sure the battery of your laptop is fully charged. This is because you may be asked to turn on your laptop to verify that it is just that, and not some other device disguised as a laptop.
- When you are on the plane, keep the laptop in the storage area under your seat, rather than in the overhead locker, so that you know where it is at all times.

At the time of printing, there are some issues with taking laptops on planes, particularly to the USA. If in doubt, contact your airline before you fly.

If there is any kind of distraction when you are going through security checks at an airport, it could be because someone is trying to divert your attention in order to steal your laptop.

When traveling through airport security, leave your laptop in Sleep mode so that it can be powered up quickly if anyone needs to check that it works properly.

Keeping in Touch

Skype has become established as one of the premier services for free voice and video calls (to other Skype users) and instant messaging for text messages. It can now be incorporated into your Windows 10 experience and used to keep in touch with family and friends, at home and around the world. To use Skype:

If the Skype button is not available from the Start menu, the app can be downloaded from the Windows Store.

1. Click on the **Skype** button on the Start menu

2. If you already have a Skype account you can sign in with these details, or with your Microsoft Account details. Click on **Create a new account** to create a new Skype account

When you create a text conversation with one of your contacts in Skype, it will continue down the page as you respond to each other.

3. Recent conversations are listed in the left-hand panel

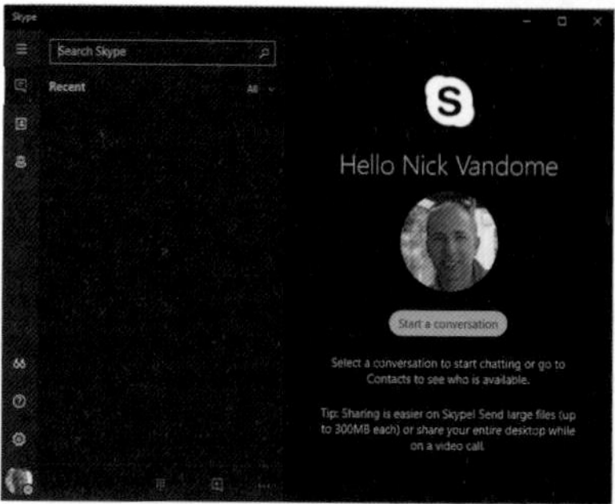

When you add someone as a contact, you have to send them a contact request, which they must accept to become one of your contacts.

4. Click on this button to view your Skype contacts, or search for new ones. Tap on one to start a voice or video call, or text message

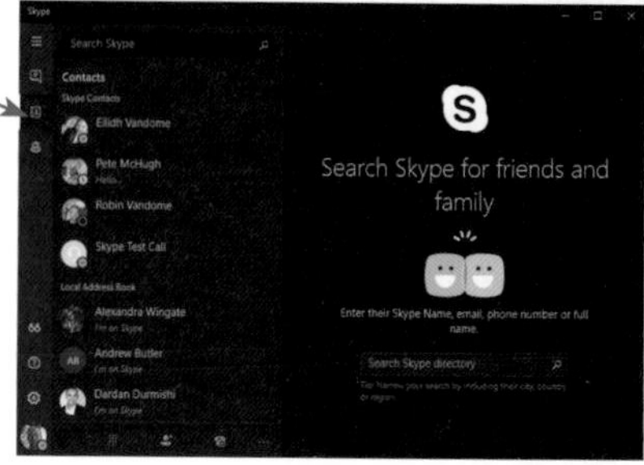

Sharing with Your Family

This chapter deals with sharing your laptop.

About Multiple Users

Because of the power and flexibility that is available in a laptop computer, it seems a waste to restrict it to a single user. Thankfully, it is possible for multiple users to use the same laptop. One way to do this is simply to let different people use the laptop whenever they have access to it. However, since everyone creates their own files and documents, and different people use different types of apps, it makes much more sense to allow people to set up their own user accounts. This creates their own personal computing area that is protected from anyone else accessing it. User accounts create a sense of personalization, and also security, as each account can be protected by a password.

Without user accounts, the laptop will display the default account automatically. However, if different user accounts have been set up on the laptop, a list of these accounts will be displayed at the top of the Start menu.

If no other user accounts have been set up, yours will be the only one, and you will be the administrator. This means that you can set up new accounts and alter a variety of settings on the laptop.

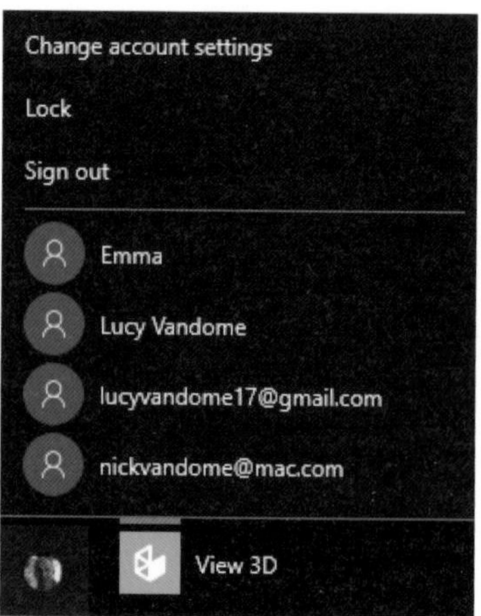

The relevant user can then click on their own account to access it. At this point they will have to enter the correct password to gain access to their account. A user can have a Local Account or a Microsoft Account. If it is the latter, the user will have access to a selection of Microsoft services, through the Windows 10 apps. A password can be specified for either a Local Account or a Microsoft one. To see how to add new user accounts, see pages 146-147.

Customization

Once individual user accounts have been set up it is possible for each user to customize their account, i.e. to set the way in which their account appears and operates. This means that each user can set their own preferences, such as for the way the Start menu and Desktop background appear, and also the items on the Taskbar:

This shows two different user accounts and the changes in Settings, Background and Taskbar apps.

The whole Desktop environment can be customized. This is done within the **Personalization** section of the **Settings** app.

Adding Users

If more than one person uses the laptop, each person can have a user account defined with a username and a password. To create a new user account, as either a Microsoft Account or a Local account:

1. Access the **Settings** app and select **Accounts**

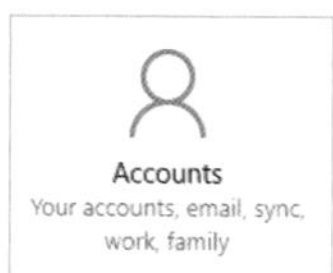

2. Click on the **Family & other people** button

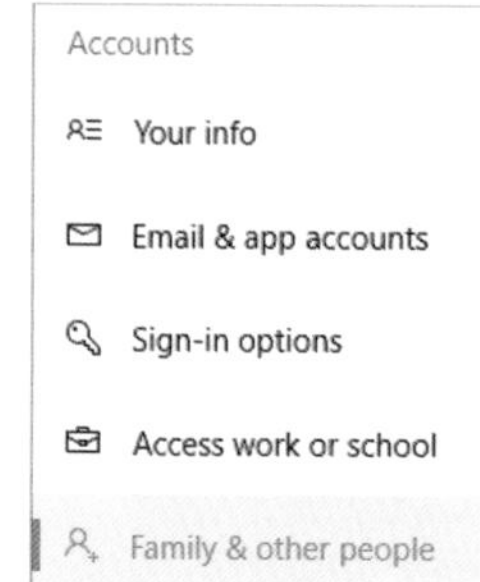

The email address is a required field when creating a new user with a Microsoft Account.

3. Click on the **Add a family member** button

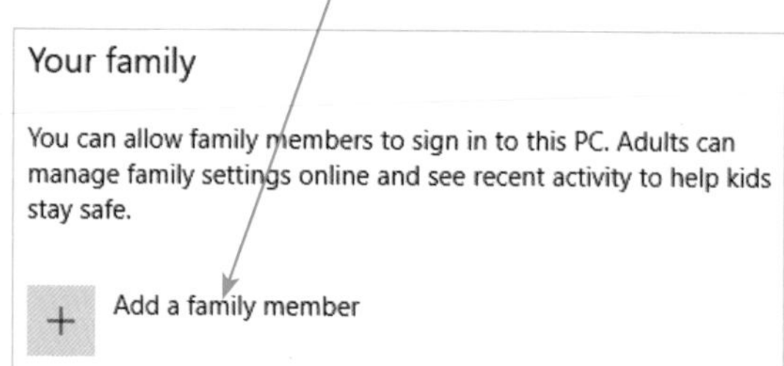

4. Select whether the account is for a child or an adult. For a child, this provides online security options. Then, click **Next**

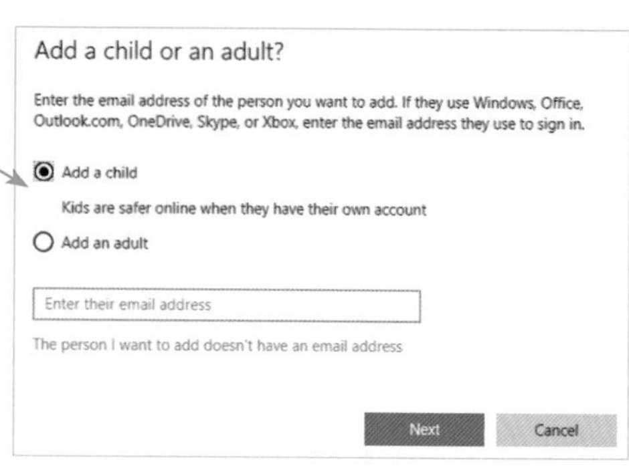

5. Enter the name of the new user, an email address and a password to create a Microsoft Account for the user

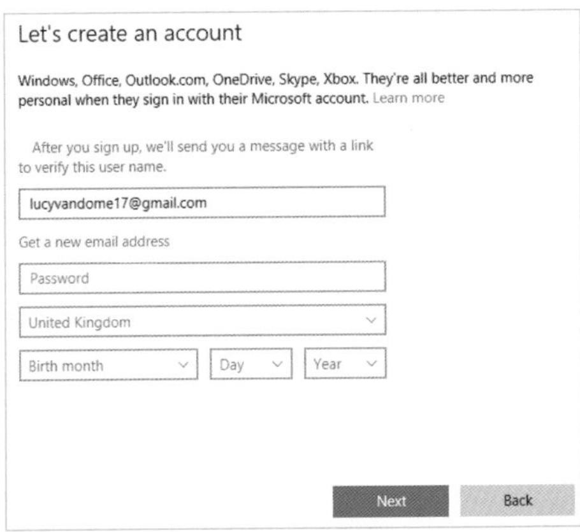

6. Click on the **Next** button to complete the setup wizard

Next

7. The user is added to the Accounts pages

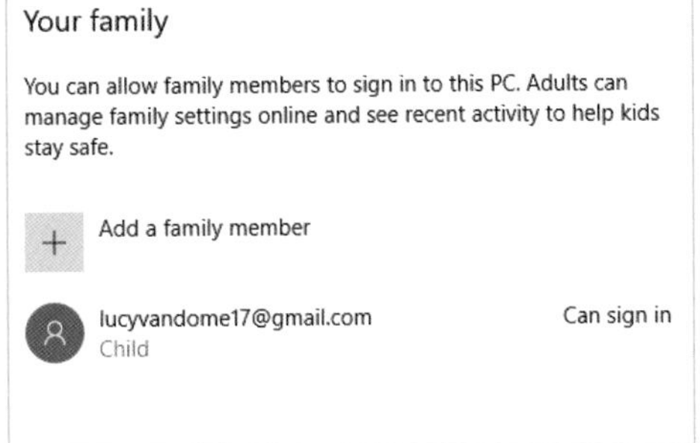

8. Click on a user to change the type of their account, e.g. from a Local account to a Microsoft Account, or to delete their account

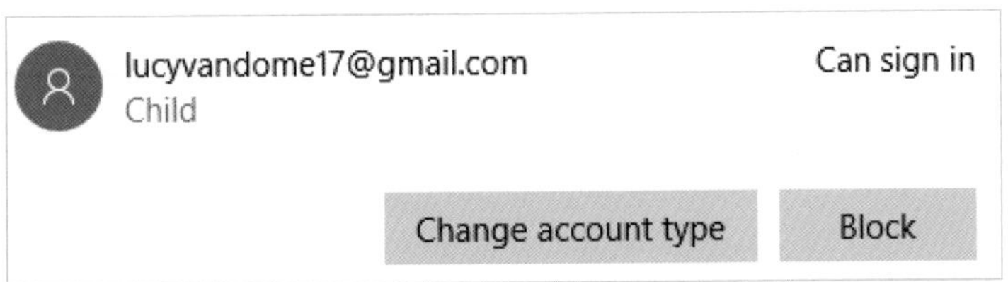

Family Safety

Once multiple user accounts have been set up, it is possible to apply separate online security settings to different accounts. This can be useful if you are going to be setting up an account for grandchildren and you want to have a certain amount of control over how they use the laptop. To do this:

1. Access the **Accounts** > **Family & other people** section of the **Settings** app
2. Select a user, and click on the **Manage family settings online** link

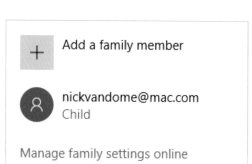

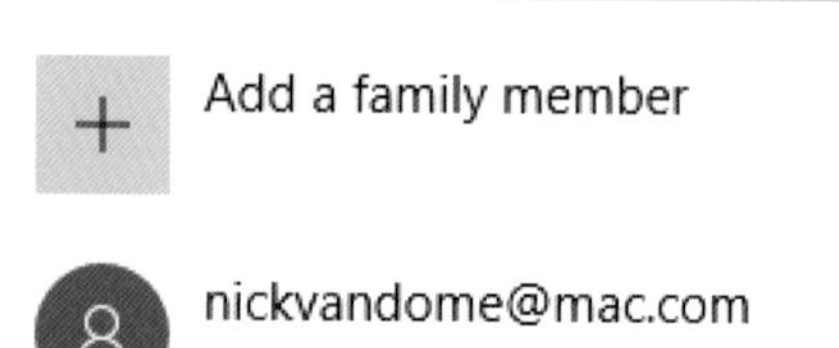

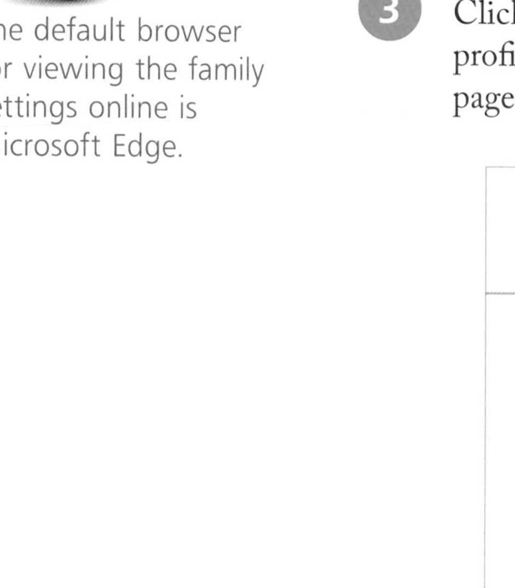

The default browser for viewing the family settings online is Microsoft Edge.

3. Click on one of the options for managing the child's profile and applying restrictions, as required (see pages 149-152)

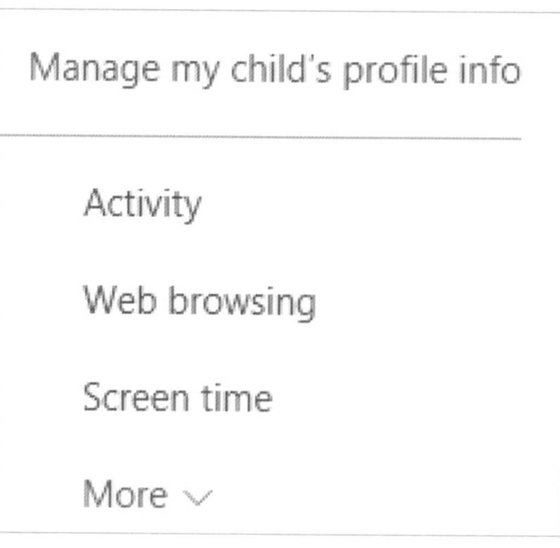

Recent activity controls

One of the options within the family safety controls is to view recent activity by a user. To view this:

1. In the Manage family settings online section, underneath Your family, select the required user

2. Click on the **Recent activity** button and drag the **Activity reporting** button to **On**

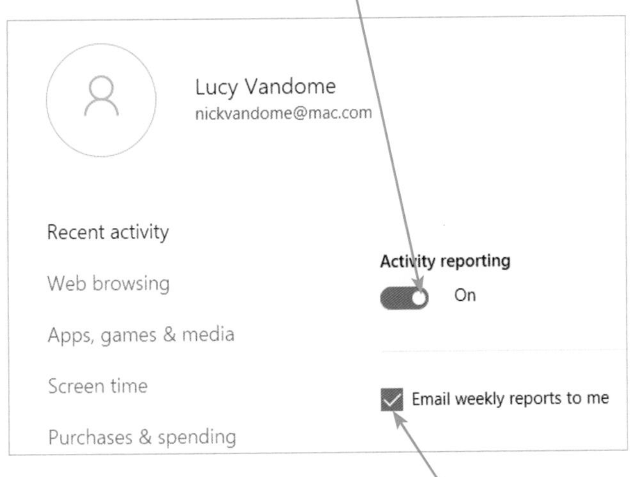

3. Check **On** the **Email weekly reports to me** button to receive a weekly report about the user's computer usage

4. Scroll down the page to view and edit the other family safety options

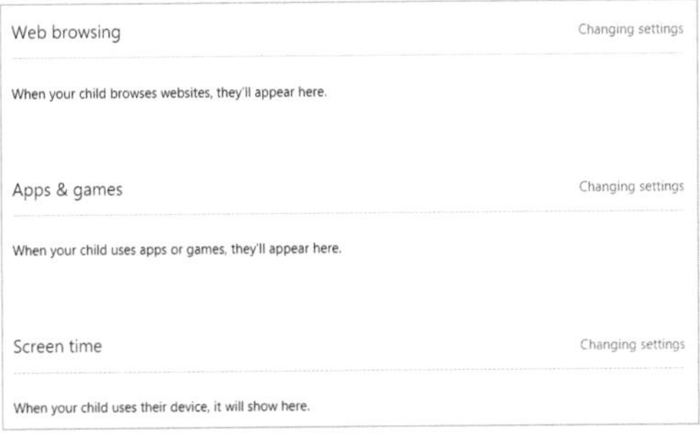

If you are setting family safety for young people, such as grandchildren, make sure you tell them what you have done so that they understand the reasons behind your actions.

...cont'd

Web browsing controls

The websites accessed by a specific user can also be controlled through family safety:

1. Click on the **Web browsing** button

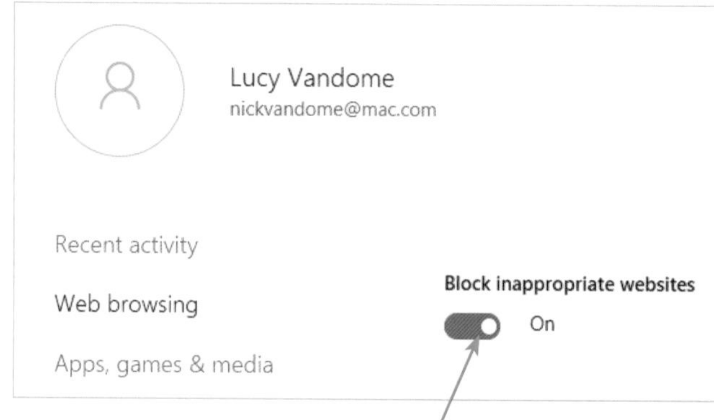

2. Drag the **Block inappropriate websites** button to **On**

3. Enter the web addresses of any websites you want to include, and click on the **Allow** button

To block specific websites, add them in the **Always block these** section, and click on the **Block** button.

Apps and games controls

Computer games and apps are another very popular pastime for young people. These include games that are downloaded from the web, and also those that are bought on CDs or DVDs. However, just as with movies, some games and apps are unsuitable for younger children and should have ratings to specify the age groups for which they are suitable. It is then possible to control which games are played. To do this:

1. From the **Manage family settings online** link (shown in the image in Step 2 on page 148), click on the **Apps, games & media** link to restrict the type of content the user can access

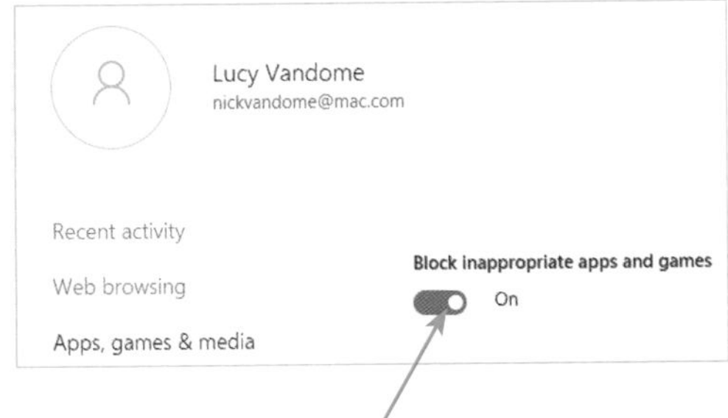

2. Drag the **Block inappropriate apps and games** button to **On**

3. Click here to select the appropriate age group, and rating, for which you want restrictions to apply

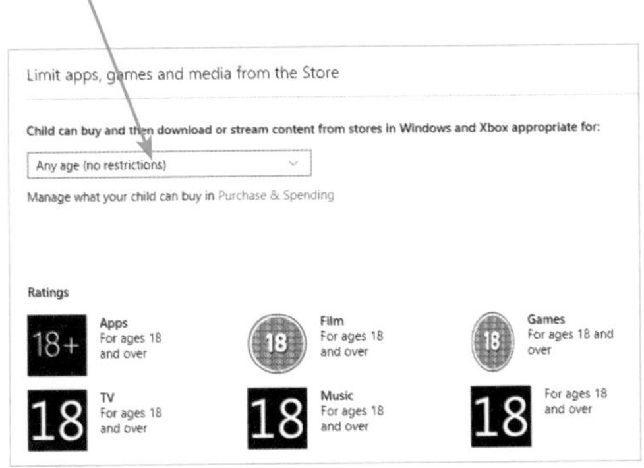

The age ratings in Step 3 will be applicable to your geographical location.

…cont'd

Screen time controls

A familiar worry when young people are using computers is the amount of time that they are spending on them. However, this can also be controlled in the Screen time controls for a selected user. To do this:

1. From the **Manage family settings online** link (shown in the image in Step 2 on page 148), click on the **Screen time** button to specify times at which a user can use the computer

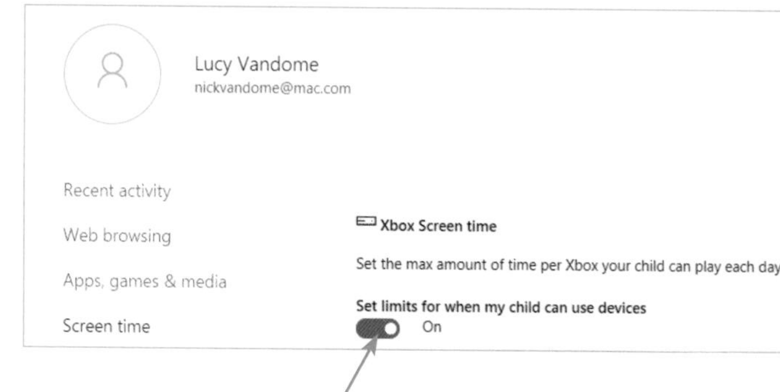

2. Drag the **Set limits for when my child can use devices** button to **On**

3. Select the times for using the laptop on specific days (each day can have its own times and also an overall limit per day)

If time controls have been set, the affected user will not be able to access their account outside the times that have been specified.

9 Networking and Wireless

This chapter shows how to use the Windows 10 networking functions, enabling you to share files and folders and use the HomeGroup file-sharing feature.

Setting Up a Network

In computing terms, a network is when a computer is connected to one or more computers, or it is connected to the internet. This means that content and files can be shared between computers.

To set up a network you must first get all of the required hardware in place. For this you will require a router, which is the device through which all of the elements of the network will communicate. To set up your network:

1. Plug in your router to the mains electricity

2. Connect your router to your internet connection, via either a phone line or an Ethernet cable. This plugs into the back of the router

3. For a Ethernet connection, attach one end of the cable to the computer and the other to the router

4. If you have a laptop with wireless connectivity, the laptop will communicate with the router wirelessly when the network software creates the network

5. Connect any other items of hardware that you want to include in the network, such as a printer. This can be done wirelessly, if the printer is equipped with a wireless card, or more commonly, with a USB or an Ethernet connection

If your network uses a wireless router, this means that anyone within the range of the router could connect to the network, even if they are outside your house. To avoid this, you have to set a password for your router, which can be done when you initially connect it and set it up.

Going Wireless

For networking, "wireless" means connecting your computer to other devices using radio waves rather than cables. These can include a router for connecting to a network, a printer, keyboard, mouse or speakers (as long as these devices also have a wireless capability). For the laptop user in particular, this gives you the ultimate freedom; you can take your laptop wherever you want, and still be able to access the internet and use a variety of peripherals.

Wireless standards

As with everything in the world of computers, there are industry standards for wireless connections: for networking devices the standard is known as IEEE 802.11. The purpose of standards is to ensure that all of the connected devices can communicate with each other.

Very few new devices use the 802.11a version of the standard, although newer devices will usually be backwards-compatible with it.

The IEEE 802.11 standard (or just 802.11) used for networks has a number of different variations (known as protocols) of the original standard. These variations have been developed since the introduction of 802.11 in 1997, with a view to making it work faster and cover a greater range. Early wireless devices used the 802.11a and 802.11b protocols, while the most widely used protocol at the time of printing is 802.11n, with 802.11ac also beginning to be used. When you are creating a wireless network it is best to have all of the devices using the same version of 802.11. For instance, if you have a wireless card in your laptop that uses 802.11n, then it is best to have the same version in your router. However, most modern wireless cards and routers have multiple compatibility, and can cater for at least the b and g versions of the standard. If two devices use different 802.11 protocols, they should still be able to communicate, but the rate of data transfer may be slower than if both of the devices used the same protocol.

Devices using the 802.11n protocol can communicate with each other via radio waves over distances of approximately 25 yards (indoors) and 75 yards (outdoors).

The Bluetooth standard is another method of connecting devices wirelessly. It does not have the same range as 802.11 and is now mainly used for connecting devices over short distances, such as a wireless mouse.

Connecting to a Network

You can connect your computers to form a network using Ethernet cables and adapters, or by setting up your wireless adapters and routers. When you start up each computer, Windows 10 will examine the current configuration and discover any new networks that have been established since the last startup. You can check this, or connect manually to a network, from within the Wi-Fi settings from the Network & Internet section of Settings. To do this:

The most common type of network for connecting to is the internet.

If your network is unavailable for any reason, this will be noted in Step 2.

1. Access the **Settings** app and click on the **Network & Internet** button

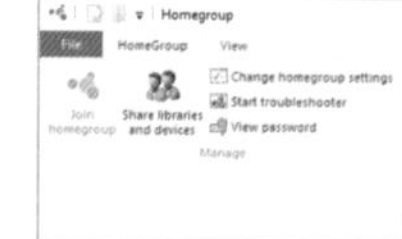

2. Drag the Wi-Fi button to **On**. Under the **Wi-Fi** heading, click on one of the available networks

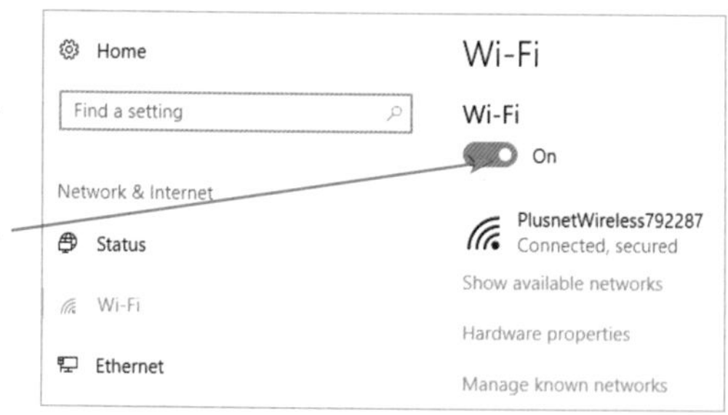

3. Click on the network and drag **On** the **Connect automatically when in range** button

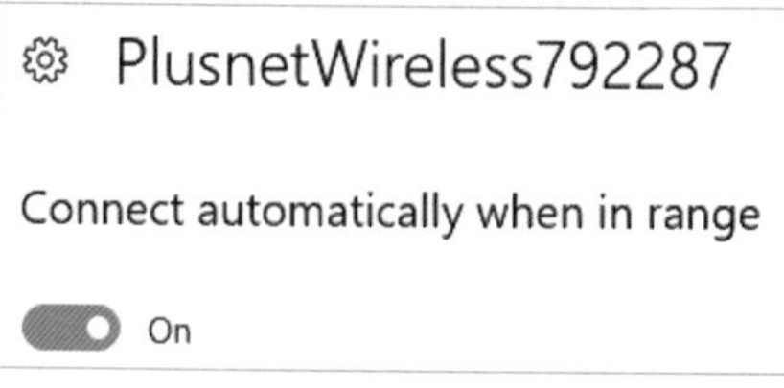

4. The selected network is shown as **Connected**. This is also shown in the Notifications area

Joining the HomeGroup

The HomeGroup is a network function that enables a Windows 10 computer to connect to another Windows 10 PC (or Windows 7/8) and share content. You can set up and connect to the HomeGroup through the Settings app:

When you add a computer to your network, Windows 10 on that computer will detect that there is a HomeGroup already created.

1. Access **Network & Internet > Status** in the Settings app and click on the **HomeGroup** link (which opens in the Control Panel)

2. Click on the **Create a homegroup** button to start setting up the HomeGroup

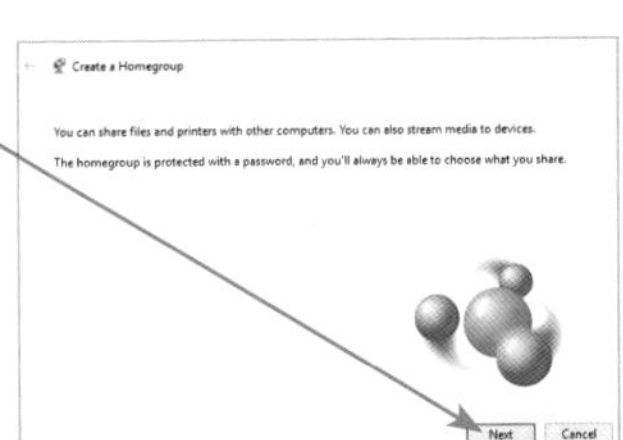

3. Click the **Next** button

A HomeGroup applies to any user with an account on the computer, so if a different user logs on, the associated files will also be accessible.

4. Select the items that you want to share in the HomeGroup, and click on the **Next** button

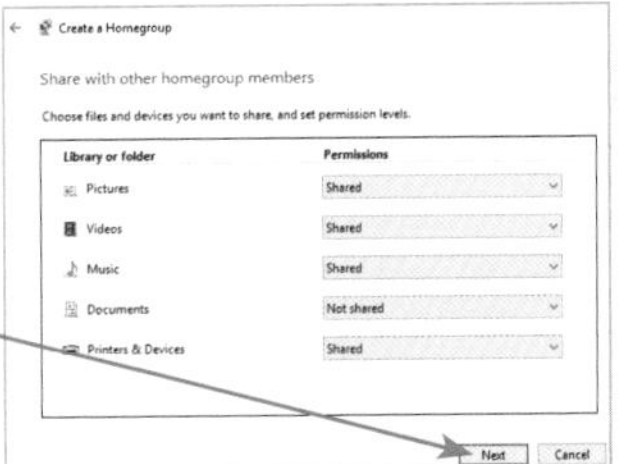

5. Enter the password from the other computer. Click on the **Finish** button. After joining the HomeGroup you will be able to share your files to the other computer, and vice versa

Windows generates the password when the HomeGroup is created.

Sharing Files and Folders

There are different ways in which you can share items once a HomeGroup has been set up:

1. Open File Explorer and select the **Homegroup** in the Navigation pane, then click on the **Share libraries and devices** button in the HomeGroup section of the File Explorer Ribbon tabs

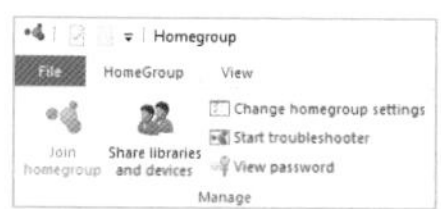

2. Select the items that you want to share with the HomeGroup. This is done automatically, i.e. if you share Pictures then all of the items in the Pictures library will be shared, as will new ones that are added in the future

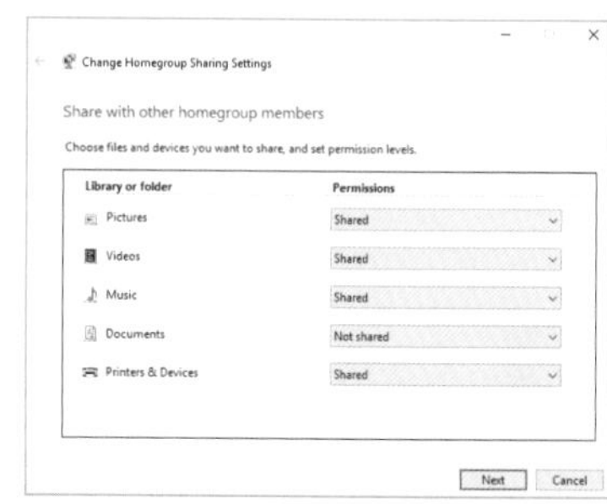

3. To share a specific item, select it in File Explorer and click on the **Homegroup (view)** button in the Share with section

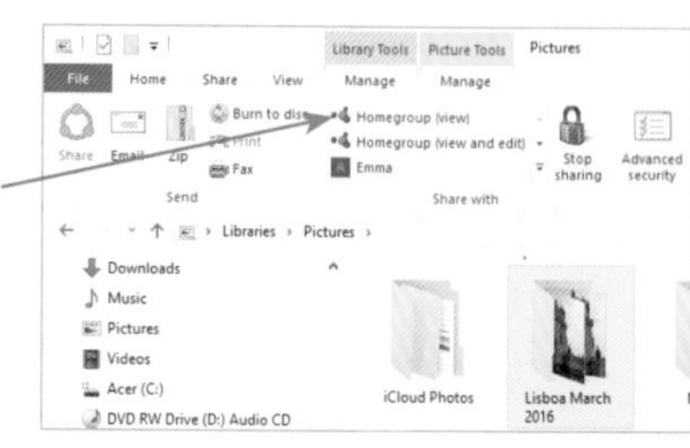

4. Select Homegroup in the Navigation pane of the File Explorer pane to view the shared item in Step 3

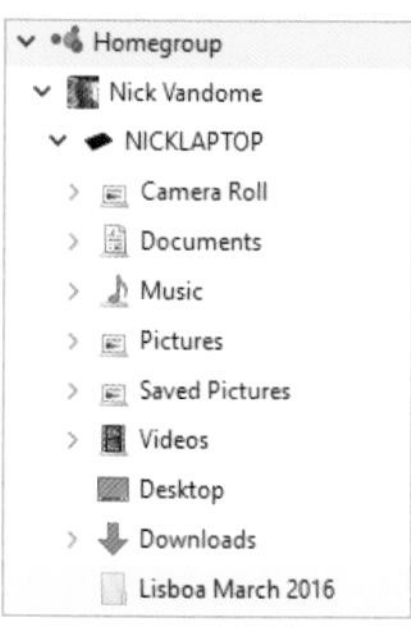

The **Share with** section in File Explorer is accessed from the Share tab on the Ribbon.

Sharing Settings

There are also options for specifying how items are shared over the network, not just in the HomeGroup. To select these:

1. Open **Settings** > **Network & Internet** > **Status** and click on the **Sharing options** link

Sharing options
For the networks you connect to, decide what you want to share.

2. Select sharing options for different networks, including Private, Guest or Public and All networks. Options can be selected for turning on network discovery so that your computer can see other computers on the network, and for turning on file and printer sharing

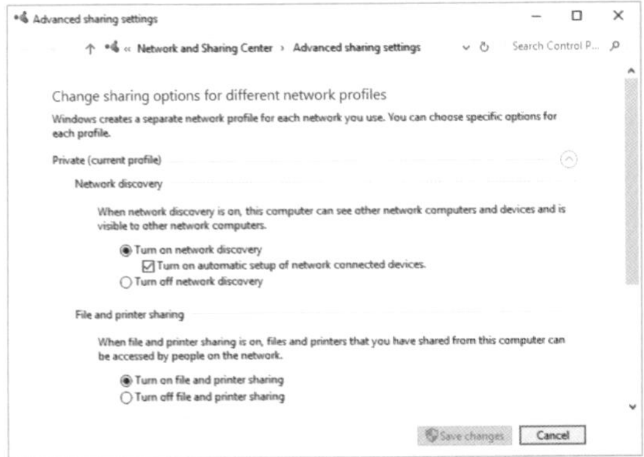

3. Click on these arrows to expand the options for each network category

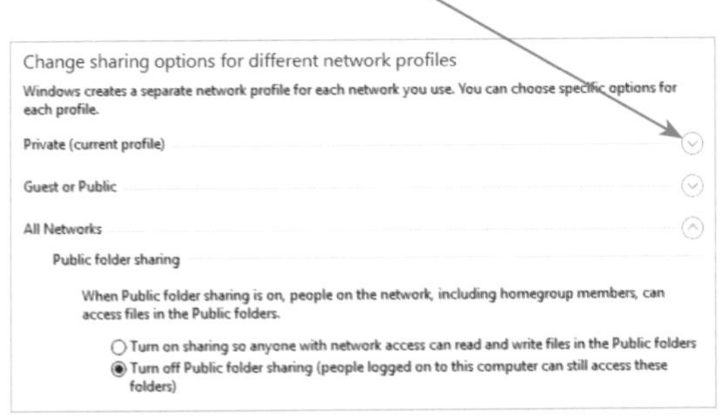

If you are sharing over a network you should be able to access the Public folder on another computer (providing that network discovery is turned on). If you are the administrator of the other computer you will also be able to access your own Home folder, although you will need to enter the required password for this.

Saving Files for Sharing

When you want to save files so that other people on your network can access them (other than with the HomeGroup), this can be done by either saving them into the Public folder on your own laptop, or saving them into the Public folder of another computer on your network. To do this:

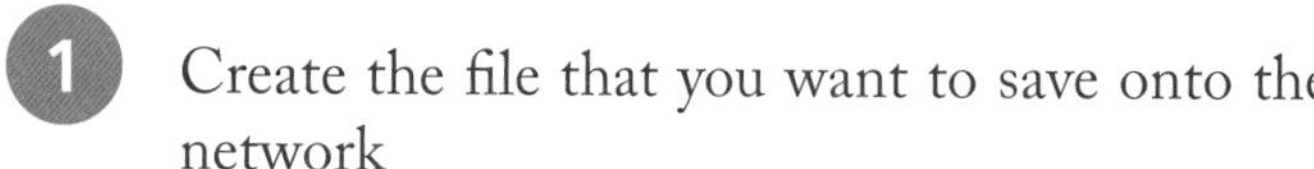

1. Create the file that you want to save onto the network

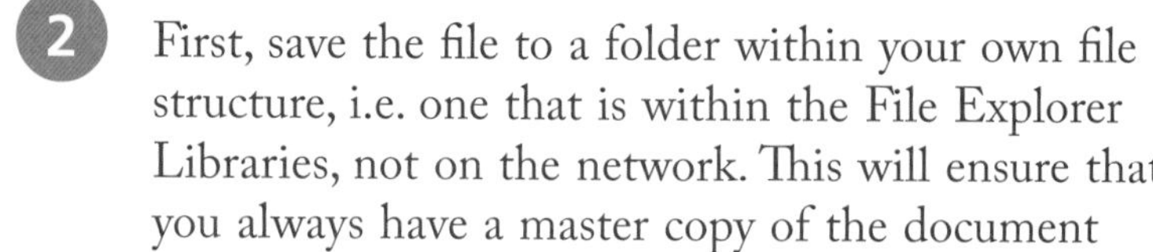

2. First, save the file to a folder within your own file structure, i.e. one that is within the File Explorer Libraries, not on the network. This will ensure that you always have a master copy of the document

3. Select **File** > **Save As** from the Menu bar (this is standard in most types of apps)

4. The Save As window has options for where you can save the file

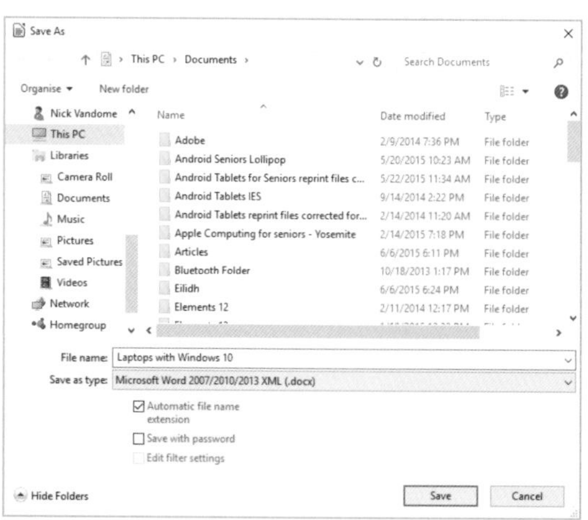

5. Click on the **Network** icon in the left-hand pane

Files can also be copied to Public folders on the network by dragging and dropping them from within your own file structure. This can be done within the File Explorer window.

6. Double-click on another computer on the network to save the file here

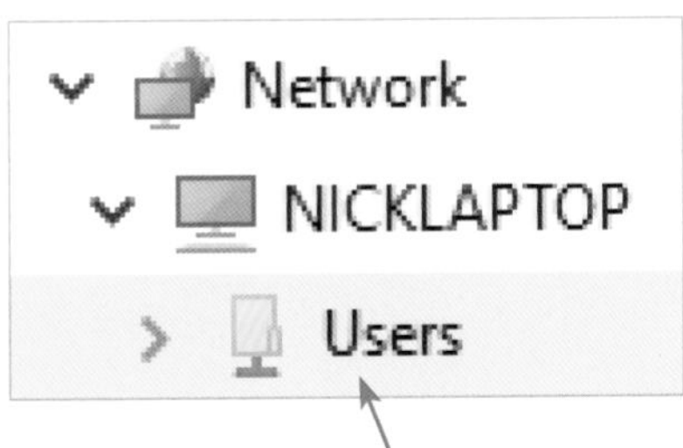

7. Double-click on the **Users** folder, then the **Public** folder

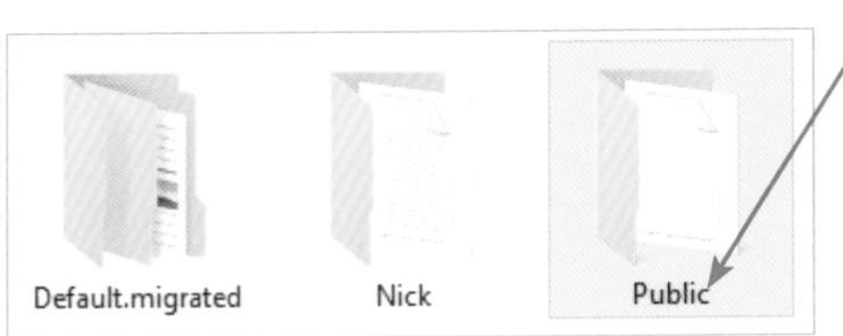

8. Double-click on the folder into which you want to save the file

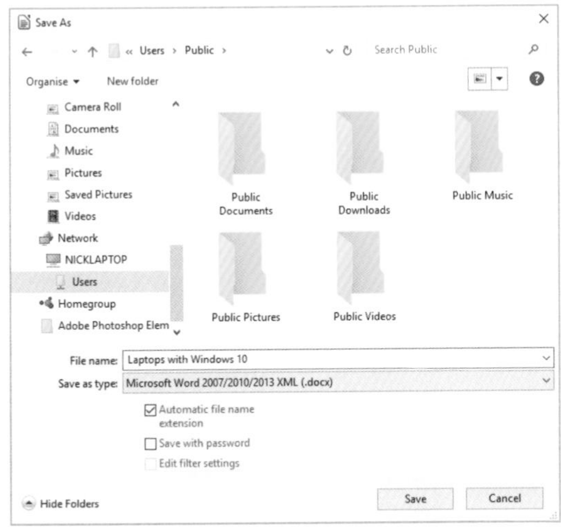

If you copy files to your own Public folder, other computers on the network will only be able to access these when your laptop is turned on.

Network Troubleshooting

1. Open **Settings** > **Network & Internet** > **Status** and click on the **Network troubleshooter** link

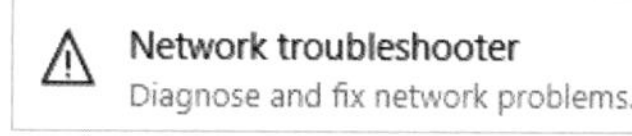

For more Windows 10 troubleshooting options, see page 175.

2. Click on the option that most closely matches your network problem

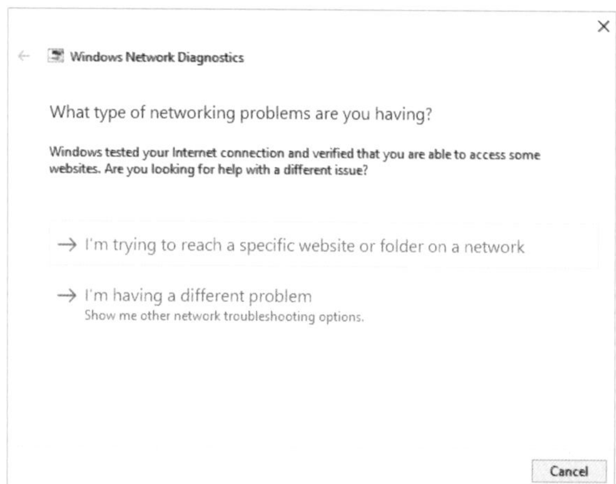

3. Most options have additional selections that can be made to try to solve the problem. Click on these as required

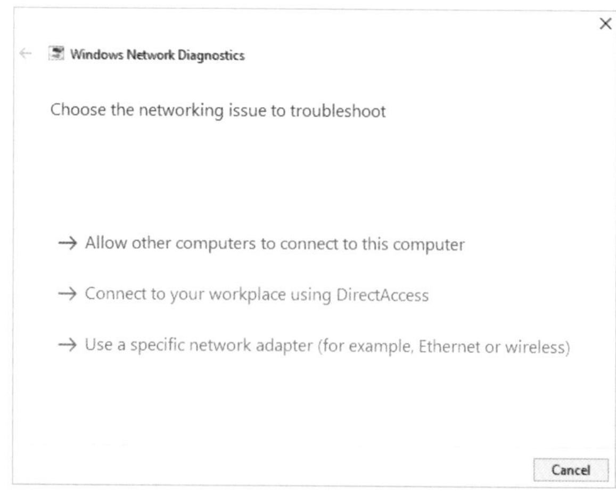

10 Battery Issues

Battery power is crucial to a laptop, and this chapter shows how to get the best out of your battery and deal with any problems.

Types of Battery

A laptop's battery is one of the items that helps to define its identity: without it, the portable nature of the laptop would be very different as it would always have to be connected with a power cable. Laptops have used a variety of different types of batteries since they were first produced, and over the years these have become smaller, lighter and more powerful. However, laptop batteries are still relatively heavy and bulky, and are one of the major sources of weight in the machine:

Don't forget

The type of battery provided with a laptop, and the approximate lifespan for each charge, should be displayed with the details about the machine on the manufacturer's website or in any promotional literature that comes with it.

The quality of laptop batteries is improving all the time. Some models currently on the market have a battery life of up to eight, or even ten, hours.

The types of batteries used in modern laptops are:

- **Lithium-ion**. This is a type of battery that has a good weight-to-power ratio and loses its charge at a relatively slow rate. However, they can be prone to overheating if they are not treated properly or are defective.
- **Lithium polymer**. This is an advanced version of the lithium-ion battery. It is generally considered to be a more stable design.

These types of batteries are rechargeable, so they can be charged and used numerous times after they initially run out. However, over time, all rechargeable batteries eventually wear out and have to be replaced.

Power Consumption

Battery life for each charge of laptop batteries is one area on which engineers have worked very hard since laptops were first introduced. For most modern laptops, the average battery life for each charge is approximately between three and five hours. However, this is dependent on the power consumption of the laptop, i.e. how much power is being used to perform particular tasks. Power-intensive tasks will reduce the battery life of each charge cycle. These types of tasks include:

- Surfing the web
- Watching a DVD
- Editing digital video
- Editing digital photographs

When you are using your laptop you can always monitor how much battery power you currently have available. This is shown by the battery icon that appears at the right-hand side of the Taskbar:

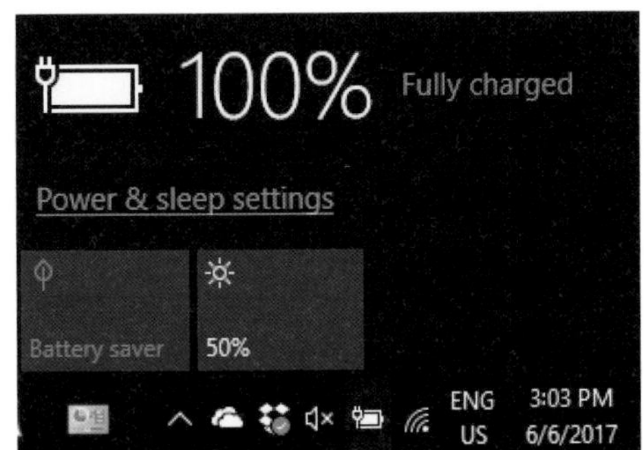

Because of the vital role that the battery plays in relation to your laptop, it is important to try to conserve its power as much as possible. To do this:

- Where possible, use the mains adapter rather than the battery when using your laptop.
- Use the Sleep function when you are not actively using your laptop.
- Use power-management functions to save battery power (see pages 166-168).

If you are undertaking an energy-intensive task, such as browsing the web, try to use the external AC/DC power cable rather than the battery, otherwise the battery may drain quickly and the laptop will close down.

Battery Management

Unlike desktop computers, laptops have options for how the battery is managed. These allow you to set things like individual power schemes for the battery and to view how much charge is left in the battery. This can be done from the Settings app. To access the options for managing your laptop's battery:

1. Access the **Settings** app and select the **System** section

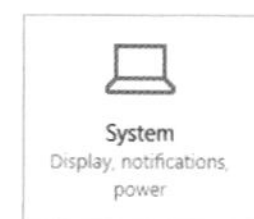

2. Click on the **Power & sleep** link

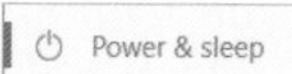

3. Under the **Power & sleep** section, click on the Screen options to make selections for the period of inactivity until the screen goes to sleep, for both on battery power and when connected to the mains

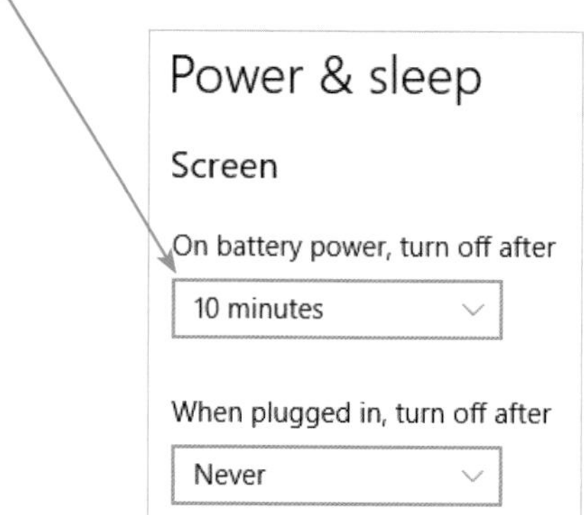

4. Select a time period for the selection made in Step 3 (this can include **Never**, in which case the screen will not be put to sleep)

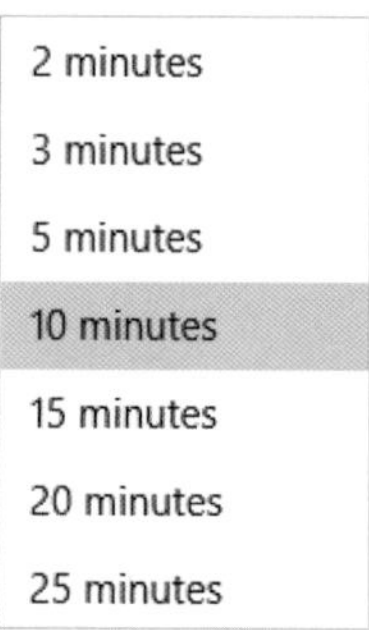

5. Under the **Sleep** section, click on options for putting the laptop to sleep after a period of inactivity, for both battery and mains power

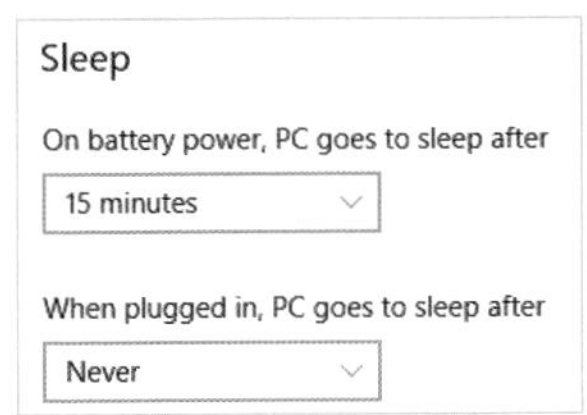

6. Select a time period for the selection made in Step 5, in the same way as for putting the screen to sleep (this can include **Never**, in which case the laptop will not be put to sleep)

If you don't protect your laptop with a password for when it is woken from sleep, anyone could access your folders and files if they wake the laptop from sleep.

Power settings

Additional power settings can be made from the link under Related settings at the bottom of the Power & sleep section.

1. Click on the **Additional power settings** link

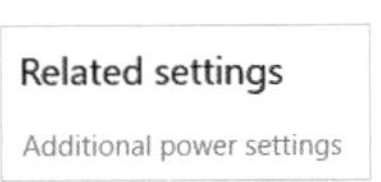

2. The link opens the Control Panel **Power Options** window for creating customized power plans

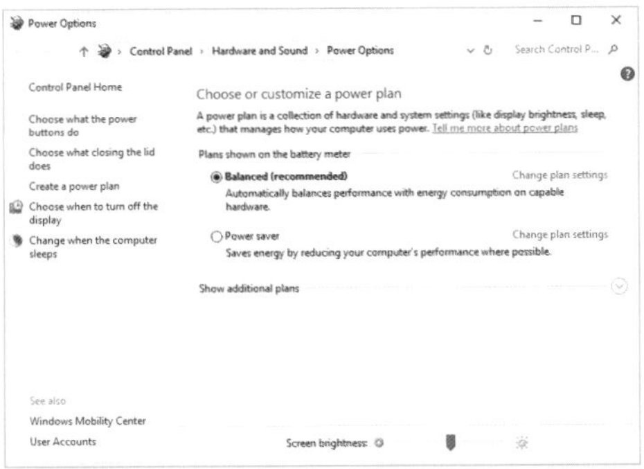

3. Click here to select power plans, for balancing performance and battery consumption

Use the links at the left-hand side of the Power Options window to access other power-management options, such as what happens when closing the lid of the laptop.

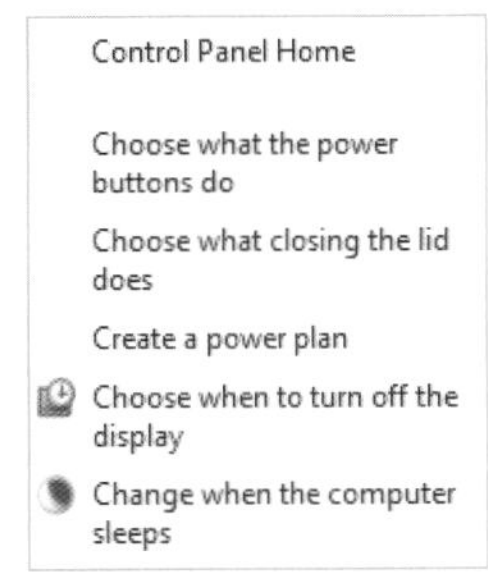

Battery saver

Within the System Settings there is also an option for viewing the current level of battery charge, the estimated time remaining on the current charge and viewing battery usage by app. There is also an option for turning the battery saver on automatically. To do this:

1. Click on the **Battery** button within **Settings** > **System**

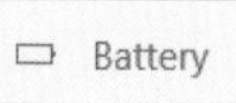

2. The current battery usage is shown here, with the estimated time remaining for the current charge shown below

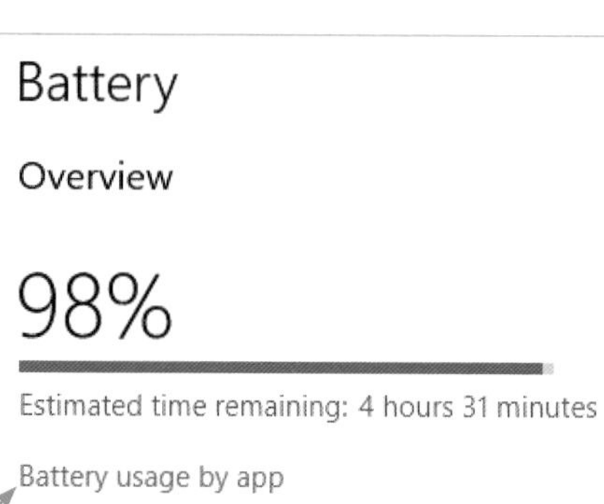

3. Click on the **Battery usage by app** link to view how much power currently-running apps are using

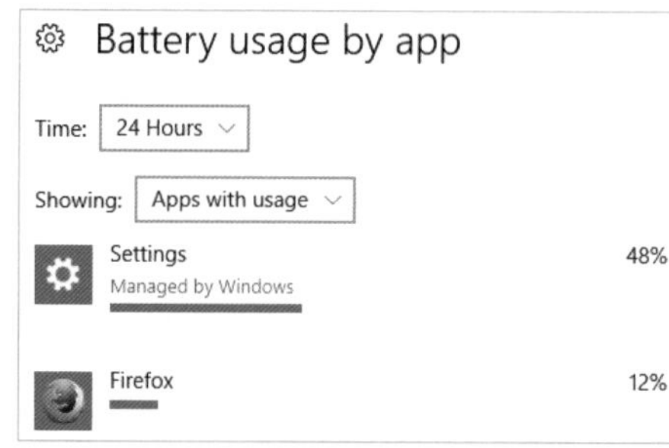

4. Under **Battery saver** check On this button and drag the slider to specify the battery level at which the battery saver will be turned on

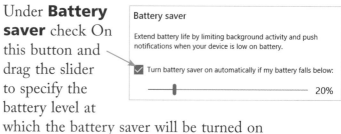

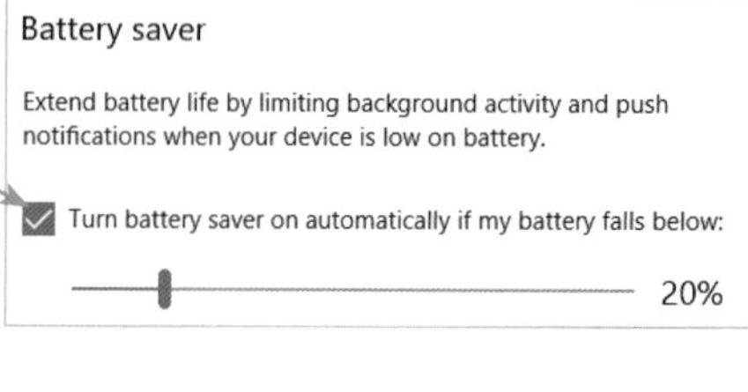

Battery saver
Extend battery life by limiting background activity and push notifications when your device is low on battery.
Turn battery saver on automatically if my battery falls below:
20%

Don't forget

When the battery saver is On, background activity (such as pushing notifications and emails) is limited in order to save power.

Charging the Battery

Laptop batteries are charged using an AC/DC adapter, which can also be used to power the laptop instead of the battery. If the laptop is turned on and being powered by the AC/DC adapter, the battery will be charged at the same time, although at a slower rate than if it is being charged with the laptop turned off.

The AC/DC adapter should be supplied with a new laptop, and consists of a cable and a power adapter. To charge a laptop battery using an AC/DC adapter:

A laptop battery can be charged whether the laptop is turned on or off.

1. Connect the AC/DC adapter to the cable and plug it into the mains socket
2. Attach the AC/DC adapter to the laptop and turn on at the mains socket
3. When the laptop is turned on, the Power Meter icon is visible at the right-hand side of the Taskbar. Click on this to view the current power details

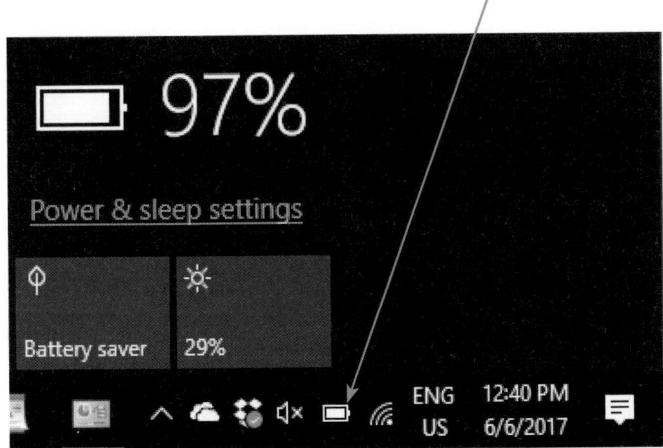

4. If the laptop is on battery power, click on the **Battery saver** button to turn this option On

Removing the Battery

Although a laptop's battery does not have to be removed on a regular basis, there may be occasions when you want to do this. These include:

- If the laptop freezes, i.e. you are unable to undertake any operations using the keyboard or mouse, and you cannot turn off the laptop using the Power button.
- If you are traveling, particularly in extreme temperatures. In situations such as this, you may prefer to keep the battery with you to try to avoid exposing it to either very hot or very cold temperatures.

To remove a laptop battery:

Some laptops, particularly slim ultrabooks, do not have removable batteries and they have to be replaced by the manufacturer.

1. With the laptop turned off and the lid closed, turn the laptop upside down
2. Locate the battery compartment and either push or slide the lock that keeps the battery in place

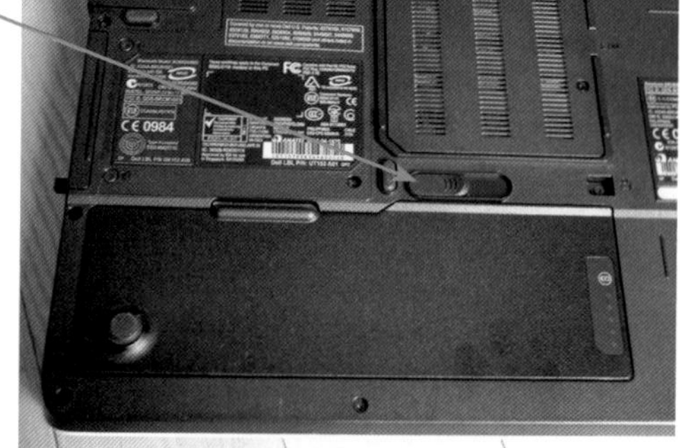

3. Slide the battery out of its compartment

To re-insert the battery, or a new battery, push it gently into the battery compartment until it clicks firmly into place.

Dead and Spare Batteries

No energy source lasts forever, and laptop batteries are no exception to this rule. Over time, the battery will operate less efficiently until it will not be possible to charge the battery at all. With average usage, most laptop batteries should last approximately five years, although they will start to lose performance before this. Some signs of a dead laptop battery are:

- Nothing happens when the laptop is turned on using just battery power.
- The laptop shuts down immediately if it is being run on the AC/DC adapter and the cord is suddenly removed.
- The Battery Meter shows no movement when the AC/DC adapter is connected, i.e. the Battery Meter remains at 0% and shows as not charging at all.

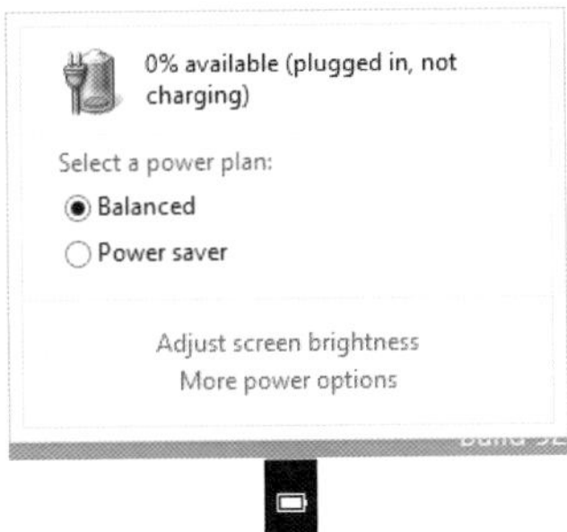

If you think that your battery may be losing its performance, make sure that you save your work at regular intervals. Although you should do this anyway, it is more important if there is a chance of your battery running out of power and abruptly turning off.

Spare battery

Because of the limited lifespan of laptop batteries, it is worth considering buying a spare battery. Although these are not cheap it can be a valuable investment, particularly if you spend a lot of time traveling with your laptop and you are not always near a source of mains electricity. In situations such as this, a spare battery could enable you to keep using your laptop if your original battery runs out of power.

When buying a spare battery, check with the laptop's manufacturer that it will be compatible: in most cases the manufacturer will also be able to supply you with a spare battery for your laptop.

Battery Troubleshooting

If you look after your laptop battery well it should provide you with several years of mobile computing power. However, there are some problems which may occur with the battery:

- **It won't keep its charge even when connected to an AC/DC adapter**. The battery is probably flat and should be replaced.
- **It only charges up a limited amount**. Over time, laptop batteries become less efficient and so do not hold their charge so well. One way to try to improve this is to drain the battery completely before it is charged again.
- **It keeps its charge but runs down quickly**. This can be caused by the use of a lot of power-hungry applications on the laptop. The more work the laptop has to do to run applications, such as those involving videos or games, the more power will be required from the battery and the faster it will run down.
- **It is fully charged but does not appear to work at all when inserted**. Check that the battery has clicked into place properly in the battery compartment and that the battery and laptop terminals are clean, and free from dust or moisture.
- **It is inserted correctly but still does not work**. The battery may have become damaged in some way, such as becoming very wet. If you know the battery is damaged in any way, do not insert it, as it could short-circuit the laptop. If the battery has been in contact with liquid, dry it out completely before you try inserting it into the laptop. If it is dried thoroughly, it may work again.
- **It gets very hot when in operation**. This could be caused by a faulty battery, and it can be dangerous and lead to a fire. If in doubt, turn off the laptop immediately and consult the manufacturer. In some cases faulty laptop batteries are recalled, so keep an eye on the manufacturer's website to see if there are any details of this if you are concerned.

If there is no response from your laptop when you turn it on in battery mode, try removing the battery and re-inserting it. If there is still no response then the battery is probably flat, and should be replaced.

If you are not going to be using your laptop for an extended period of time, remove the battery and store it in a safe, dry, cool place.

11 System and Security

Windows 10 includes tools to help protect your online privacy, troubleshoot common problems, maintain your hard drive, guard against malicious software and keep your system up-to-date.

Privacy

Online privacy is a major issue for all computer users, and the Windows 10 Creators Update has a number of options for viewing details about your personal online privacy.

The **Privacy** options have been enhanced in the Windows 10 Creators Update and there is a range of privacy settings that can be applied when the Creators Update is first installed.

1. Open the **Settings** app and click on the **Privacy** button

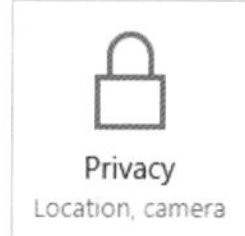

2. Drag these buttons **On** or **Off** to allow advertising more specific to you, let websites provide local content based on the language being used by Windows, and let Windows track apps that are launched to make the search results more specific

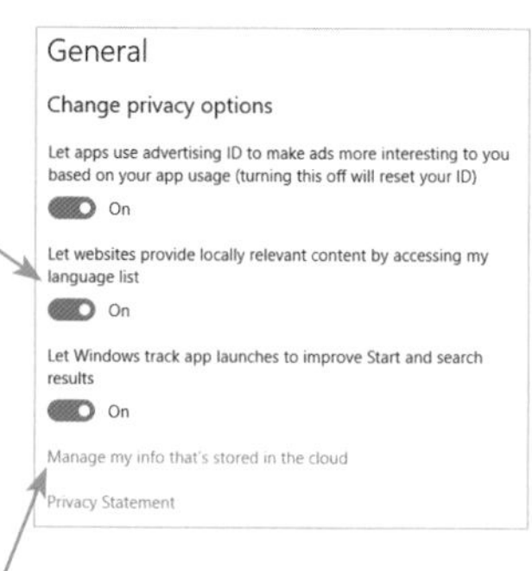

Click on **Privacy Statement** in Step 2 to view Microsoft's Privacy Statement (this is an online statement and, by default, is displayed within the Edge browser).

3. Click on **Manage my info that's stored in the cloud** to view details on the Microsoft website about how ads are used online and in Windows 10 apps

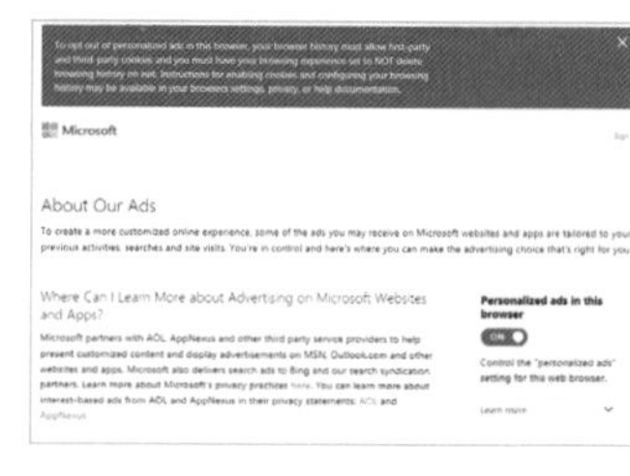

4. Drag the **Personalized ads in this browser** button to **On** to control the types of ads that are displayed in your browser

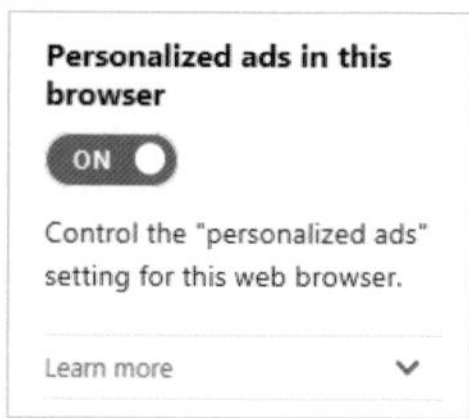

The Privacy Settings also have a range of options for enabling, or disabling, location access to specific apps.

5. Click on **Learn more** in Step 2 to view further details about general privacy settings and options within Windows 10

Know your privacy options
Learn how this setting impacts your privacy.
Learn more

Troubleshooting

On any computing system there are always things that go wrong or do not work properly. The Windows 10 Creators Update is no different, but there are comprehensive troubleshooting options for trying to address a range of problems. To use this:

The **Troubleshooting** options have been enhanced in the Windows 10 Creators Update.

1. Open the **Settings** app, select **Update & security** and click on the **Troubleshoot** button

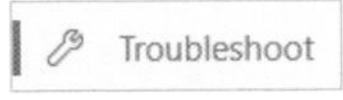

2. The range of troubleshooting options is displayed within the main window

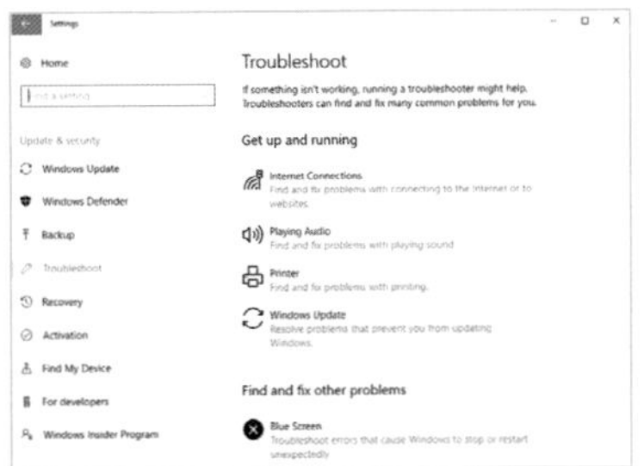

3. The top troubleshooting categories are displayed at the top of the window (other options are shown further down the window)

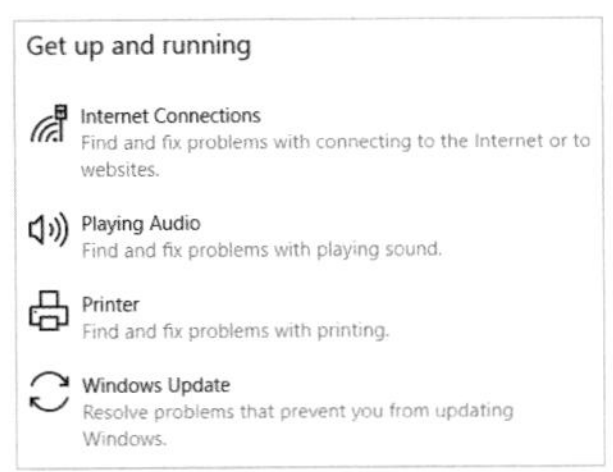

4. Click on one of the categories to select it, and click on the **Run the troubleshooter** button

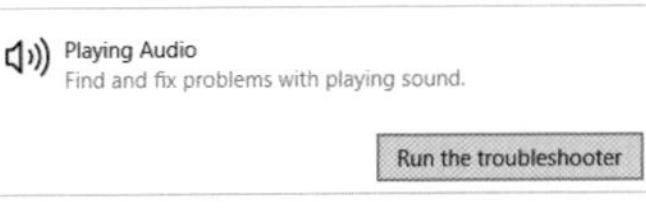

5. Any issues for the selected item are displayed along with options for trying to fix the issue

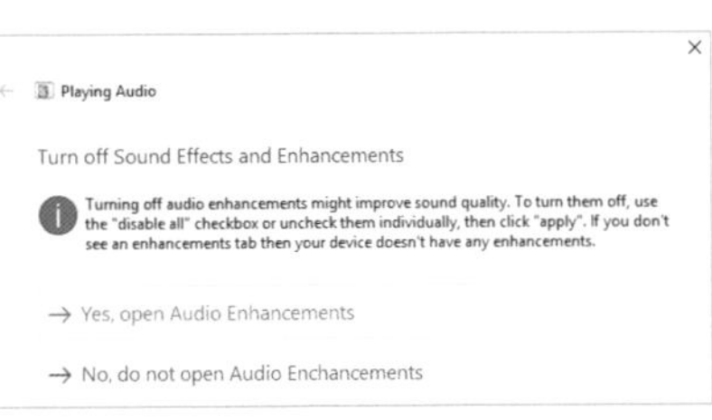

System Properties

There are several ways to open the System Properties, and view information about your laptop:

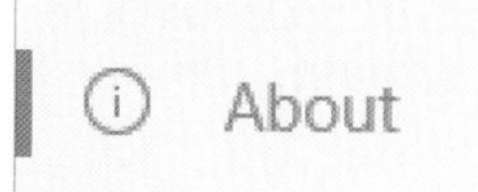

- Select **Settings** > **System** > **About**.
- Press the **WinKey** + the **Pause/Break** keys (this opens the System page within the Control Panel).
- Right-click **This PC** in the File Explorer Navigation pane, and select **Properties** from the menu.
- Right-click on the **Start** button and select **System** from the Power User menu.

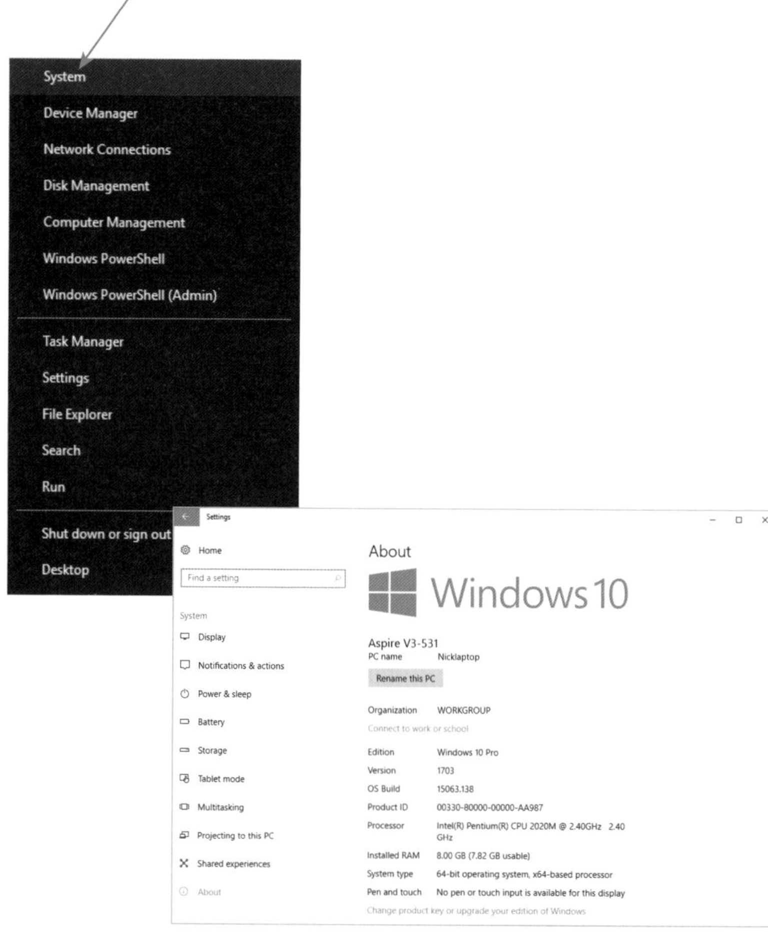

The main System panel provides the Windows 10 edition, processor details, memory size, computer and network names, and Windows 10 activation status. There are also links to the Device Manager and to more advanced settings (under the **Related settings** heading at the bottom of the page).

Device Manager

1. Select **Settings** > **System** > **About** > **Device Manager** to list all of the hardware components that are installed on your computer

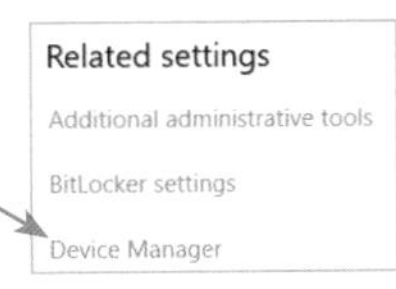

2. Select the › symbol to expand that entry to show details

3. Double-click any device to open its properties

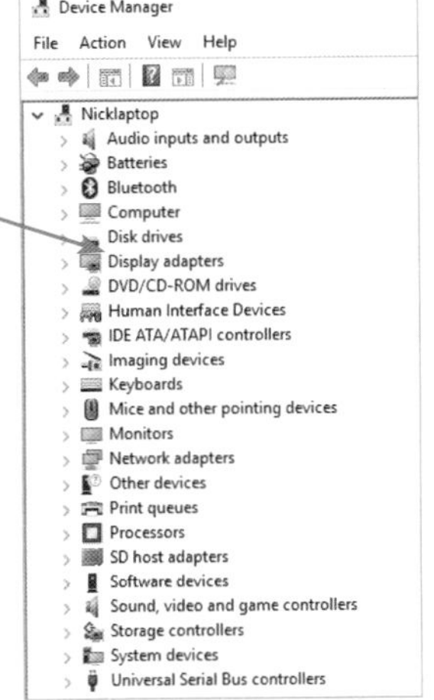

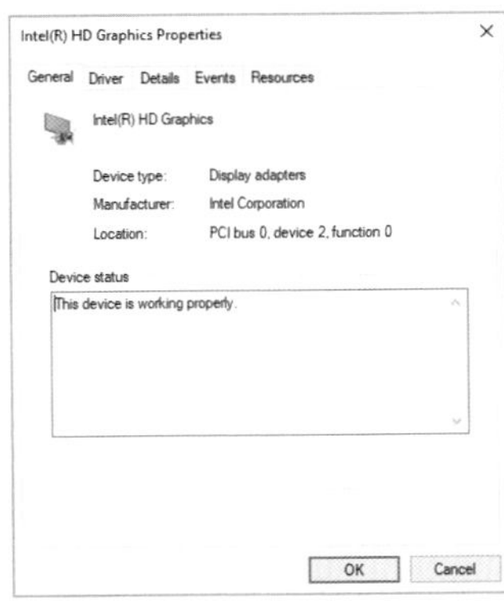

You may be prompted for an administrator password or asked for permission to continue, when you select some Device Manager entries.

4. Select the ⌄ symbol to collapse the expanded entry

5. Select the Driver tab and select **Update Driver** to find and install new software

6. Select **Disable Device** to put the particular device offline. The button changes to **Enable Device**, to reverse the action Enable Device

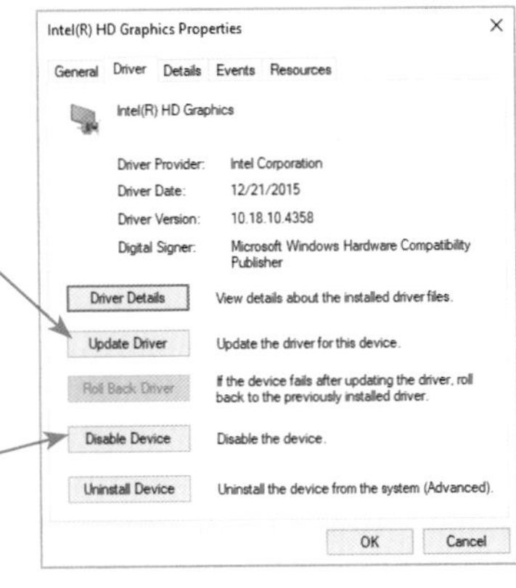

Click on the **Roll Back Driver** button to switch back to the previously-installed driver for that device, if the new one fails.

Clean Up Your Disk

1. In File Explorer, right-click the **C:** drive and click on the **Properties** option

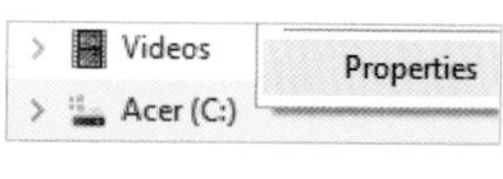

2. Click on the **Disk Cleanup** button

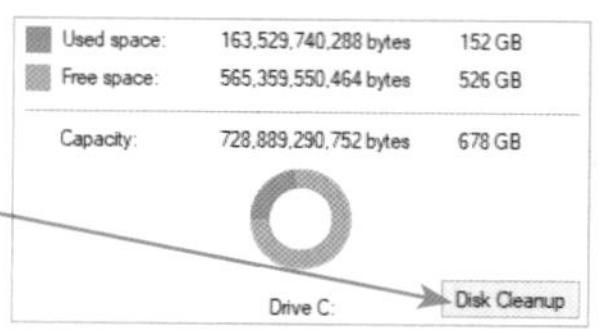

3. Disk Cleanup scans the drive to identify files that can be safely removed

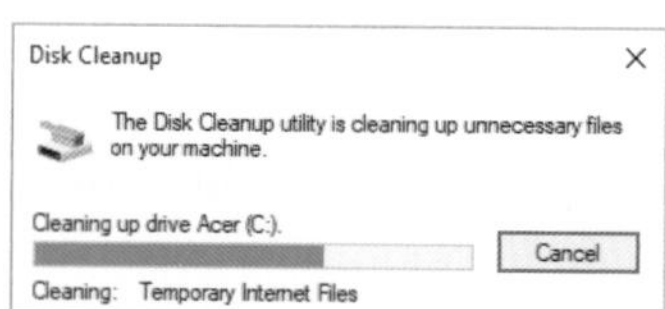

4. All of the possible files are listed by category, and the sets of files recommended to be deleted are marked with a tick symbol

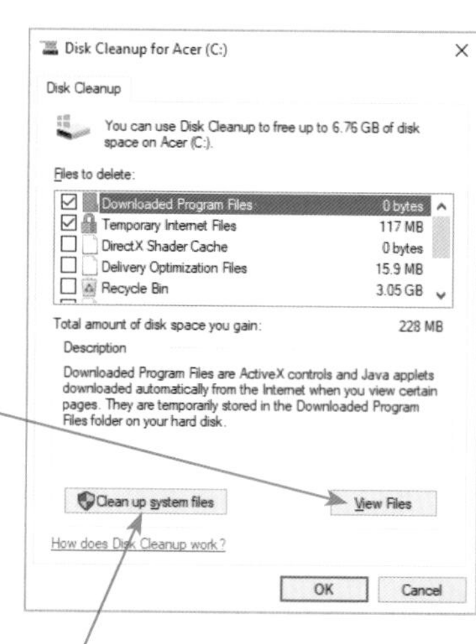

5. Make changes to the selections, clicking **View Files** if necessary to help you choose

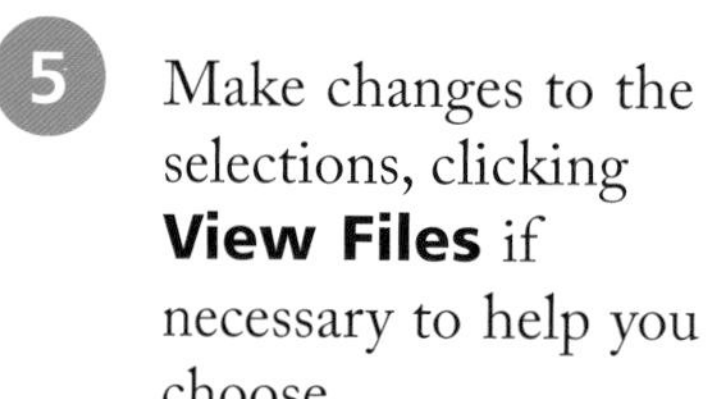

6. Select the button **Clean up system files**, to also include these, then select **OK**

7. Deleted files will not be transferred to the Recycle Bin, so confirm that you do want to permanently delete all of these files. The files will be removed and the disk space will become available

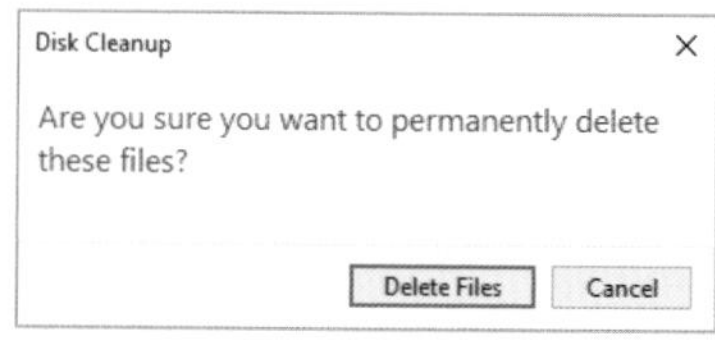

When a file is written to the hard disk, it may be stored in several pieces in different places. This fragmentation of disk space can slow down your computer. Disk Defragmenter rearranges the data so the disk will work more efficiently.

1. In the File Explorer, right-click on the **C:** drive and click on the **Properties** option

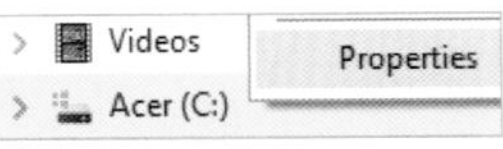

Spellings are localized.

2. Select the **Tools** tab and click on the **Optimize** button

3. The process runs as a scheduled task, but you can select a drive and select **Analyze** to check out a new drive

Only disks that can be fragmented are shown. These can include USB drives that you add to your system.

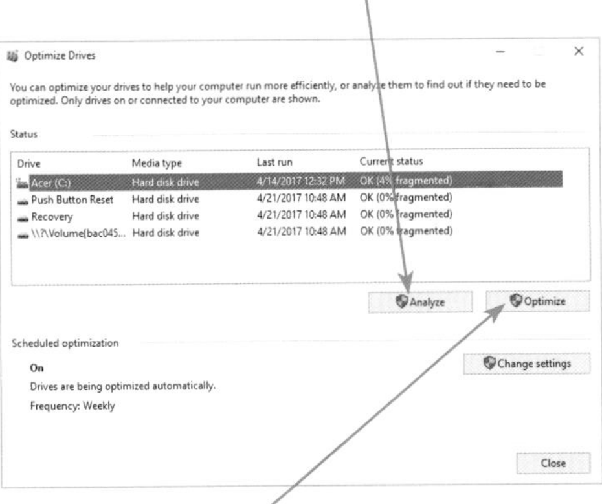

4. Click the **Optimize** button to process the selected disk drive. This may take between several minutes to several hours to complete, depending on the size and state of the disk, but you can still use your computer while the task is running

Windows Update

Updates to Windows 10 and other Microsoft products are supplied regularly, to help prevent or fix problems, improve security or enhance performance. The way in which they are downloaded and installed can be specified from the Settings app:

Click on the **Windows Insider Program** link within the **Update & security** settings to access pre-release versions of the latest Windows 10 updates.

1. Access the **Settings** app and click on the **Update & security** button

2. Click on **Windows Update**

Update & security

Windows Update

3. Click on the **Check for updates** button to see details of any updates that are waiting to be installed

Update status

Your device is up to date. Last checked: Today, 12:47 PM

Check for updates

Pausing updates (see below) is a new feature in the Windows 10 Creators Update.

4. Click on the **Advanced options** button and make a selection under **Choose how updates are installed** to specify how updates are installed

Advanced options

To avoid being inundated with updates, under **Pause Updates** in Step 4 drag the button to **On** to prevent updates being installed for up to 7 days. However, updates should still be installed regularly to ensure that the latest security updates are installed.

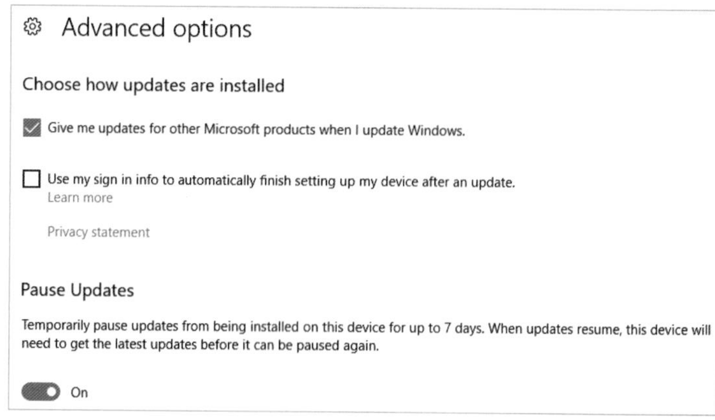

Backing Up

Backing up your data is an important task in any computer environment, and in the Windows 10 Creators Update this can be done from within the Settings app. To do this:

1. Access the **Settings** app and click on the **Update & security** button

2. Click on the **Backup** button

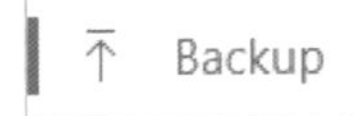

3. Click on the **Add a drive** button to select an external drive for the backup

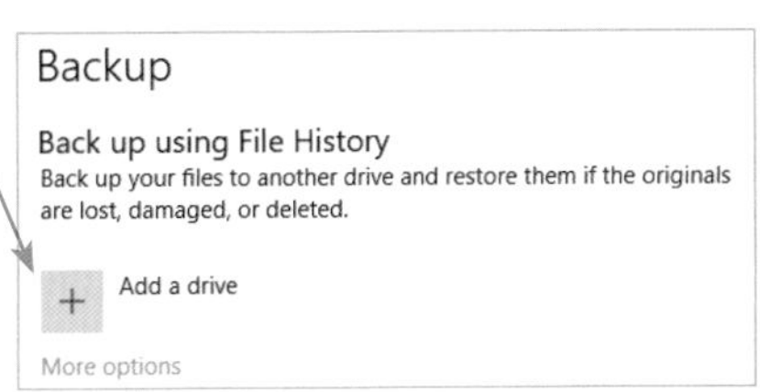

4. Click on the required external drive

Select a drive

Seagate Slim Drive (E:)
63.6 GB free of 465 GB

5. Drag the **Automatically back up my files** button to **On** to back up your files whenever the external drive is connected. After the initial backup, each further one will be incremental, i.e. only new files that have been added, or changed, will be backed up, not the whole system

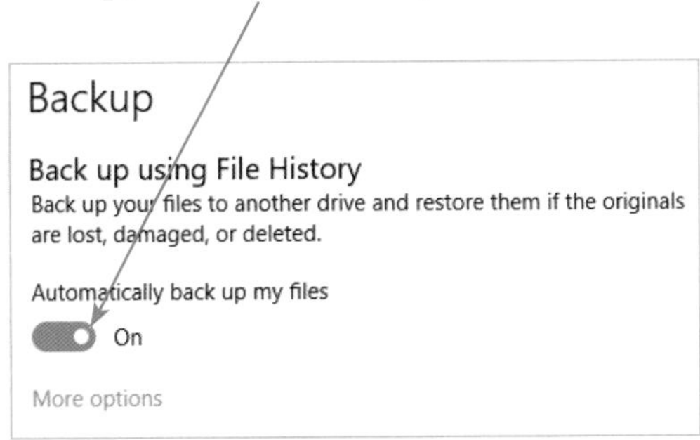

You can create a system image (an exact copy of a drive) and also back up data files in the libraries and other folders on your system. To select items to be backed up, click on **More options** in Step 3.

The **Recovery** option in **Update & security** has a **Reset this PC** option that can be used to reinstall Windows and select which files you want to keep.

System Restore

Windows 10 takes snapshots of the system files before any software updates are applied, or in any event once every seven days. You can also create a snapshot manually. The snapshots are known as "restore points" and are managed by System Restore.

System Restore returns system files to an earlier point in time, allowing you to undo system changes without affecting your documents, email, and other data files.

1. From the Control Panel, open **System** under **System and Security** and select **System protection**

System
Control
Control Panel Home
Device Manager
Remote settings
System protection
Advanced system settings

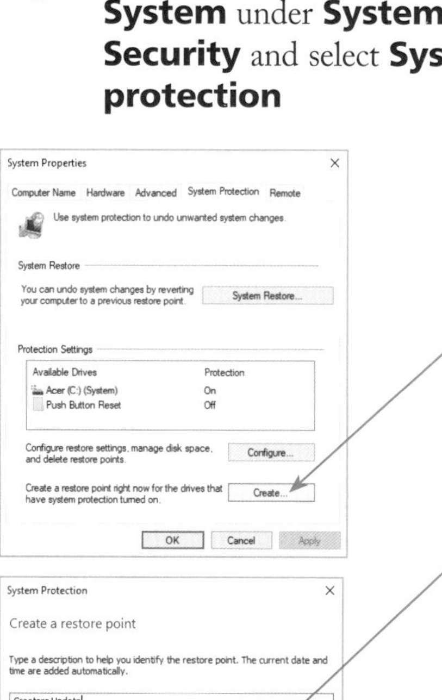

2. Select the **Create...** button, to create a restore point manually

3. Provide a title for the restore point and click **Create**

4. The required data is written to disk and the manual restore point is set up

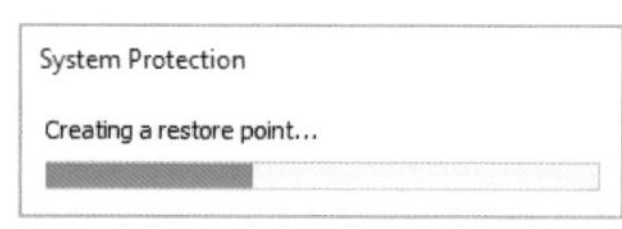

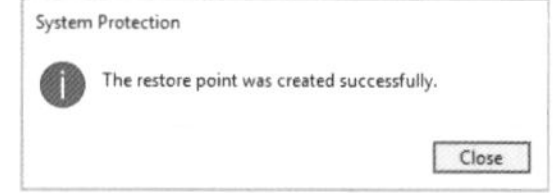

System Restore is not intended for protecting personal data files. For these you should use Windows Backup (see page 181).

Using restore points

The installation of a new app or driver software may make Windows 10 behave unpredictably. Usually, uninstalling the app or rolling back the driver will correct the situation. If this does not fix the problem, use an automatic or manual restore point to reset your system to an earlier date when everything worked correctly.

1. Select **System protection** and click the **System Restore...** button

System Restore...

2. By default, this will offer to undo the most recent change. This may fix the problem

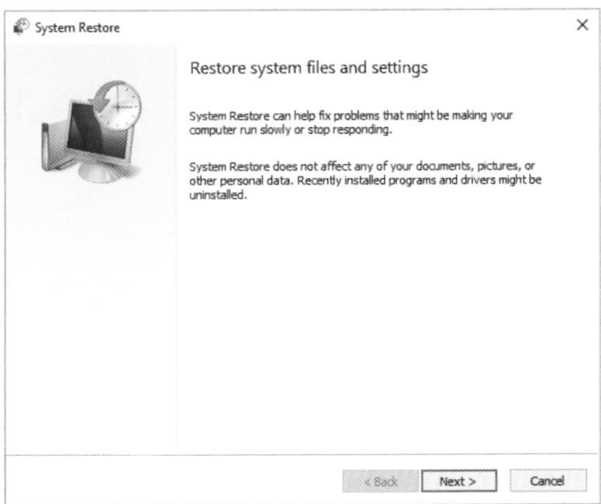

3. Otherwise, click a suitable item to use as the restore point

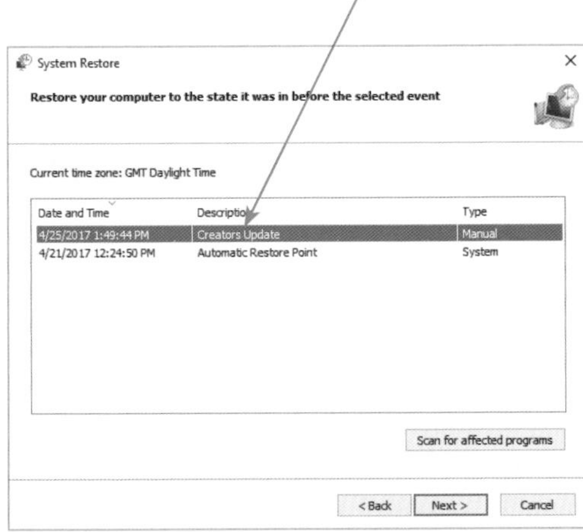

4. Follow the prompts to restart the system using system files from the selected date and time

You can also run **System Restore from Safe Mode**, the troubleshooting option. Start up the laptop and press **F8** repeatedly as your laptop reboots, to display the boot menu, then select **Safe Mode**.

If the selected restore point does not resolve the problem, you can try again, selecting another restore point.

Security and Maintenance

The Security and Maintenance section in the Control Panel monitors security and delivers alerts for security features.

1. In the Control Panel, click on the **Security and Maintenance** link in **System and Security**

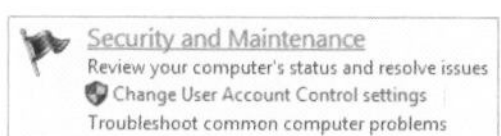

2. Select the **Change Security and Maintenance settings** link

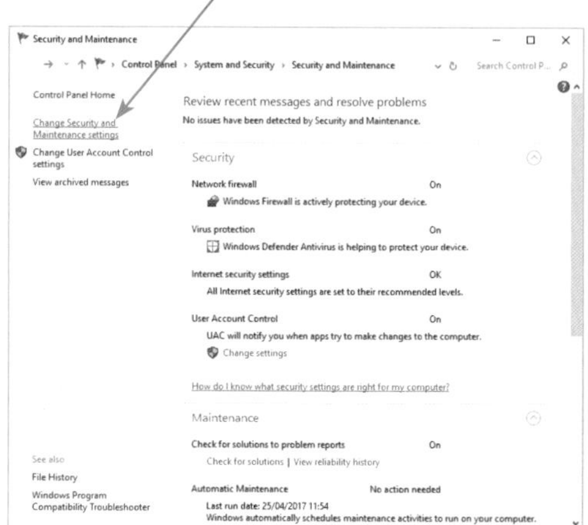

3. Check the settings **On** or **Off** as required

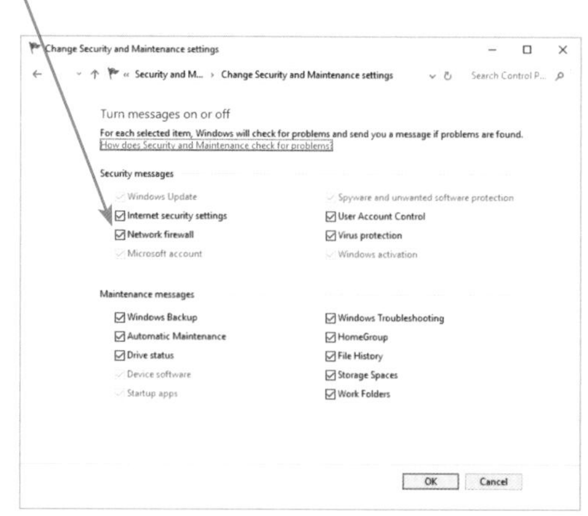

In the Security and Maintenance settings you can also **Change User Account Control settings**, from a link at the side of the window.

Windows Firewall

1. Open the Control Panel, select the **System and Security** category and select **Windows Firewall**

Windows Firewall
Check firewall status
Allow an app through Windows Firewall

2. Select **Turn Windows Firewall on or off** to customize settings for private (home and work) and public networks

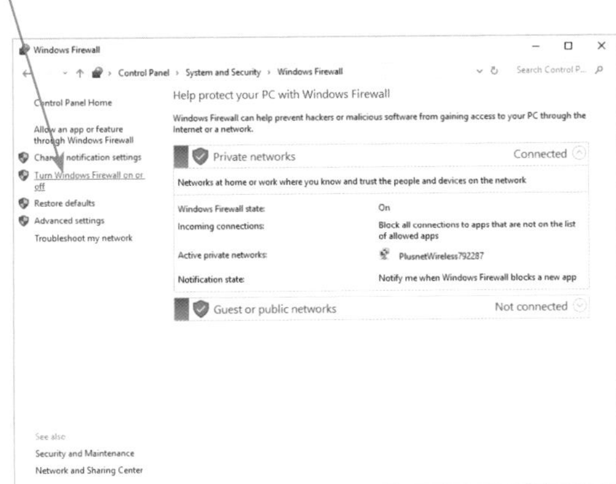

3. Select **Allow an app or feature through Windows Firewall**, to view the allowed apps

Allow an app or feature through Windows Firewall

4. Click on the **Change settings** button to allow or restrict apps

Change settings

5. Check apps **On** or **Off** to allow or remove them from the allowed list. Click on the **OK** button to apply the changes

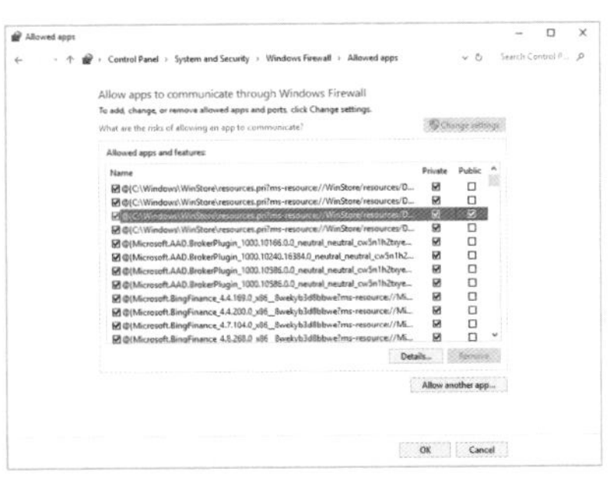

Windows Firewall can be used to provide a level of protection against malicious software and viruses.

Firewall is on by default in Windows 10, but you can turn it off if you have another firewall installed and active.

Only add apps to the allowed list if you are advised to do so by a trusted advisor, or if you trust their origins.

Malware Protection

The Windows Defender app, which is pre-installed with Windows 10, can be used to give a certain amount of protection against viruses and malicious software. To use it:

Malware (malicious software) is designed to deliberately harm your computer. To protect your system, you need up-to-date antivirus and anti-spyware software. Windows Defender provides the latter, but you should install a separate antivirus app.

The Windows Defender version in the Windows 10 Creators Update has been enhanced to provide more robust virus protection than earlier versions.

1. Select **Settings** > **Update & security** > **Windows Defender**

2. Click on **Open Windows Defender Security Center**

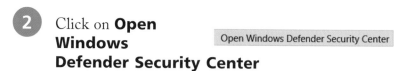

Open Windows Defender Security Center

3. The Windows Defender window contains options for scanning your PC for viruses

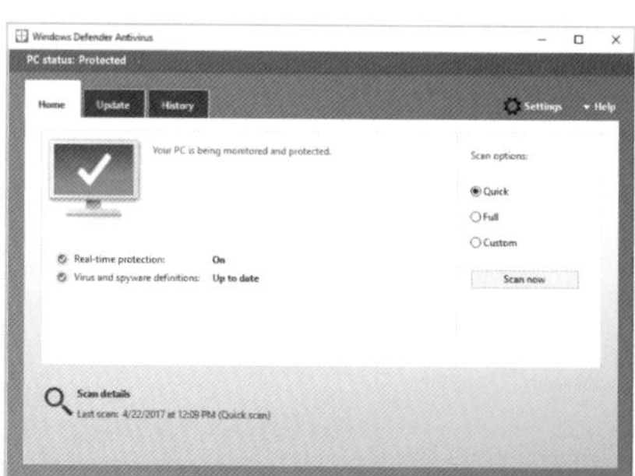

4. Select one of the scan options and click on the **Scan now** button

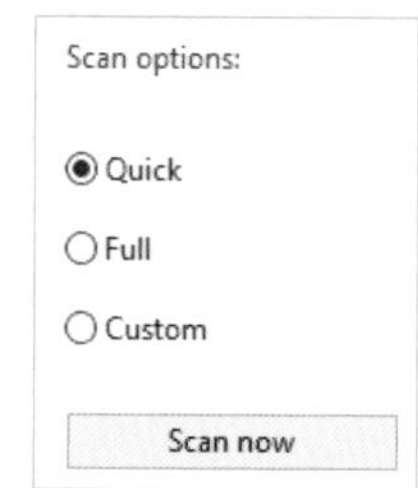

5. The progress of the scan is indicated by the green bar. When the scan is completed, any issues will be listed, along with suggested action to take

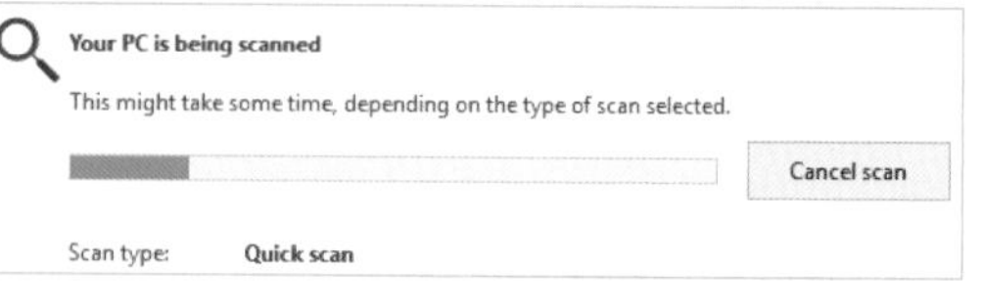

Symbols

A

B

C

L

M

N

O

P

Q

R

S

T

U

V

W

X